THE ANTIQUE
COLLECTOR'S GUIDES

A DICTIONARY OF MARKS

THE ANTIQUE COLLECTOR'S GUIDES

A
DICTIONARY
OF MARKS

Compiled and edited by
MARGARET MACDONALD-TAYLOR

Revised by
LUCILLA WATSON

BARRIE & JENKINS
LONDON

Published by Barrie & Jenkins Ltd
20 Vauxhall Bridge Road, London SW1V 2SA

First published in hardback 1962
Copyright © 1962 George Rainbird Ltd
Revised editions 1966, 1973, 1976
Reprinted 1963, 1965, 1967, 1968, 1970, 1978, 1983, 1989, 1993

Copyright © 1989 The National Magazine Company Ltd
First published in paperback 1990
Revised edition 1992

ISBN 0 7126 5303 1

Typeset by Deltatype Limited, Ellesmere Port

Printed and bound in England by Clays Ltd, St Ives, plc

Contents

Preface to Fifth Edition

It is thirty years since this dictionary was originally compiled and well over a decade since it was last revised and updated. In that time not only have most of the standard works on which it is based been revised, in some cases more than once. Tastes and attitudes among collectors have also evolved; where, for example, anything more recent than about 1830 was once given scarcely more than a second glance, almost everything from Victorian silver to studio ceramics is now rightly accepted as having its own interest and its own worth.

This dictionary has been updated accordingly. Little has been subtracted but a certain amount of new material has been added and corrections to almost all sections made as a result of information that has recently come to light. The metalwork section has been expanded, first to take in a selection of silversmiths working up to the Edwardian period, and secondly to include provincial silversmiths, who today are no longer thought to be of negligible importance by comparison with those of London.

Notable advances in research into marks, signatures and labels on English furniture have called for that section to be rewritten, although given their sheer diversity it was impractical to include more than a representative selection. The section dealing with marks on European ceramics now includes a greater spread of makers active between the mid-19th and early 20th centuries and beyond. Marks on Chinese and Japanese ceramics, possibly the most difficult of all to interpret, are also described in fuller detail.

Finally, the list of books for further reading now includes the most recent editions of acknowledged standard works, others that have appeared since 1976, and books – for the most part recently published – chosen for their wider coverage of each aspect of marks dealt with in this volume.

The publishers would like to thank the following for their advice on the revision of this dictionary: David Beasley, Librarian, Goldsmiths Hall; Christopher Gilbert, Temple Newsam House, Leeds City Art Galleries; and John Sandon, Phillips Fine Art Auctioneers. The publishers also extend their thanks to John Fallon, who drew additional marks for the ceramics section.

L. W.

Preface to Fourth Edition

The interest in pictures and antiques of all kinds has gathered increasing momentum of recent years, and books and articles of generalised or particular interest continue to delight and inform a wide public. It is not necessary to be rich to indulge one's taste for fine things. Many people today can see objects of the highest quality in the surroundings most fitted to show them to advantage, especially in the many country houses open to visitors. More people than ever before are appreciating the great store of beauty housed in museums and art galleries, and by frequent visits learn to train the eye to see quality and to remember shapes and ornamentation. At previews of auction sales, and in the more intimate atmosphere of antique dealers' shops, even the most diffident enthusiast can find opportunities to go further than simply looking. The experience of actually touching a piece of Chippendale or of holding in the hand some fine piece of porcelain or silver brings closer acquaintance with its character, and stimulates the desire for even more detailed knowledge. For some people this particular interest may be encouraged by having a good eye for fine design and workmanship, and perhaps by being able to acquire a few antiques to add grace to their homes. Others, again, may be happy in the possession of some heirlooms, such as family silver, which has been lovingly cherished from one generation to the next, or old porcelain, carefully preserved. In the case of inherited treasures, some intimate story connected with them will doubtless also be handed down; in very fortunate circumstances there may exist the original bills which record the name of the maker and details of the purchase. Here there is not only valuable documentary proof, so much prized by the art historian and the connoisseur, but, for everyone interested, expert and amateur alike, an additional savour given to appreciation of the pieces concerned.

Where such documentary proof is lacking, knowledge of the provenance, period, and maker's name may be gained by other means, notably by deduction from marks, especially in ceramics and metalwork. To search out these marks and identify them is a detective exercise which brings both pleasure and reward, but the hunt may be rather protracted and full of complications, if reference works are out of print or otherwise inaccessible; and not everyone has time for lengthy research in reference libraries.

Signatures, or other inscriptions, on pictures and prints do not here concern us, but rather the marks of differing kinds and purposes on ceramics, metalwork, furniture and tapestry. These marks are now put into one book, although they are kept in separate sections. Each category receives the particular form of presentation felt to be best suited to it.

Metalwork is a complex subject and has therefore been subdivided, for the convenience of the reader, into several sections. On old English silver, of course, several marks will be found, including the standard mark, town mark, and date mark. These are grouped in historical sequence under the chief towns, and can be checked easily from the object being studied. English silversmiths were further required to identify their wares by using initials. A selective list of such initials (including compound initials indicating more than one person) has been compiled, in alphabetical order, including those silversmiths whose work is most commonly met with. The reader can run his finger down the list, and find the name of the person given alongside, with approximate dates, and brief indication of the shape in which the initials are enclosed. Taking together the initials, the town mark and its date letter, the maker can be traced with reasonable confidence. Where two different makers with the same initials are found, the year mark is a useful counter-check. Changes of initials are recorded separately, even where they refer to the same silversmith. In English pewter, an enormous number of makers' "touches", as they are called, have been officially recorded. Lack of space did not permit of depicting these here by drawings. To aid the enquirer, however, a selective list of English pewterers, arranged alphabetically by surname, has been included, with approximate dates and a brief description of the touch. Reference to the metalwork index for the emblems will lead the reader to the page, but most touches have readily identifiable names still to be seen, where not partially erased by domestic polishing. Entries recorded under Sheffield plate need no comment.

Many people now take a keen interest in American silver; it was not normally required to bear standard or other marks, but the makers' marks often consist of the straightforward use of the name. Numbers of American silversmiths, however, not only had a taste for imitating the shapes of English silver, but, copying from choice a practice that was followed by regulation in England, used initials only, to mark their work. A selective list of such initials given here follows the method of entry used for English silversmiths, and the selective list of American pewter touches is again in line with that used for English pewter.

Marks on furniture and tapestry also have their appeal for the connoisseur, although in regard to furniture the French claim the largest share of attention. Since, by regulation, the various French master craftsmen, cabinet-makers, clockmakers, bronze workers and others (except those holding special royal privilege) were required to "sign" their pieces, this category takes the form of a selective list, arranged in alphabetical order, with a brief note of dates, together with those few emblems which occur. Marks on tapestry, a practice initiated in Brussels and soon imitated elsewhere, sometimes take almost cabalistic forms, which are therefore not susceptible of being put in an index. The chief English and European centres, and some makers, appear, with their marks, in alphabetical order.

On ceramics, i.e. pottery and porcelain, all kinds of marks are found, sometimes in the form of emblems, anchor, crossed swords, and so on; these may be tracked down by using the ceramic index. Except in the case of Oriental marks, the entries are not separated; English and European appear together in alphabetical order, according to the name of the factory, with a separate entry for an artist if conspicuously famous. Each ceramics entry gives a brief note on date, country, type of ware (i.e. maiolica, porcelain, etc.), with, wherever possible, a facsimile representation of known marks, whether name or emblem. In the case of much English nineteenth-century work, however, an entry giving the firm's name in type only has been deemed sufficient. Decorators' marks, where known and identified, and thought useful to record, are normally here included under the factory entry. In using this book, therefore, the reader should first check the factory mark; if an emblem is used, this will be traced by the ceramics index. Once the factory mark has been identified, it is a simple matter to trace under the particular entry any additional mark (e.g. date letter, artists's initials, etc.) which may occur on the piece being examined. As regards Oriental marks, the dynasty marks of China and the year marks of Japan have been illustrated. Although so foreign in appearance to Western eyes, constant study soon makes them familiar, especially since their number is not large. As some European and English factories have used imitation Oriental marks, it is interesting to refer to the genuine, original mark, and to note the differences between the two.

In short the essential marks to be recognised when studying or collecting antiques have been included in this book, and no claim to be all-embracing is made. To extend his knowledge yet further, the reader is referred to those specialised books listed in the bibliography. All such study will contribute greatly to the appreciation of those works of the past which were such a source of pride and pleasure to the original owners, and which continue to delight us today.

New material now includes two important entries relating to British metalwork: firstly, the new usages arising from the Hallmarking Act of 1973; secondly, the formation of the Association of British Pewter Craftsmen in 1970, and their introduction of a special quality mark in 1971. Then in the United States the American Revolution Bicentennial symbol has been introduced for use on new objects for a limited period. All the foregoing, it is hoped, record useful information for future collectors. Finally, in the Ceramics section the entries relating to English objects of the Victorian and Edwardian periods have been expanded.

M.M.T.

Acknowledgements

The editor would like to record sincere appreciation of the work done by Mrs Mary Platford who drew, with great care and precision, the metalwork marks and those relating to Oriental pottery and porcelain, and who brought unfailing patience to the lengthy task of deciphering the editor's notes, sketches, and directions. In this present revised edition, a debt of gratitude is owed to Mr Geoffrey Godden, the distinguished writer on British ceramics, who has revised and updated entries relating to this field, and has also given the publishers permission to reproduce a number of new drawings from his *Encyclopaedia of British Pottery and Porcelain Marks* (Barrie & Jenkins) and from his *Handbook of British Pottery and Porcelain Marks* (Barrie & Jenkins). His help is warmly acknowledged.

Metalwork

British Metalwork

Precious metals include gold and silver, and for each a standard mark has long applied. Since 1 January 1975 some slight changes were introduced. Also since 1 February 1975, following the Hallmarking Act 1973, platinum was included as a precious metal and therefore has its own standard mark. Imported articles have also been subject to hallmarking according to standard, and again these marks have been slightly changed since 1 January 1975. Also as from 1 January 1975 there have been some slight changes in Town Marks (Assay Office Marks), whether on the work of native craftsmen or on imported articles.

Tables for Comparison

Standard Mark   BRITISH ARTICLES

PRIOR TO 1975	FROM 1975	PRIOR TO 1975	FROM 1975
22 carat gold Marked in England Marked in Scotland	916	9 carat gold 375	375
18 carat gold Marked in England Marked in Scotland	750	Sterling silver Marked in England Marked in Scotland	
14 carat gold ·585	585	Britannia silver Platinum —	

Standard Mark   IMPORTED ARTICLES

PRIOR TO 1975	FROM 1975	PRIOR TO 1975	FROM 1975
22 carat gold 916	916	18 carat gold 750	750

PRIOR TO 1975	FROM 1975	PRIOR TO 1975	FROM 1975
14 carat gold ⚓ 585	585	Britannia silver 9584	958
9 carat gold 375	375	Platinum —	950
Sterling silver 925	925		

BRITISH ARTICLES

Assay Office Mark

PRIOR TO 1975		FROM 1975	PRIOR TO 1975	FROM 1975
London			**Edinburgh**	
Gold & sterling silver	Britannia silver	Gold, silver & platinum	Gold & silver	Gold & silver
Birmingham			**Sheffield**	
Gold	Silver	Gold & platinum / Silver	Gold / Silver	Gold & silver

IMPORTED ARTICLES

Assay Office Mark

PRIOR TO 1975		FROM 1975		PRIOR TO 1975		FROM 1975	
Gold	Silver	Gold & silver	Platinum	Gold	Silver	Gold & silver	Platinum
London				**Edinburgh**			
Ω	Ω	unchanged	Ω	X	X	unchanged	—
Birmingham				**Sheffield**			
△	△	unchanged	△	Ω	Ω	unchanged	—

NOTE Hallmarking is done in Austria, France, Holland and Sweden. No hallmarking is done in Germany or in the United States or Canada.

British Silver

Four marks are usually found stamped on silver, namely: the hall, or town, mark, indicating the assay office; the maker's mark; the annual mark or date letter, indicating the year of assay; the standard mark, indicating sterling quality. Other marks are: the Britannia mark, used 1697 to 1719, to indicate the higher standard of silver required during that period; the Sovereign's head or duty mark, used 1784 to 1890, to indicate duty had been paid on the piece so stamped; the Jubilee mark, used in addition to other marks, on pieces with date letters from 1933/4 to 1935/6, celebrating the silver jubilee of King George V and Queen Mary; the Coronation mark of 1953 (the head of Queen Elizabeth II) to mark her accession. The Hallmarking Act 1973 ensured that from 1 January 1975 all British Assay Offices (London, Birmingham, Edinburgh and Sheffield) use the same date letter cycle, beginning with the letter A on 1 January 1975 and being changed annually on 1 January in each succeeding year.

The following is a guide to the letters at the head of each table: **LH** Leopard's head; **DL** Date letter; **LP** Lion passant; **LHC** Leopard's head crowned; **B** Britannia; **LHE** Lion's head erased; **TM** Town mark; **RC** Rose crowned; **DM** Deacon's mark; **AM** Assay mark; **T** Thistle; **LR** Lion rampant; **SH** Sovereign's head.

London

Goldsmiths' Company empowered to assay and stamp gold or silver articles in 1327. Marks: the **leopard's head** (i.e. a lion's face) at first uncrowned; crowned 1478–1697; not used during "Britannia" period (1697–1719); crowned 1720–1823, thereafter uncrowned; the **lion passant**, indicating sterling standard, at first "guardant", and crowned until 1550; disused during "Britannia" period (1697–1719); the **Britannia figure**, and the **lion's head erased** (profile head, cut off at neck), both used during Britannia period (1697–1719); **Sovereign's head**, as duty mark, 1784–1890; **date letter**, formerly changed annually in May; from 1975 changed 1 January; **maker's mark**.

1558–1578

LHC	LP	DL		LHC	LP	DL	
		a	1558/59			g	1564/65
		b	1559/60			h	1565/66
		cc	1560/61			i	1566/67
		d	1561/62			kk	1567/68
		e	1562/63			l	1568/69
		ff	1563/64			mm	1569/70

16

LHC	LP	DL		LHC	LP	DL	
⬡	🦁	𝕹	1570/71	⬡	🦁	𝑷	1592/93
		𝖔	1571/72			𝑸	1593/94
		𝖕	1572/73			𝑹	1594/95
		𝖖	1573/74			𝑺	1595/96
		𝖗	1574/75			𝑻	1596/97
		𝖘	1575/76			𝑽	1597/98
		𝖙	1576/77				
		𝖚	1577/78				

1578–1598

LHC	LP	DL	
⬡	🦁	A	1578/79
		B	1579/80
		C	1580/81
		D	1581/82
		E	1582/83
		F	1583/84
		G	1584/85
		H	1585/86
		I	1586/87
		K	1587/88
		L	1588/89
		M	1589/90
		N	1590/91
		O	1591/92

1598–1618

LHC	LP	DL	
⬡	🦁	𝕬	1598/99
		𝕭	1599/1600
		𝕮	1600/1
		𝕯	1601/2
		𝕰	1602/3
		𝕱	1603/4
		𝕲	1604/5
		𝕳	1605/6
		𝕴	1606/7
		𝕶	1607/8
		𝕷	1608/9
		𝕸	1609/10
		𝕹	1610/11
		𝕺	1611/12
		𝕻	1612/13

METALWORK

LHC	LP	DL		LHC	LP	DL	
		O	1613/14			r	1634/35
		R	1614/15			s	1635/36
		S	1615/16			t	1636/37
		T	1616/17			v	1637/38
		V	1617/18				

1638–1658

LHC	LP	DL	
		a b	1638/39
		b	1639/40
		c	1640/41

1618–1638

LHC	LP	DL	
		a	1618/19
		b b	1619/20
		c	1620/21
		d	1621/22
		e	1622/23
		f	1623/24
		g	1624/25
		h	1625/26
		i	1626/27
		k k	1627/28
		l	1628/29
		m	1629/30
		n	1630/31
		o	1631/32
		p	1632/33
		q	1633/34

	d	1641/42
	e	1642/43
	f	1643/44
	g	1644/45
	h	1645/46
	i	1646/47
	k	1647/48
	l	1648/49
	m	1649/50
	n	1650/51
	o	1651/52
	p	1652/53
	q	1653/54
	r	1654/55

LHC	LP	DL		LHC	LP	DL	
🛡	🦁	O	1655/56	🛡	🦁	L	1676/77
		d	1656/57			B	1677/78
		B	1657/58				

1678–1697

LHC	LP	DL	
🛡	🦁	a	1678/79

1658–1678

LHC	LP	DL		DL	
🛡	🦁	A	1658/59	b	1679/80
		B	1659/60	c	1680/81
		C	1660/61	d	1681/82
		D	1661/62	e	1682/83
		E	1662/63	f	1683/84
		F	1663/64	g	1684/85
		G	1664/65	h	1685/86
		H	1665/66	k	1686/87
		I	1666/67	k	1687/88
		K	1667/68	l	1688/89
		L	1668/69	m	1689/90
		M	1669/70	n	1690/91
		N	1670/71	o	1691/92
		O	1671/72	p	1692/93
		P	1672/73	q	1693/94
		Q	1673/74	r	1694/95
		R	1674/75	s	1695/96
		S	1675/76	t	1696/97

1697–1716

LHC	LP	DL		B	LHE	DL	
![LHC]	![LP]	![a]	1697	![B]	![LHE]	**A**	1716/17
B	**LHE**	![b]	1697/98			**B**	1717/18
![B]	![LHE]	![c]	1698/99	**LHC**	**LP**	**C**	1718/19
		![d]	1699/1700	![LHC]	![LP]	**D**	1719/20
		![e]	1700/1			**E**	1720/21
		![f]	1701/2			**F**	1721/22
		![g]	1702/3			**G**	1722/23
		![h]	1703/4			**H**	1723/24
		![i]	1704/5			**I**	1724/25
		![k]	1705/6			**K**	1725/26
		![l]	1706/7			**L**	1726/27
		![m]	1707/8			**M**	1727/28
		![n]	1708/9			**N**	1728/29
		![o]	1709/10			**O**	1729/30
		![p]	1710/11			**P**	1730/31
		![q]	1711/12			**Q**	1731/32
		![r]	1712/13			**R**	1732/33
		![s]	1713/14			**S**	1733/34
		![t]	1714/15			**T**	1734/35
		![u]	1715/16			**V**	1735/36

1716–1736

1736–1756

LHC	LP	DL	
		a	1736/37
		b	1737/38
		c	1738/39
		d	1739/40
		d	1739/40
		e	1740/41
		f	1741/42
		g	1742/43
		h	1743/44
		i	1744/45
		k	1745/46
		l	1746/47
		m	1747/48
		n	1748/49
		o	1749/50
		p	1750/51
		q	1751/52
		r	1752/53
		s	1753/54
		t	1754/55
		u	1755/56

1756–1776

LHC	LP	DL	
		A	1756/57
		B	1757/58
		C	1758/59
		D	1759/60
		E	1760/61
		F	1761/62
		G	1762/63
		H	1763/64
		I	1764/65
		K	1765/66
		L	1766/67
		M	1767/68
		N	1768/69
		O	1769/70
		P	1770/71
		Q	1771/72
		R	1772/73
		S	1773/74
		T	1774/75
		U	1775/76

1776–1796

LHC	LP	DL	
		a	1776/77

LHC	LP	DL	SH	Year
👑	🦁	b		1777/78
		c		1778/79
		d		1779/80
		e		1780/81
		f		1781/82
		g		1782/83
		h		1783/84
		i	👤	1784/85
		k		1785/86
		l	👤	1786/87
		m		1787/88
		n		1788/89
		o		1789/90
		p		1790/91
		q		1791/92
		r		1792/93
		s		1793/94
		t		1794/95
		u		1795/96

1796–1816

LHC	LP	DL	SH	Year
👑	🦁	A	👤	1796/97
		B		1797/98
		C		1798/99

LHC	LP	DL	SH	Year
👑	🦁	D	👤	1799/1800
		E		1800/1
		F		1801/2
		G		1802/3
		H		1803/4
		I		1804/5
		K		1805/6
		L		1806/7
		M		1807/8
		N		1808/9
		O		1809/10
		P		1810/11
		Q		1811/12
		R		1812/13
		S		1813/14
		T		1814/15
		U		1815/16

1816–1836

LHC	LP	DL	SH	Year
👑	🦁	a	👤	1816/17
		b		1817/18
		c		1818/19
		d		1819/20
		e	👤	1820/21

LH	LP	DL	SH	
🦁	🦁	f	👤	1821/22
		g		1822/23
		h		1823/24
		i		1824/25
		k		1825/26
		l		1826/27
		m		1827/28
		n		1828/29
		o		1829/30
		p		1830/31
		q	👤	1831/32
		r		1832/33
		s		1833/34
		t		1834/35
		u		1835/36

1836–1856

LH	LP	DL	SH	
🦁	🦁	A	👤	1836/37
		B	👤	1837/38
		C		1838/39
		D		1839/40
		E		1840/41
		F		1841/42

LH	LP	DL	SH	
🦁	🦁	G	👤	1842/43
		H		1843/44
		J		1844/45
		K		1845/46
		L		1846/47
		M		1847/48
		N		1848/49
		O		1849/50
		P		1850/51
		Q		1851/52
		R		1852/53
		S		1853/54
		T		1854/55
		U		1855/56

1856–1876

LH	LP	DL	SH	
🦁	🦁	a	👤	1856/57
		b		1857/58
		c		1858/59
		d		1859/60
		e		1860/61
		f		1861/62
		g		1862/63

LH	LP	DL	SH	
🛡	🛡	h	●	1863/64
🛡	🛡	i		1864/65
		k		1865/66
		l		1866/67
		m		1867/68
		n		1868/69
		o		1869/70
		p		1870/71
		q		1871/72
		r		1872/73
		s		1873/74
		t		1874/75
		u		1875/76

LH	LP	DL	SH	
🛡	🛡	I	●	1884/85
		K		1885/86
		L		1886/87
		M		1887/88
		N		1888/89
		O		1889/90
		P		1890/91
		Q		1891/92
		R		1892/93
		S		1893/94
		T		1894/95
		U		1895/96

1876–1896

LH	LP	DL	SH	
🛡	🛡	A	●	1876/77
		B		1877/78
		C		1878/79
		D		1879/80
		E		1880/81
		F		1881/82
		G		1882/83
		H		1883/84

1896–1916

LH	LP	DL	
🛡	🛡	a	1896/97
		b	1897/98
		c	1898/99
		d	1899/1900
		e	1900/1
		f	1901/2
		g	1902/3
		h	1903/4
		i	1904/5

24

LH	LP	DL			LH	LP	DL	SH	
🐱	🦁	**K**	1905/6		🦁	🦁	**o**		1929/30
		l	1906/7				**p**		1930/31
		m	1907/8				**q**		1931/32
		n	1908/9				**r**		1932/33
		o	1909/10		🦁	🦁	**s**	●	1933/34
		p	1910/11				**t**		1934/35
		q	1911/12				**u**		1935/36
		r	1912/13						
		s	1913/14						
		t	1914/15						
		u	1915/16						

1936–1956

LH	LP	DL		
🐱	🦁	**A**	1936/37
		B	1937/38
		C	1938/39
		D	1939/40
		E	1940/41
		F	1941/42
		G	1942/43
		H	1943/44
		I	1944/45
		K	1945/46
		L	1946/47
		M	1947/48
		N	1948/49
		O	1949/50
		P	1950/51
		Q	1951/52

1916–1936

LH	LP	DL		
🐱	🦁	**a**	1916/17
		b	1917/18
		c	1918/19
		d	1919/20
		e	1920/21
		f	1921/22
		g	1922/23
		h	1923/24
		i	1924/25
		k	1925/26
		l	1926/27
		m	1927/28
		n	1928/29

LH	LP	DL	SH	
🐾	🦁	**R**	🙂	1952/53
		S		1953/54
		T		1954/55
		U		1955/56

LH	LP	DL	
🐾	🦁	**S**	1973/74
		t	May–Dec 1974

1956–1974

LH	LP	DL	
🐾	🐕	**a**	1956/57
		b	1957/58
		c	1958/59
		d	1959/60
		e	1960/61
		f	1961/62
		g	1962/63
		h	1963/64
		i	1964/65
		k	1965/66
		l	1966/67
		m	1967/68
		n	1968/69
		o	1969/70
		p	1970/71
		q	1972/73
		r	1973/74

1975–

LH	LP	DL	
🙂	🦁	**A**	1975
		B	1976
		C	1977
		D	1978
		E	1979
		F	1980
		G	1981
		H	1982
		I	1983
		K	1984
		L	1985
		M	1986
		N	1987
		O	1988
		P	1989
		Q	1990
		R	1991
		S	1992

British Silversmiths' Marks

Dates refer to the year in which each mark was entered by the maker at the assay office. Dates of marks for which no record exists are prefixed by 'found in . . .', indicating the earliest known instance of an unrecorded mark on a piece of silver.

London

Ab **Abercromby, Robert**
(in flattened oval punch, 1739)

A Bros Ltd **Adie Bros Ltd**
(in lozenge-shaped punch, 'Bros' and 'Ltd' each side of 'A', 1914)

AC **Augustine Courtauld**
(with fleur-de-lis over, in plain punch with rounded top, entered 1729; in italics over fleur-de-lis, in trefoil-shaped punch, 1739)

AC
EF **Alex Coates** and **Edward French**
(in quatrefoil-shaped punch, 1734)

A&CoLtd **Asprey & Co. Ltd**
(in rectangular punch, 1909)

AF
SG **Andrew Fogelberg** and **Stephen Gilbert**
(in quatrefoil-shaped punch with crown over, 1780)

A·F **Andrew Fogelberg**
(in rectangular punch, found in 1777)

AL **Augustin Le Sage**
(crowned, in oval punch, found in 1769; with pellet between, chalice above and star below, in quatrefoil-shaped punch, found in 1774)

AN **Anthony Nelme**
(AN italic caps in monogram in cartouche, 1722)

ANe **Anthony Nelme**
(AN in monogram with "e", in shield-shaped punch, 1697)

AR **Archambo, Peter**
(between crown and fleur-de-lis, in shaped punch, 1720)

AS
JS
AS **Savory, Adey, Joseph** and **Albert**
(in upright rectangular punch, 1833)

AT **Ann Tanqueray**
(with sun above and escallop below, in lozenge-shaped punch, c.1725)

AV   **Aymé Videau**
(with pellet above in rhomboid punch; italic caps with star over and pellet below, in near-quatrefoil punch, 1739)

A·Z·J·Z·   **Arthur and John Zimmerman**
(in rectangular punch, 1889)

Ba   **Bamford, Thomas**
(Gothic or Roman letters in small oval punch, 1719)

Ba   **Barnard, John**
(Gothic letters over fleur-de-lis (?) in heart-shaped punch, 1697; also "Ba" over pellet, in heart-shaped punch, 1720)

BA   **Barnett, Edward**
(in shaped punch, 1715)

B·H·M·   **Berthold Hermann Muller** (importer of German silver)
(in rectangular punch, 1912)

BI   **Bignell, John**
(in shield-shaped punch, 1718)

BM   **Berthold Hermann Muller** (importer of German silver)
(letters separate or conjoined, in rectangular punch, 1897)

BN   **Bowles Nash**
(over fleur-de-lis in heart-shaped punch, 1721)

BS   **Benjamin Smith**
(in rectangular punch, 1812)

B·S   **Benjamin Smith** and **James Smith**
I·S   (in plain rectangle, 1809)

Bu   **Burridge, Thomas**
(with rosette and two pellets over and one pellet below, in cartouche, 1706)

BU   **Burridge, Thomas**
(with star over, in trefoil-shaped punch, 1717)

CA   **Aldridge, Charles**
(in plain rectangular punch, 1786)

CA   **Charles Asprey**
(in nipped rectangular punch, 1855)

C·A   **Charles Asprey Snr** and **Jnr**
C·A   (in rectangular punch, 1878)

CA·GA   **Charles** and **George Asprey**
(in oval punch, 1891)

CB   **Charles Bellassyse**
(with mitre over, in cinquefoil-shaped punch, 1740)

CF   **Charles Fabergé**
(in oval punch, 1911)

CF   **Charles Fox**
(in plain oval punch, 1822)

C·F·H·   **Charles Frederick Hancock**
(crowned, in rectangular punch, 1850; crowned in curved punch,
    1870)

C·F·H· & Co   **Hancocks & Co.**
(before lion rampant, in cartouche, 1899; crowned, 1890)

CH   **Charles Hatfield**
(with pellet above and below, in quatrefoil-shaped punch, 1727; italic
    letters with fleur-de-lis above in trefoil-shaped punch, 1739)

CH   **Chartier, John**
(initials surmounted by fleur-de-lis, with or without crown, in shaped
    punch, 1698)

CK   **Charles Kandler**
(in oval punch, 1778)

Co   **Cole, John**
(over star in heart-shaped punch, 1697)

Co   **Coles, Lawrence**
(in shaped punch, 1697)

Co   **Collins, Henry**
(crowned C enclosing "o" in narrow rectangular shield-shaped punch,
    1698)

Co   **Cooke, John**
(crowned letters in shaped punch, 1699)

CO   **Cornock, Edward**
(in bordered oval punch, 1707)

CO   **Courtauld, Augustine**
(with fleur-de-lis over in trefoil-shaped punch, 1708)

CR   **Crespin, Paul**
(italic caps in shaped oblong punch, 1740)

C R
A   **Charles Robert Ashbee**
(in shield-shaped punch, 1896)

CSH   **Charles Stuart Harris**
(in rectangular punch, 1891; in nipped oval punch, 1871, and others
    similar 1884 and 1891)

C
T W   Probably **Thomas** and **William Chawner**
(in square punch, found 1764)

C
T·W
W   **Thomas Whipman** and **Charles Wright**
(in upright oval or circular punch, 1757)

CW   **Charles Woodward**
(in rectangular punch; 1741)

C & W Pt.   **Charles** and **Walter Padgett**
(in rectangular punch, 1902)

DH   **David Hennell**
(with or without pellet between, in plain rectangle, 1736; with pellet between and fleur-de-lis over in shaped punch, 1739)

Do   **Downes, John**
(with fleur-de-lis above and below, in upright oval punch, 1697)

DS
BS   **Digby Scott** with **Benjamin** and **James Smith**
(in upright rectangular punch, found in 1810s)
IS

DT   **David Tanqueray**
(with sunburst over and pellet below, in quatrefoil-shaped punch, 1720)

DW   **David Willaume I**
(with two stars over and trefoil (?) below, shaped shield, 1720)

DW   **David Willaume II**
(italic letters with a six-point star above and below, in quatrefoil-shaped punch, 1739; in rectangular punch, 1728)

DY   **Dymond, Edward**
(with star above and below, in diamond-shaped punch, 1722)

EA   **Edward Aldridge**
(in rectangular punch, 1724; italic letters with pellet between, in shaped square punch, 1739; with star between, in rectangular punch, found 1762; with pellet between, found 1763)

E & Co   **Elkington & Co Ltd**
(in nipped oval punch, 1890; '&' surmounting 'E' and 'Co', in trilobed punch, 1913)

EC   **Eckfourd, John**
(in nipped oval punch, 1698)

EC   **Edward Cornock**
(in bordered oval punch, 1723)

ED   **Edward Dymond**
(with pellet above and below, in diamond-shaped punch, 1722)

E E
B   **Edward Barnard** with **Edward jr, John & William**
(in quatrefoil-shaped punch, 1829)
J W

EF   **Edith Fletcher**
(with fleur-de-lis above and pellet below, in diamond-shaped punch, entered between 1729 and 1732)

EF   **Edward Feline**
(with bird over and star under, in shaped punch, 1720; italic caps with pellet over, in cinquefoil punch, 1739; the same in almost shield-shape punch, 1739)

EH   **Edward Hutton**
(Gothic letters in shaped square punch, 1880)

E·I   **Edward Jennings**
(crowned in shaped oval punch, 1720)

E J
B   **E. J. Barnard** and **W. Barnard**
& W   (in quatrefoil-shaped punch, 1846)

EL   **Edward Lambe**
(italic caps over a ring, in rounded punch, 1740)

EM   **Edward** and **Joseph Mappin**
JM   (in rectangular punch, 1863)

E T   **Elizabeth Tuite**
(with ewer between initials, in square punch, 1741)

EV   **Edward Vincent**
(with crescent above and ring below, 1720)

EW   **Edward Wakelin**
(Gothic caps under feathers in shaped punch, 1747)

EW   **Edward Wood**
(with pellet above and below, in oval punch, 1722; with star above and pellet (?) under, in oval punch, 1722; crowned EW in Gothic caps, in oval punch, 1740)

F   **Fawdery, Hester**
(in lozenge-shaped punch, 1727)

FA   **Farren, Thomas**
(with fleur-de-lis over and star below, in rectangle with semicircular top and bottom, 1707)

Fa   **Fawdery, John**
(in rectangular punch with canted corners, 1697)

FA   **Fawdery, William**
(in bordered circular punch, found 1708; in circular punch, 1707)

Fa   **Fawler, Thomas**
(in shield-shaped punch, 1707)

F·B·T·   **Francis Boone Thomas**
(with feathers over in shaped rectangular punch, 1887)

Fe   **Feline, Edward**
(with bird over and star below, in quatrefoil-shaped punch, 1720; in trefoil-shaped punch, found 1720)

F
G·S   **Francis Crump** and **Gabriel Sleath**
C   (in upright rectangle with canted corners, 1753)

FG   **Francis Garthorne**
(over star in shield-shaped punch, found 1725)

FK   **Charles Frederick Kandler**
(with crown over and mullet below, in shaped rectangular punch, 1735; italic caps under fleur-de-lis in shaped punch, 1739; with pellet between, ascribed to him, found 1776)

FL   **Fleming, William**
(crowned, in shield-shaped punch, 1697)

FN   **Francis Nelme**
(italic caps in monogram, in shaped shield, 1722; initials FN in
cartouche, 1739)

GA   **Garthorne, George**
(with crown above and crescent below, in semi-shield-shaped punch,
1697)

G   **Garthorne, Francis**
enclosing A   (in shield-shaped punch, 1697)

GA   **George W. Adams**
(in shaped punch, 1840)

GH   **George Heming** and **William Chawner**
WC   (in rectangle, recorded 1781)

GI   **George Jones**
(under crowned rose, in shaped punch, 1726; in italic caps in
rectangular punch, 1739)

GJ   **George Jackson** and **David Fullerton**
DF   (in shield-shaped punch, 1897)

GM   **Gilbert Marks**
(cursive letters, in rectangular punch with canted corners, 1896)

G of H Ltd   **Guild of Handicrafts Ltd**
(G enclosing 'of', in rectangular punch with canted corners, 1900)

G   **George Hindmarsh** and **Robert Abercromby**
R·A   (rectangular punch with canted corners, 1731)
H

GR   **Green, Samuel**
(with animal above and pellet below, in shield-shaped punch, 1721)

GR   **Greene, Henry**
(with two pellets above and a ring below, in roughly shield-shaped
punch, 1700)

Gr   **Green, David**
(Gothic caps with crown over, in shaped punch, 1701)

Gr   **Greene, Nathaniel**
(Gothic letters over fleur-de-lis in shield-shaped punch, 1698)

G   **Green, Richard**
enclosing R   (the G large, enclosing the R small, in shield-shaped punch, 1703)

GRE   **George Richards Elkington**
(in nipped oval punch, 1851)

GS   **Gabriel Sleath**
(with mullet below, in shaped rectangular punch, 1720; italic letters in
oval punch, 1739)

G·S **George Smith**
(in plain rectangular punch, 1732; in italic caps in rectangular punch, 1739)

G & S Co Ltd **Goldsmiths and Silversmiths Co. Ltd**
(in heart-shaped punch, 1899, with later variations; in rectangular punch, 1906)

GS **George Smith** and **Thomas Hayter**
TH (in square punch, 1792)

GU **Gulliver, Nathaniel**
(in diamond-shaped punch, 1722)

GW **George Wickes**
(with crown above, in shaped rectangular punch, 1735; italic letters with feathers above, 1739)

G **George Wickes**
enclosing W (large G enclosing small W in square punch with canted corners, 1722)

H & Co. Ltd **Heming & Co. Ltd**
(in trefoil-shaped punch, 1912)

H & R **Hunt & Roskell**
Ltd (crowned, 1897; in shield-shaped punch, 1901)

H & A **Holland, Aldwinkle & Slater**
S (in trefoil-shaped punch, 1902; in triangular punch with canted corners, 1905)

HA **Hanet, Paul**
(with (?) pellet above and below, in shield-shaped punch, 1717)

HA **Harache, Pierre**
(initials under crown and crescent, in shaped punch, 1697)

HA **Hatfield, Charles**
(with pellet above and rose or mullet (?) below, in rectangular punch with semicircular top and bottom, 1727)

HB **Hester Bateman**
(italic initials in plain or shaped rectangular punch, between 1761 and 1787)

HC **Henry Cowper**
(italic letters in small rectangular punch, 1782)

HC **Henry Chawner** and **John Emes**
IE (in oval, 1796)

HG **Henry Greene**
(with pellet above and below, in quatrefoil-type punch, 1720)

H·G **Henry Greenway**
(in plain rectangular punch, 1775)

HH **Henry Hayens**
(initials conjoined, in nearly square punch, 1749)

H·H   **Henry Hebert**
(in plain rectangle, 1733; with three crowns over, in shaped punch, 1734; italic HH crowned in shaped rectangle, 1739; HH with fleur-de-lis and crown over, in shaped punch, 1739)

HN   **Henry Nutting**
(in oblong punch, 1809)

HN
RH   **Henry Nutting** and **Robert Hennell**
(in square punch, 1808)

H
S·H   **Samuel Herbert & Co**
B   (in quatrefoil-shaped punch, 1750)

I·A   **John Allen**
(with fleur-de-lis over, in shaped rectangular punch, 1761)

IB   **John Bignell**
(in small oval punch, 1720)

I·B   **John Bridge**
(in plain rectangular punch; or crowned in shaped rectangular punch; both 1823)

IC   **John Chartier**
(with trefoil or fleur-de-lis over, in shaped punch, 1723)

IC
TH   **John Cotton** and **Thomas Head**
(in plain upright rectangular punch, 1809)

I·C
T·H   **John Crouch** and **Thomas Hannam**
(in shaped rectangle, 1773)

IC
WR   **Joseph Craddock** and **William Reid**
(in quatrefoil-shaped punch, 1812)

IE   **John Eckfourd I**
(in small rectangular punch, c.1720)

IE   **John Eckfourd II**
(under five-point star, in shaped punch, 1725)

I
EA   **John Stamper** and **Edward Aldridge**
S   (in cartouche-shaped punch, or quatrefoil-shaped punch, both 1753)

I+F   **John Fawdery**
(in square punch with canted corners, 1728)

IG   **James Gould**
(crowned in shaped rectangular punch, 1747; in Gothic letters with star over in shaped punch, 1739)

IG   **James Gould**
(monogram, in heart-shaped punch, 1722; with crown over in rectangular punch, c.1732–4)

IH
&   **John Hunt** and **Robert Roskell**
RR   (crowned, in rectangular punch or shaped oval punch, both 1865)

I·I   **James Jenkins**
(crowned in shaped rectangular punch, 1738; italic II with fleur-de-lis over, in shaped rectangular punch, 1731)

I·I   **John Jacob**
(with crown over and rosette below, in shaped rectangular punch, 1739)

I·I   **John Jones**
(crowned initials in tall shaped rectangular punch, 1729)

IL   **Jane Lambe**
(with paschal lamb over, in lozenge-shaped punch, entered between c.1719 and c.1722)

IL
HL   **John, Henry** and **Charles Lias**
CL   (in upright rectangular punch, 1823)

I·L   **John** and **Henry Lias**
H·L   (in square punch with canted corners, 1819)

I·M   **Jacob Marsh**
(in cartouche-shaped punch, 1744)

IO   **Jones, John**
(in oval punch, 1723)

IO   **Jones, Lawrence**
(italic letters, with crown over, in shield-shaped punch, 1697; crowned with mullet below, found 1697)

Io   **Jones, Edward**
(in heart-shaped punch with star above and below 'o', 1697)

I·P   **John Preist**
(in cartouche, 1748)

IP   **Joseph Preedy**
(with mullet between, in rectangular punch, 1800)

I·P   **John Parker** and **Edward Wakelin**
E·W   (with large fleur-de-lis over, in cartouche, after 1758)

IS   **James Smith**
(italic caps in plain rectangular punch, 1744)

IS   **James Smith**
(under a star, in shaped rectangular punch, 1720)

IS   **John Le Sage**
(italic letters with crown over and rosette below, in cartouche-shaped punch, 1739; Roman letters with chalice and crown over and pellet below, in trilobed punch, 1722)

I·S   **Joseph Smith**
(in oval punch, 1728)

ISH   **John S. Hunt**
(with crown over, in trefoil-shaped punch, 1844)

I T   **John Tuite**
(with ewer emblem between, in shaped punch, 1739)

IW   **J. Wisdome**
(with half-rosette (?) over, in shaped rectangular punch, 1720)

IW   **John White**
(italic caps under a pellet, in shaped punch, 1739)

I·W
R·G   **J. Wakelin** and **Robert Garrard**
(in rectangular punch, 1792)

I·W
W·T   **John Wakelin** and **William Taylor**
(with fleur-de-lis over, in shaped punch, 1776)

IWS
WE   **J. W. Story** and **W. Elliott**
(in rectangular punch, 1809)

J·A   **Jonathan Alleine**
(italic caps in plain rectangular punch, entered by 1771; JA in rectangular punch, 1777)

J·A
I·A   **John** and **Joseph Angell**
(with star between the two sets of initials, in quatrefoil-shaped punch, 1831)

JB   **James Beebe**
(in rectangular punch with slightly canted corners, 1811)

J·C   **John Crouch**
(in small rectangular punch with canted corners, 1808)

J.C.E   **James Charles Edington**
(in plain rectangular punch, 1828)

JE   **John Eckfourd**
(italic caps in rough quatrefoil-shaped punch, 1739)

J·E   **John Emes**
(in nipped oval punch, 1798; in italic caps, in quatrefoil-shaped punch, 1798)

JG   **James Garrard**
(italic letters, with crown over, in rectangular punch, 1881)

JH   **Joseph Heming**
(with pellet below, in trefoil-shaped punch, 1890)

JJ   **James Jenkins**
(italic caps under fleur-de-lis in shaped rectangular punch, 1731)

JJ   **James Jones**
(italic caps in shaped rectangular punch, 1755)

JJ   **John Jacobs**
(crowned italic letters over a mullet, in shaped punch, 1739)

JJ   **John Jones**
(italics in small plain rectangular punch, 1733)

Jo   **Jones, Lawrence**
(with coronet over, in shield-shaped punch, 1697)

J·W   **John Wirgman**
(italic letters in plain oblong punch, 1751)

KA   **Kandler, Charles**
(with mitre over and pellet below, in shaped punch, probably 1727)

KA
MU   **Kandler, Charles,** and **Murray, James**
(in shield-shaped punch with pellet below, 1727)

LA   **Lambe, George**
(with lamb over and ring below, in shaped rectangular punch, 1713)

LA   **Lambe, George,** widow of
(in lozenge-shaped punch, with lamb over, entered between 1719 and 1722)

LA   **Lamerie, Paul de**
(initials crowned between mullet and fleur-de-lis, in shaped punch, 1712)

LC   **Louisa Courtauld**
(initials in lozenge-shaped punch, found 1766)

LC
GC   **Louisa Courtauld** and **George Cowles**
(in rectangular or quatrefoil-shaped punch, both found 1772)

LC
SC   **Louisa** and **Samuel Courtauld**
(in rectangular punch, 1777)

le   **Ley, Petley**
(Gothic letters with pellet below, in square bordered punch with canted corners, 1715)

L·E   **Ley, Timothy**
(surrounded by a ring of six pellets and two stars, in a circular punch, 1697)

LL   **Louis Laroche**
(italic letters with coronet over and star below, in rectangular punch with rounded corners, 1739)

LP   **Lewis Pantin**
(in near-square rectangular punch, 1733; also LP in italic caps with pellet over, in shaped rectangular punch, 1739)

L
S*I   **Samuel Laundy** and **Jeffery Griffith**
G   (in oval punch, 1731)

Lu   **Lukin, William**
(Gothic letters over a pellet, in shield-shaped punch, 1699)

Ly & Co.   **Liberty & Co.**
(in rectangular punch with canted corners, 1899)

MA	**Margas, Jacob** (with anchor above, in trefoil-shaped punch, 1706. Marks ascribed to him: MA with crown over and crescent below, in shaped punch, found 1702; MA with crown over and (?) fleur-de-lis below, in shaped punch, found 1710)
MA	**Margas, Samuel** (crowned over fleur-de-lis in shaped punch, 1715)
MC	**Mark Cripps** (in small rectangular punch, 1767)
MC	**Mary Chawner** (in rectangular punch, 1834)
MC GA	**Mary Chawner** and **George W. Adams** (in quatrefoil-shaped punch, 1840)
MF	**Magdalen Feline** (italic letters conjoined, with pellet above and below, in lozenge-shaped punch, 1753)
MI	**Middleton, William** (with two pellets over and one under, in shield-shaped punch, 1700)
Mɴ Wʙ &	**Mappin & Webb Ltd** (in shield-shaped punch, 1889; in rectangular punch, 1898)
MP	**Mary Pantin** (initials with peacock over, in lozenge with semicircular head, 1733)
MS ES	**Mary** and **Elizabeth Sumner** (in broad oval punch, 1809)
N·G	**Nathaniel Gulliver** (in diamond-shaped punch, 1722)
NS	**Nicholas Sprimont** (italic letters with star over, in shaped punch, 1742)
P	**Pyne, Benjamin** (crowned in a cartouche-shaped punch, found 1726)
PA	**Pantin, Simon** (surmounted by peacock, in shaped punch, 1701)
PA	**Peter Archambo** (crowned in shaped punch, recorded 1722; italic letters in shaped punch, 1739)
PB AB	**Peter** and **Ann Bateman** (in square punch, 1791)
PB IB	**Peter** and **Jonathan Bateman** (in rectangular punch, 1790)
PB WB	**Peter** and **William Bateman** (in plain rectangular punch, 1805)

PC **Paul Crespin**
(with scallop above and star below, in shaped rectangular punch, c.1720; in oval punch, 1757; italic letters in nipped oval punch, 1739)

PE **Penstone, Henry**
(with two pellets over and one below, in shield-shaped punch, 1697)

PE **Penstone, William I**
(with star above and pellet below, in dot-bordered circular punch, 1697)

PE **Penstone, William II**
(with pellet above and below, in quatrefoil-shaped punch, 1717)

PE **Petley, William**
(with crown and pellet over and bird (?) under, upright rectangle with semicircular top and bottom, 1717; with crown over in circular bordered punch, 1699)

P·G **Peter Gillois**
(in rectangular punch, 1782)

I
P·G **Pierre Gillois**
(with crown over in shaped punch, 1754)

PH **Paul Hanet**
(with two pellets (?) over, in shaped punch, 1721)

PI **Pilleau, Pezé**
(with fleur-de-lis over in shaped punch, entred after 1720)

PL **Paul de Lamerie**
(with crowned star over and fleur-de-lis below, incised, 1732; italic caps between crown and pellet, in shaped punch, 1739)

PL **Platel, Pierre**
(with crown and mullet over, and fleur-de-lis under, 1699)

P·P **Pezé Pilleau**
(under fleur-de-lis in shaped rectangular punch, 1720; PP in italic caps under a star, in rounded punch, 1739)

PP **Philip Platel**
(in decorative oval, 1737)

PR *or* **P.R** **Philip Rundell**
(in plain rectangle, 1819)

PS *or* **P·S** **Paul Storr**
(in rectangular or nipped oval punch, 1793)

PY **Pyne, Benjamin**
(under crowned rose, in shaped punch, 1697; Gothic letters "Py" in dotted oval punch, 1697)

R·A **Robert Andrews**
(in shaped punch, 1745)

R·A **Robert Abercromby**
(under a coronet, in plain shaped punch, 1731; in nipped oval punch, with two pellets between, 1739)

RB   **Richard Beale**
(italic letters with crown over, in rectangular punch, 1739; with two
pellets above and one below, in heart-shaped punch, 1733; in
rectangular punch, found 1732)

RB&R   **Rundell, Bridge & Rundell**
(with crown centrally over, in rectangle with semicircular top
arranged to include the crown, found early 19th century)

R   **D. & R. Hennell**
D·H   (in cross-shaped rectangle, 1768)
H

RE   **Rebecca Emes** and **Edward Barnard**
EB   (in quatrefoil-shaped punch, 1808)

RG   **Richard Green**
(over star in heart-shaped punch, 1726)

R·G   **Robert Garrard**
(in rectangular punch with canted corners, 1802; cursive caps with
crown over, in shaped rectangular punch, 1822)

RG   **Garrard**
(with crown over in shaped rectangular punch, 1801)

RH   **Robert** and **David Hennell**
DH   (in rectangular punch, 1795)

R·H   **Robert Hennell**
(in oval punch, 1773; also RH in rectangular punch)

R·M   **Richard Mills**
(in plain rectangular punch, 1755)

RN & CR   **Ramsden, Omar,** and **Carr, Alwyn**
(in oval punch, 1910)

RR   **Robert Ross**
(italic letters in plain rectangular punch, 1774)

R·R   **Richard Rugg**
(in oblong punch, 1754; in nipped oval punch, 1775)

R·R   **Robert Rew**
(in rectangular punch, 1754)

R.R   **Hunt & Roskell**
A·R   (crowned, in rectangular punch, 1882)
I·M·H

RS   **Richard Sibley**
(italic letters in rectangular punch, 1812)

R·S   **Richard Sibley**
(in rectangular punch, 1805; in curvilinear punch, 1837)

R·W   **Robert Williams**
(with mitre over, in shaped rectangular punch, 1726)

SA   **Le Sage, John**
(crowned, with star above and pellet below, in shaped punch, 1718)

S·C   **Samuel Courtauld**
(with sun above, in trefoil-shaped punch, 1756; in oval punch 1751)

S
G·S   **G. and S. Smith**
S   (in quatrefoil-shaped punch, 1751)

SH   **Samuel Hennell**
(in concave-sided rectangular punch, 1811)

SL   **Samuel Lee**
(crowned initials in shaped shield, 1720)

SL   **Sleamaker, Daniel**
(with crown over and mullet below, in shaped punch, 1704)

SL   **Sleath, Gabriel**
(with chalice over, in shaped punch; over pellet in cartouche; 1706)

S.L   **Samuel Laundy**
(crowned in shaped rectangle: S:L in oval punch. Both 1727)

S·L   **Simon Le Sage**
(italic caps with goblet over and star below, in shaped cartouche
punch, 1754; italic letters in rectangular punch, 1754)

SM   **Samuel Margas**
(with crown over and mitre below, in shaped punch, 1721)

SM   **Smith, James**
(with mullet over in oval punch, 1718)

SM   **Smith, Samuel**
(with rosette over and fleur-de-lis below, in quatrefoil-shaped punch,
1719)

SM   **S. Mordan**
(in rectangular punch, 1843)

SM & Co   **S. Mordan & Co. Ltd**
(in rectangular or square punch, 1890)

SP *or* **S·P**   **Simon Pantin**
(with peacock over, in rectangle with semi-circular head, 1701 and
1717; a variant has the peacock predominantly larger, over SP in
small space, 1720)

SQ   **Squire, George**
(in flattened oval punch, 1720)

S·S   **Samuel Smith**
(in quatrefoil-shaped punch, 1754)

S·W   **Samuel Wood**
(in flattened oval punch, 1733; in shaped oblong punch, 1737; italic
letters in shaped punch, 1739; in flattened oval punch, 1756)

TA	**Tanqueray, Anne** (with mullet above and scallop below, in lozenge-shaped punch, c.1726)
TA	**Tanqueray, David** (with star above and scallop below, in rectangular punch with semicircular top and bottom, 1713)
TB	**Thomas Bamford** (in small oval punch, 1720; italic letters in shaped rectangular punch, 1739)
TC	**Thomas Chawner** (in rectangular punch, 1773 and 1775; with pellet between, 1782)
T·C·S	**Thomas Cox Savory** (in plain rectangular punch, 1827 and 1832)
T·C **W·C**	**T. & W. Chawner** (in square punch, 1765; mark ascribed)
TE	**Tearle, Thomas** (with mullet over and fleur-de-lis under, in lozenge-shaped punch, 1719)
T·H	**Thomas Heming** (italic caps with crown over, in shaped rectangular punch, 1767; TH in oval punch, 1745)
TH **GH**	**Thomas** and **George Hayter** (in square punch with canted corners, 1816; in quatrefoil-shaped punch, 1821)
TH **IC**	**Thomas Hannan** and **John Crouch** (in quatrefoil-shaped punch, 1799)
T·H **I·C**	**Thomas Hannan** and **John Carter** (in quatrefoil-shaped punch, c.1765)
TL	**Timothy Ley** (in ring of two stars and six pellets in a circular punch, 1728)
T.P **E.R**	**T. Phipps** and **E. Robinson** (in quatrefoil-shaped punch, 1783)
T **R·G** **C**	**Thomas Cooke** and **Richard Gurney** (in quatrefoil-shaped punch, 1727; punch as cross; 1734 without pellet, 1739)
TS **WS** **HH**	**Thomas, Walter** and **Henry Holland** (in nipped oval punch, 1895)
TT	**Thomas Tearle** (crowned with rosette over in shaped punch, 1720; italic T.T crowned, in curved shaped punch, 1739)
TW	**Thomas Whipham** (italic letters in shaped rectangular punch, 1739; with pellet between and rosette above, in shaped rectangular punch, 1737)

T.W   **Thomas Wallis** and **Jonathan Hayne**
J.H   (in square punch, 1810)

Wa   **Ward, Joseph**
(in plain rectangular punch, 1717; WA with anchor between, 1697)

WB   **William Bateman**
(cursive letters, in shaped rectangular punch, 1815)

WB   **William Bellassyse**
(with mitre over, in shaped rectangular punch, 1723)

W·B   **William Bateman**
(in curved punch, 1815)

W·B   **Walter Brind**
(in plain rectangular punch, 1749; also WB in shaped rectangular punch, 1757)

WB   **William Bateman** and **Daniel Ball**
DB   (in quatrefoil-shaped punch, 1839)

WBJ   **Walter** and **John Barnard**
(in shield-shaped punch, 1877)

W J   **Edward Barnard & Sons** (Walter, John and Stanley Barnard)
B   (in shield-shaped punch, 1896)
M S

W·B   **William Burwash** and **Richard Sibley**
R·S   (in plain rectangle, 1805)

WC   **William Cafe**
(Gothic caps with rosette over, in trefoil-shaped punch, 1758)

WC   **William Chawner**
(with pellet over, in rectangle with shaped top, 1817; in plain rectangle, 1815)

W.C   **William Cripps**
(in shaped rectangular punch, 1743)

W·E   **William Elliott**
(in plain rectangular punch, 1813)

W.F   **William Frisbee**
(in rectangular punch, 1792 and 1798; WF in shaped rectangular punch, 1801)

W.F   **William Frisbee** and **Paul Storr**
P.S   (in rectangular punch, 1792)

W   **George Heming** and **William Chawner**
G·H   (in vase-shaped punch, 1774)
C

Wh   **White, John**
(letters "Wh" conjoined, with pellet above and six-point star below, in cartouche, 1719)

WI   **Wickes, George**
(with fleur-de-lis over, in shaped rectangular punch, 1721)

WI   **Willaume, David**
(with two stars above, and fleur-de-lis under, in shield-shaped punch, 1697; another similar 1719; in plain rectangle, 1728)

WI   **Wisdome, J.**
(over fleur-de-lis, in cartouche, 1704; another similar 1717)

WI   **Williams, Robert**
(with mitre over, in shaped rectangle, 1726)

WL   **William Lukin**
(over a pellet, in shield-type punch, 1725)

W.O   **Wood, Edward**
(with pellet above and fleur-de-lis below, in circular punch, 1718)

WP   **William Penstone**
(in rectangular punch, the right end curved, 1772)

WP   **William Petley**
(with crowned mullet over, in near-heart-shaped punch, 1720)

WP
JP   **William and James Priest**
(intersected by cross in square punch with canted corners, 1768)

W.P
J.P   **William Pitts and Joseph Preedy**
(in circular punch, 1791)

W.T   **William Traies**
(in plain rectangular punch, 1822)

WT   **William Tuite**
(in flattened shield-shaped punch, 1756; W·T in oblong punch ascribed to him, 1758–72)

W
T C   **Thomas and William Chawner**
C   (in rectangular punch, ascribed, 1760s.)

WT
RA   **William Theobalds and Robert Atkinson**
(in plain square punch, 1838)

W
T·W   **Thomas Whipham and William Williams**
W   (in quatrefoil-shaped punch, 1740)

W.W   **William Woodward**
(with mullet above and below, in square punch with canted corners, 1731; initials W:W. in italic caps in oblong punch, 1743)

W
W·S   **William Shaw and William Preist**
P   (in punch resembling Maltese cross, 1749)

British Silversmiths – Birmingham

A   **Adie Brothers**
(with 'Bros Ltd', in diamond-shaped punch, 1907)

A.E.J.   **A. E. Jones**
(in oval punch, 1902)

BGHLd   **Birmingham Guild of Handicraft**
(in diamond-shaped punch, 1897)

C&B   **Cocks & Bettridge**
(in rectangular punch, 1806)

C.J.S   **Cyril Shiner**
(in rectangular punch, 1930)

D&H   **Deykin & Harrison**
(in Gothic letters, in rectangular punch or three separate punches, 1895; in Roman letters in three separate punches, 1924)

E&Co   **Elkington & Co. Ltd**
(in shield-shaped punch, 1843)

GN   **Nathan & Hayes**
RH   (in shield-shaped punch, 1894)

GU   **George Unite**
(in rectangular punch, 1838)

H & H   **Hukin & Heath Ltd**
(in separate oval or rectangular punches, 1875 and 1877; in oval punch, 1909)

HM   **H. Matthews**
(in separate square punches, 1896)

IB   **John Bettridge**
(in oval punch, 1822)

IT   **Joseph Taylor**
(in oval punch, 1787)

JB   **Joseph Bettridge**
(in oval or rectangular punch, 1829)

JH.&C?   **John Hardman & Co.**
(in elongated oval punch, 1863)

JTH   **Heath & Middleton**
JHM   (in quatrefoil-shaped punch, 1887)

J.W   **Joseph Willmore**
(with or without pellet, in oval punch, 1832)

L&Co   **Liberty & Co.**
(in three diamond-shaped punches conjoined, 1903)

MB   **Matthew Boulton**
(in rectangular punch, 1790)

45

MB IF   **Matthew Boulton & John Fothergill**
(in two separate punches, 1773)

MB   **Matthew Boulton & John Fothergill**
IF   (in square punch, 1773–1801)

ML   **Matthew Linwood**
(in rectangular punch; ML monogram in oval punch, 1807)

N&H   **Nathan & Hayes**
(in oval punch, 1891)

NM   **Nathaniel Mills**
(in rectangular punch, 1826)

SP   **Samuel Pemberton**
(italic letters in rectangular punch, 1783); in oval punch, 1784)

T&P   **Taylor & Perry**
(in rectangular punch, 1834)

Y&W   **Yapp & Woodward**
(in rectangular punch, 1846)

British Silversmiths – Chester

GL   **George Lowe I**
(in rectangular punch, 1791)

G.L   **George Lowe II**
(in nipped oval punch, 1820)

GL   **George Lowe** jnr
(in rectangular punch, 1853)

J.L   **John Lowe**
(in rectangular punch, 1826)

Ri   **Richard Richardson I**
(in shield-shaped punch, recorded 1701)

RL   **Robert Lowe**
(in oval punch)

ЯR   **Richard Richardson I and II**
(in shield-shaped punch, 1730)

R.R.   **Richard Richardson**
(in shield-shaped punch, 1739; without pellet, in rectangular punch, 1730; in shaped rectangular punch, 1730)

RR   **Richrd Richardson II and III**
(in shaped rectangular punch, 1769)

RR   **Richard Richardson IV**
(letters conjoined, in rectangular punch, 1778)

British Silversmiths – Edinburgh

AU   **Archibald Ure**
(in rectangular punch, 1715)

AZ   **Alexander Zeigler**
(in rectangular punch, 1792)

B&S   **Brook & Son**
(in rectangular punch, 1902)

E.L   **Edward Lothian**
(with crown over, 1734)

H&I   **Hamilton & Inches**
(italic letters in rectangular punch, 1880; Roman letters in rectangular punch, 1884)

HB   **Harry Beathune**
(in shaped oval punch, 1704)

HG   **Hugh Gordon**
(in shaped oval punch, 1731)

ID   **James Dempster**
(in oval punch, 1777)

I.K   **James Ker**
(in shaped rectangular punch, 1738)

IM   **James Mitchellsone**
(in shaped square punch, 1710)

IZ   **John Zeigler**
(in rectangular punch, 1798)

J&WM   **James** and **William Marshall**
(in rectangular punch, 1816)

JC&C   **James Crichton & Co.**
(italic letters in rectangular punch, 1891)

JC&Co.   **J. Crichton & Co.**
(first C enclosing &, in shaped rectangular punch, 1896)

JN   **James Nasmyth**
(in shaped rectangular punch, 1833)

JM   **J. McKay**
(in rectangular punch, 1813)

JN&Co   **James Nasmyth & Co.**
(in rectangular punch, 1840)

K&D   **Ker & Dempster**
(in rectangular punch, 1755)

L&R   **Lothian & Robertson**
(in rectangular punch, 1758)

M&C   **Mackay & Chisholm**
(in rectangular punch with undulating outline, 1849)

M&S   **Marshall & Sons**
(in rectangular punch, 1832)

MK   **Colin McKenzie**
(with pellet below in heart-shaped punch, 1700)

MY   **Mungo Yorstoun**
(in heart-shaped punch, 1702)

PC
&S   **P. Cunningham & Son**
(in square punch, 1807)

PM   **Patrick Murray**
(monogram in oval punch, 1705)

PR   **Patrick Robertson**
(in rectangular punch, 1768)

RG   **Robert Gordon**
(italic letters with crown over, in shaped punch, 1742)

RG
&S   **Robert Gray & Son**
(in square punch, 1810)

T   **James Taitt**
(with pellet above, in shield-shaped punch, 1704)

T.K   **Thomas Ker**
(in cinquefoil-shaped punch, 1715)

W&
PC   **William** and **Patrick Cunningham**
(in square punch, 1780)

WA   **William Auld**
(in nipped oval punch, 1803)

WA   **William Aytoun**
(in nipped oval punch, 1729)

W.C
PC   **William** and **Patrick Cunningham**
(in square punch, 1776)

WPC   **W. & P. Cunningham**
(in rectangular punch, 1797)

WZ   **William Zeigler**
(in rectangular punch, 1815)

EI **John Elston I**
(Gothic letters with crown over, in circular punch, 1701)

GF **George Ferris**
(in nipped oval punch, 1816)

JE **John Elston II**
(italic letters in shield-shaped punch, 1723)

JE **Thomas Eustace**
(italic letters in shaped punch, 1775)
See also **TE**

J.S. **John Stone**
(in rectangular punch, 1856; in nipped oval punch, 1840)

JW **James Williams**
(in rectangular punch, 1861)

J.W **Josiah Williams & Co.**
&Co (in quatrefoil-shaped punch)

JW **James and Josiah Williams**
& (in quatrefoil-shaped punch, 1866)
JW

PS **Pentecost Symonds**
(in shaped square punch, 1746)

RW **Robert, James and Josiah Williams**
JW (in rectangular punch, 1847)
JW

SB **Samuel Blachford**
(with crown over, in shaped punch, 1722)

SOBEY **W. R. Sobey**
(in rectangular punch, 1837)

Sp **Pentecost Symonds**
(Gothic letters, in oval punch, 1717)

TE **Thomas Eustace**
(in rectangular punch, 1785)

WRS **William Rawlings Sobey**
(in shaped oval punch, 1835)

British Silversmiths – Newcastle

A.R **Ann Robertson**
(in rectangular punch with canted corners, 1801)

Ba **Francis Batty**
(with star over, in semi-shield-shaped punch, 1703)

CJR **Reid & Sons** (mostly retailers rather than makers from mid-19th century)
(in oval punch with crown over, in shaped punch, 1868)

CR **Reid & Son**
DR (in square punch, 1819; in quatrefoil-shaped punch, 1828)

CR **Reid & Sons**
DR (in sexfoil punch, 1833)
CR

D.L **Dorothy Langlands**
(in oval punch, 1804)

DR **Reid & Sons**
(with crown over, in trefoil-shaped punch, 1845; in rectangular punch)

I.C **Isaac Cookson**
(with ring over, in trefoil-shaped punch, 1728)

JC **Isaac Cookson**
(italic letters, with ring over, in trefoil-shaped punch, 1738; italic letters in oval punch, 1746)

I.K **James Kirkup**
(in rectangular punch, 1722)

I.L **John Langlands I**
(with ring over, in rectangular punch, 1758)

I.L. **John Langlands II**
(in oval punch, 1795)

I.L **John Langlands** and **John Robertson**
I.R (in square punch with canted corners, 1778; with ring over, in rectangular punch, 1784)

IR **James Kirkup**
(Gothic letters in rectangular punch, 1720)

J:L **John Langlands I**
(with ring over in shaped punch, 1757)

Ki **James Kirkup**
(with two pellets above and star below, in shaped punch, 1719)

RM **Robert Makepeace**
(Gothic letters in rectangular punch, 1728); Roman letters with pellet between, in oval punch, 1738)

T.W. **Thomas Watson**
(in rectangular punch, 1793; TW in rectangular punch, 1816)

WB **William Beilby**
(with ring above in rectangular punch, 1738)

British Silversmiths – Glasgow

AG **Adam Graham**
(in rectangular punch, 1763)

AM **Alex Mitchell**
(in rectangular punch, 1822)

GLN **James Glen**
(in rectangular punch, 1743)

HM **Henry Muirhead**
(in rectangular punch, 1841)

IG **James Glen**
(in square punch, 1743)

IL **John Luke**
(in shield-shaped punch; with or without pellet between, in heart-shaped punch; all 1699)

JM **John Mitchell**
(in rectangular punch, 1834)

J&WM **J. & W. Mitchell**
(in rectangular punch, 1834)

M&C **Milne & Campbell**
(in rectangular punch, 1757)

M&R **Mitchell & Russell**
(in rectangular punch, 1803)

RG **Robert Gray**
(in plain or shaped rectangular punch, 1776)

**RG
&S** **Robert Gray & Son**
(in square punch, 1802; also as one line in rectangular punch, 1802)

WA&S **W. Alexander & Son**
(in rectangular punch, 1858)

British Silversmiths – Norwich

AH   **Arthur Hazelwood I**
(in shield-shaped punch, 1633; in shaped square punch, 1650)

AH   **Arthur Hazelwood II**
(letters conjoined, in shield-shaped punch, 1661)

EH   **Elizabeth Hazelwood**
(with crown over, in domed rectangular punch, 1688; in square punch with canted corners, 1691)

ID   **James Daniel**
(monogram in shaped square punch, 1691; with pellet between and two pellets and star below, 1696)

TH   **Thomas Havers**
(With mullet below in shield-shaped punch, 1675)

TS   **Timothy Skottowe**
(Monogram in shaped rectangular punch, 1626; monogram semi-shield-shaped punch, 1637)

British Silversmiths – Sheffield

AG&Co.   **Alex Goodman & Co.**
(in rectangular punch, 1801)

DH&Co.   **Daniel Holy & Co.**
(in rectangular punch, 1783)

EM&Co   **Elkington Mason & Co.**
(in oval punch, 1859)

G.A. &Co.   **George Ashworth**
(in square punch, 1772)

GE &Co   **George Eadon & Co**
(in rectangular punch, 1795)

H&H   **Howard & Hawksworth**
(in rectangular punch, 1835)

HE &Co   **Hawkesworth, Eyre & Co.**
(in quatrefoil punch, 1833)

HT&Co   **Henry Tudor & Co.**
(in rectangular punch, 1797)

HT TL   **Tudor & Leader**
(in square punch, 1773)

HW &Co   **Henry Wilkinson & Co.**
(in quatrefoil or shield-shaped punch, 1831)

IG&Co	**John Green & Co.** (in rectangular punch, 1793)
I.K.W&Co	**Kirkby, Waterhouse & Co.** (in rectangular punch, c.1813)
I.P. &Co.	**John Parsons & Co.** (in rectangular punch, 1783)
I.R.& Co.	**John Roberts & Co.** (in rectangular punch, 1805)
ITY **&Co.**	**J. T. Younge & Co.** (in rectangular punch, 1797)
ITY&Co.	**John Younge & Sons** (in rectangular punch, 1788)
IW&Co.	**John Winter & Co.** (in rectangular punch, 1773)
J.D **&S**	**James Deakin & Sons** (in shield-shaped punch, 1894)
J.D&S	**James Dixon & Son** (in shaped rectangular punch, 1867)
JD **WD**	**James Deakin & Sons** (in shield-shaped punch, 1878)
JR	**John Round & Son Ltd** (in oval, bordered punch, 1874)
M&W	**Mappin & Webb** (in shaped rectangular punch, 1892)
MB	**Mappin Bros** (in rectangular punch with rounded corners, 1859)
MF **&Co**	**M. Fenton & Co.** (in square punch, c.1790)
MF **RC**	**Fenton Creswick & Co.** (in square punch, 1773)
MH **&Co**	**Martin Hall & Co.** (in shield-shaped punch, 1854)
MW&Co	**Mappin & Webb** (Gothic letters in shaped rectangular punch, 1864)
N.S&Co.	**Nathaniel Smith & Co.** (in rectangular punch, 1780)
R&B	**Roberts & Belk** (in rectangular punch, 1892)
R.M	**Richard Morton & Co.** (in rectangular punch, 1773 and 1781; with '&Co' below in square punch, 1773)

RM EH	**Martin Hall & Co.** (in quatrefoil punch, 1863; in diamond-shaped punch, 1880)
SR&Co	**S. Roberts & Co.** (in rectangular punch, 1773)
ST N&H	**Smith, Tate & Co (Nicholson & Hoult)** (in rectangular punch, 1812)
TB &S	**Thomas Bradbury & Sons** (in shield-shaped punch, 1892)
TI NC	**T. J. & N. Creswick** (in square punch with canted corners, c.1827)
TJ&NC	**T. J. & N. Creswick** (in rectangular punch, 1819)
T.LAW	**Thomas Law** (in rectangular punch, 1773)
TW&Co	**Thomas Watson & Co.** (in rectangular punch, c.1801)
W&H	**Walker & Hall** (in rectangular punch, 1862; in flag-shaped punch, 1896)
WS GS	**W. & G. Sissons** (in quatrefoil-shaped punch, 1858)

British Silversmiths – York

H&P	**John Hampston** and **John Prince** (in rectangular punch with canted corners, 1784)
HP &C	**Hampston, Prince & Cattles** (in square punch, 1799)
I.H. I.P.	**John Hampston** and **John Prince** (in rectangular punch, 1779)
I I . H P	**John Hampston** and **John Prince** (in quatrefoil-shaped punch, 1787; in hexagonal punch, 1793)
JB	**James Barber** (in nipped oval punch, 1847)
JB GC WN	**James Barber, George Cattle** and **William North** (in rectangular punch, 1829)
JB WN	**James Barber** and **William North** (in square punch, 1836)

JB
WW   **James Barber** and **William Whitewell**
       (in square punch, 1812)

LA   **John Langwith**
       (in shield-shaped punch, 1702)

RC   **Robert Cattle** and **James Barber**
JB   (in square punch with canted corners, 1809)

Birmingham

Assay marking begun here 1773, and continues. Marks: an **anchor**, for "town" mark; **lion passant**, as standard mark; **Britannia figure**, for silver of 11 oz. 10 dwts; **Sovereign's head** as duty mark (1784–1890); **date letter**, formerly changed annually in July, from 1975 changed 1 January; **maker's mark**.

		1773–1798						1773–1798		
TM	LP	DL	SH		TM	LP	DL	SH		
🔱	🦁	A		1773/74	🔱	🦁	U	◆	1792/93	
		B		1774/75			V		1793/94	
		C		1775/76			W		1794/95	
		D		1776/77			X		1795/96	
		E		1777/78			Y		1796/97	
		F		1778/79			Z		1797/98	
		G		1779/80						

				1798–1824		
		H		1780/81	TM	LP	DL	SH	
		I		1781/82	🔱	🦁	a	👤	1798/99
		K		1782/83			b		1799/1800
		L		1783/84			c		1800/1
		M	◆	1784/85			d		1801/2
		N		1785/86			e		1802/3
		O		1786/87			f		1803/4
		P		1787/88			g		1804/5
		Q		1788/89			h		1805/6
		R		1789/90			i		1806/7
		S		1790/91			j		1807/8
		T		1791/92			k		1808/9

TM	LP	DL	SH		TM	LP	DL	SH	
⚓	🦁	l	🐦	1809/10	⚓	🦁	K	●	1833/34
		m		1810/11			L		1834/35
		n		1811/12			M		1835/36
		o		1812/13			N		1836/37
		p		1813/14			O		1837/38
		q		1814/15			P	●	1838/39
		r		1815/16			Q		1839/40
		s		1816/17			R		1840/41
		t		1817/18			S		1841/42
		u		1818/19			T		1842/43
		u		1819/20			U		1843/44
		v		1819/20			U		1843/44
		w		1820/21			V		1844/45
		x		1821/22			W		1845/46
		y		1822/23			X		1846/47
		z		1823/24			Y		1847/48
							Z		1848/49

1824–1849

TM	LP	DL	SH	
⚓	🦁	A	●	1824/25
		B		1825/26
		C		1826/27
		D		1827/28
		E		1828/29
		F		1829/30
		G		1830/31
		h		1831/32
		J		1832/33

1849–1875

TM	LP	DL	SH	
⚓	🦁	A	●	1849/50
		B		1850/51
		C		1851/52
		D		1852/53
		E		1853/54
		F		1854/55
		G		1855/56
		H		1856/57

TM	LP	DL	SH	
⚓	🦁	I	●	1857/58
		J		1858/59
		K		1859/60
		L		1860/61
		M		1861/62
		N		1862/63
		O		1863/64
		P		1864/65
		Q		1865/66
		R		1866/67
		S		1867/68
		T		1868/69
		U		1869/70
		V		1870/71
		W		1871/72
		X		1872/73
		Y		1873/74
		Z		1874/75

TM	LP	DL	SH	
⚓	🦁	h	●	1882/83
		i		1883/84
		k		1884/85
		l		1885/86
		m		1886/87
		n		1887/88
		o		1888/89
		p		1889/90
		q		1890/91
		r		1891/92
		s		1892/93
		t		1893/94
		u		1894/95
		v		1895/96
		w		1896/97
		x		1897/98
		y		1898/99
		z		1899/1900

1875–1900

TM	LP	DL	SH	
⚓	🦁	a	●	1875/76
		b		1876/77
		c		1877/78
		d		1878/79
		e		1879/80
		f		1880/81
		g		1881/82

1900–1925

TM	LP	DL	
⚓	🦁	a	1900/1
		b	1901/2
		c	1902/3
		d	1903/4
		e	1904/5
		f	1905/6
		g	1906/7

TM	LP	DL		TM	LP	DL	SH	
⚓	🦁	h	1907/8	⚓	🦁	H		1932/33
		i	1908/9			J	🛡	1933/34
		k	1909/10			K		1934/35
		l	1910/11			L		1935/36
		m	1911/12			M		1936/37
		n	1912/13			N		1937/38
		o	1913/14			O		1938/39
		p	1914/15			P		1939/40
		q	1915/16			Q		1940/41
		r	1916/17			R		1941/42
		s	1917/18			S		1942/43
		t	1918/19			T		1943/44
		u	1919/20			U		1944/45
		v	1920/21			V		1945/46
		w	1921/22			W		1946/47
		x	1922/23			X		1947/48
		y	1923/24			Y		1948/49
		z	1924/25			Z		1949/50

1925–1950

TM	LP	DL	
⚓	🦁	A	1925/26
		B	1926/27
		C	1927/28
		D	1928/29
		E	1929/30
		F	1930/31
		G	1931/32

1950–1974

TM	LP	DL	SH	
⚓	🦁	A		1950/51
		B		1951/52
		C	🛡	1952/53
		D		1953/54

TM	LP	DL		TM	LP	DL	
⚓	🦁	*E*	1954/55	⚓	🦁	*Z*	July–Dec 1974
		F	1955/56				
		G	1956/57			1975–	
		H	1957/58	TM	LP	DL	
		I	1958/59	⚓	🦁	*A*	1975
		K	1959/60			*B*	1976
		L	1960/61			*C*	1977
		M	1961/62			*D*	1978
		N	1962/63			*E*	1979
		O	1963/64			*F*	1980
		P	1964/65			*G*	1981
		Q	1965/66			*H*	1982
		R	1966/67			*I*	1983
		S	1967/68			*K*	1984
		T	1968/69			*L*	1985
		U	1969/70			*M*	1986
		V	1970/71			*N*	1987
		W	1971/72			*O*	1988
		X	1972/73			*P*	1989
⚓		*Y*	1973/74			*Q*	1990
						R	1991
						S	1992

The Anchor with two Cs was struck in 1973 to mark Birmingham's bicentenary year. It was used only on silver and for marks down to a certain size so that the two Cs would be apparent.

Chester

Plate assayed here from early 15th century; marks regulated about end 17th century; the Chester assay office re-established 1701; closed end 1961. Marks: **three wheatsheaves** with **sword**, as "town" mark (1686–1701, and 1779 onward); LING recorded between 1683 and 1700; **three wheatsheaves/three lions halved**, from 1701 to 1779; **leopard's head**, crowned 1719–1823, uncrowned 1823–39, then disused; **lion's head erased** and **Britannia**, 1701–19; **Sovereign's head**, as duty mark, 1784–1890; **date letter**, changed annually in July; **lion passant**, after 1719; **maker's mark**.

STER

1686/90

1701–1726				
TM	B	LHE	DL	
			A	1701/2
			B	1702/3
			C	1703/4
			D	1704/5
			E	1705/6
			F	1706/7
			G	1707/8
			H	1708/9
			I	1709/10
			K	1710/11
			L	1711/12
			M	1712/13
			N	1713/14
			O	1714/15
			P	1715/16
			Q	1716/17
			R	1717/18
			S	1718/19

TM	LP	LHC	DL	
			T	1719/20
			U	1720/21
			V	1721/22
			W	1722/23
			X	1723/24
			Y	1724/25
			Z	1725/26

1726–1751				
TM	LP	LHC	DL	
			A	1726/27
			B	1727/28
			C	1728/29
			D	1729/30
			E	1730/31
			F	1731/32
			G	1732/33
			H	1733/34
			I	1734/35

TM	LP	LHC	DL		TM	LP	LHC	DL	
🛡	🦁	👤	K	1735/36	🛡	🦁	👤	K	1760/61
			L	1736/37				L	1761/62
			M	1737/38				m	1762/63
			N	1738/39				n	1763/64
			O	1739/40				O	1764/65
			P	1740/41				P	1765/66
			Q	1741/42				Q	1766/67
			R	1742/43				R	1767/68
			S	1743/44				S	1768/69
			T	1744/45				T	1769/70
			U	1745/46				U	1771/72
			V	1746/47				V	1773
			W	1747/48				W	1774
			X	1748/49				X	1775
			Y	1749/50				Y	1775/76
			Z	1750/51					

1751–1776

TM	LP	LHC	DL	
🛡	🦁	👤	a	1751/52
			b	1752/53
			c	1753/54
			d	1754/55
			e	1755/56
			f	1756/57
			G	1757/58
			h	1758/59
			I	1759/60

1776–1797

TM	LP	LHC	DL	SH	
🛡	🦁	👤	a		1776/77
			b		1777/78
			c		1778/79
👤			d		1779/80
			e		1780/81
			f		1781/82
			g		1782/83
			h		1783/84
			i		1784/85
			i	👤	1784/85

TM	LP	LHC	DL	SH	
			K		1785/86
			l		1786/87
			m		1787/88
			n		1788/89
			o		1789/90
			p		1790/91
			q		1791/92
			r		1792/93
			s		1793/94
			t		1794/95
			u		1795/96
			v		1796/97

1797–1818

TM	LP	LHC	DL	SH	
			A		1797/98
			B		1798/99
			C		1799/1800
			D		1800/1
			E		1801/2
			F		1802/3
			G		1803/4
			H		1804/5
			I		1805/6
			K		1806/7
			L		1807/8
			M		1808/9
			N		1809/10

TM	LP	LHC	DL	SH	
			O		1810/11
			P		1811/12
			Q		1812/13
			R		1813/14
			S		1814/15
			T		1815/16
			U		1816/17
			V		1817/18

1818–1839

TM	LP	LHC	DL	SH	
			A		1818/19
			B		1819/20
			C		1820/21
			D		1821/22/23
		LH	E		1823/24
			F		1824/25
			G		1825/26
			H		1826/27
			I		1827/28
			K		1828/29
			L		1829/30
			M		1830/31
			N		1831/32
			O		1832/33
			P		1833/34
			Q		1834/35
			R		1835/36

TM	LP	LH	DL	SH	
			S		1836/37
			T		1837/38
			U		1838/39

1839–1864

TM	LP	DL	SH	
		A		1839/40
		B		1840/41
		C		1841/42
		D		1842/43
		E		1843/44
		F		1844/45
		G		1845/46
		H		1846/47
		I		1847/48
		K		1848/49
		L		1849/50
		M		1850/51
		N		1851/52
		O		1852/53
		P		1853/54
		Q		1854/55
		R		1855/56
		S		1856/57
		T		1857/58
		U		1858/59
		V		1859/60

TM	LP	DL	SH	
		W		1860/61
		X		1861/62
		Y		1862/63
		Z		1863/64

1864–1884

TM	LP	DL	SH	
		a		1864/65
		b		1865/66
		c		1866/67
		d		1867/68
		e		1868/69
		f		1869/70
		g		1870/71
		h		1871/72
		i		1872/73
		k		1873/74
		l		1874/75
		m		1875/76
		n		1876/77
		o		1877/78
		p		1878/79
		q		1879/80
		r		1880/81
		s		1881/82
		t		1882/83
		u		1883/84

		1884–1903		
TM	LP	DL	SH	
🛡	🦁	**A**	👤	1884/85
		B		1885/86
		C		1886/87
		D		1887/88
		E		1888/89
		F		1889/90
		G		1890/91
		H		1891/92
		I		1892/93
		K		1893/94
		L		1894/95
		M		1895/96
		N		1896/97
		O		1897/98
		P		1898/99
		Q		1899/1900
		R		1900/1
		A		1901/2
		B		1902/3

	1903–1926		
TM	LP	DL	
🛡	🦁	**C**	1903/4
		D	1904/5
		E	1905/6
		F	1906/7

TM	LP	DL	
🛡	🦁	*G*	1907/8
		H	1908/9
		I	1909/10
		K	1910/11
		L	1911/12
		M	1912/13
		N	1913/14
		O	1914/15
		P	1915/16
		Q	1916/17
		R	1917/18
		S	1918/19
		T	1919/20
		U	1920/21
		V	1921/22
		W	1922/23
		X	1923/24
		Y	1924/25
		Z	1925/26

	1926–1951		
TM	LP	DL	
🛡	🦁	**a**	1926/27
		b	1927/28
		c	1928/29
		d	1929/30
		e	1930/31

TM	LP	DL	SH		TM	LP	DL	
▦	▦	ff		1931/32	▦	▦	W		1947/48
		G		1932/33			X		1948/49
		H	●	1933/34			Y		1949/50
		J		1934/35			Z		1950/51

TM	LP	DL	SH	
		K		1935/36

1951–1961

TM	LP	DL	SH	
		L		1936/37
▦	▦	A		1951/52

TM	LP	DL	SH	
		W		1937/38
		B	●	1952/53
		N		1938/39
		C		1953/54
		O		1939/40
		D		1954/55
		P		1940/41
		E		1955/56
		Q		1941/42
		F		1956/57
		R		1942/43
		G		1957/58
		S		1943/44
		H		1958/59
		T		1944/45
		J		1959/60
		U		1945/46
		K		1960/61
		V		1946/47

Edinburgh

Plate marked here from 1457 onwards. Marks: **three-towered castle** as "town" mark (from 1485 onwards); **deacon's mark** (1457–1681); **Assay Master's mark** (1681–1759); **thistle mark** (1759–1974); **lion rampant** (1975 onwards); **Sovereign's head**, as duty mark (1784–1890); **date letter** (from 1681) formerly changed annually in October; from 1975 changed 1 January; **maker's mark**.

TM	DM		TM	DM	
🯄	🯄	1552/62	🯄	🯄	1642
	🯄 IC	1563/64			
	🯄	1570		🯄	1644/46
	🯄	1576		🯄 GG	1649
	🯄 M	1585/86		🯄	1651/59
	🯄	1590/91		🯄 B	1660
	🯄	1591/92		🯄 S	1665/67
	🯄	1591/94		🯄 S	1665
	🯄	1596/1600		🯄	1669/75
	🯄	1609/10		🯄 E	1663/81
🯄	🯄	1611/13		🯄 W	1675/77
	🯄 IL	1617/19			

	🯄 G	1617
	🯄	1613/21
	🯄 G	1616/35
	🯄 R	1633

1681–1705

TM	AM	DL	
🯄	🯄 B	🯄	1681/82
	🯄 B	🯄	1682/83
		🯄 C	1683/84
		🯄 D	1684/85
		🯄 E	1685/86
		🯄 F	1686/87
		🯄 G	1687/88

1637–1677

TM	DM	
🯄	🯄	1637/39
	🯄	1640/42

TM	AM	DL	
🏰	𝐵	h	1688/89
		i	1689/90
		k	1690/91
		l	1691/92
		m	1692/93
		n	1693/94
		o	1694/95
		p	1695/96
	♥P	q	1696/97
		r	1697/98
		s	1698/99
		t	1699/1700
		u	1700/1
		w	1701/2
		x	1702/3
		y	1703/4
		z	1704/5

TM	AM	DL	
🏰	EP	K	1714/15
		L	1715/16
		M	1716/17
		N	1717/18
	EP	N	1717/18
		O	1718/19
		P	1719/20
	EP	P	1719/20
		Q	1720/21
		R	1721/22
		S	1722/23
		T	1723/24
		U	1724/25
		V	1725/26
		W	1726/27
		X	1727/28
		Y	1728/29
		Z	1729/30
	AU	Z	1729/30

1705–1730

TM	AM	DL	
🏰	♥T	A	1705/6
		B	1706/7
	EP	C	1707/8
		D	1708/9
		E	1709/10
		F	1710/11
		G	1711/12
		H	1712/13
		I	1713/14

1730–1755

TM	AM	DL	
🏰	AU	A	1730/31
		B	1731/32
		C	1732/33
		D	1733/34
		E	1734/35
		F	1735/36
		G	1736/37

TM	AM	DL		TM	T	DL	
🏰	AU	𝕳	1737/38	🏰	🗦	𝕴	1763/64
		𝕴	1738/39			𝕶	1764/65
		𝕶	1739/40			𝕷	1765/66
	GED	𝕷	1740/41			𝕸	1766/67
		𝕸	1741/42			𝕹	1767/68
	EL	𝕹	1742/43			𝕺	1768/69
		𝕺	1743/44			𝕻	1769/70
	HG	𝕻	1744/45			𝕼	1770/71
		𝕼	1745/46			𝕽	1771/72
		𝕽	1746/47			𝕾	1772/73
		𝕾	1747/48			𝕿	1773/74
		𝕿	1748/49			𝖀	1774/75
		𝖀	1749/50			𝖁	1775/76
		𝖀	1750/51			𝖂	1776/77
		𝖂	1751/52			𝖃	1777/78
		𝖃	1752/53			𝖅	1778/79
		𝖄	1753/54			𝖀	1779/80
		𝖅	1754/55				

1755–1780

TM	AM	DL	
🏰	HG	𝕬	1755/56
		𝕭	1756/57
		𝕮	1757/58
	T	𝕯	1758/59
	🗦	𝕰	1759/60
		𝕱	1760/61
		𝕲	1761/62
		𝕳	1762/63

1780–1806

TM	T	DL	SH	
🏰	🛡	A		1780/81
		B		1781/82
		C		1782/83
		D		1783/84
		E	🖐	1784/85
		F		1785/86
		G	🖐	1786/87/88
		H		1788/89
		IJ		1789/90

TM	T	DL	SH	
丗	疹	**K**	❷	1790/91
		L		1791/92
		M		1792/93
		N		1793/94
		O		1794/95
		P		1795/96
		Q		1796/97
		R	❀	1797/98
		S		1798/99
		T		1799/1800
		U		1800/1
		V		1801/2
		W		1802/3
		X		1803/4
		Y		1804/5
		Z		1805/6

TM	T	DL	SH	
丗	疹	**j**	❷	1815/16
		k		1816/17
		l		1817/18
		m		1818/19
		n		1819/20
		o		1820/21
		p		1821/22
		q		1822/23
		r	❀	1823/24
		S		1824/25
		t		1825/26
		u		1826/27
		v		1827/28
		w		1828/29
		x		1829/30
		y		1830/31
		Z		1831/32

1806–1832

TM	T	DL	SH	
丗	疹	**a**	❷	1806/7
		b		1807/8
		c		1808/9
		d		1809/10
		e		1810/11
		f		1811/12
		g		1812/13
		h		1813/14
		i		1814/15

1832–1857

TM	T	DL	SH	
丗	疹	**A**	❷	1832/33
		B		1833/34
		C		1834/35
		D		1835/36
		E		1836/37
		F		1837/38
		G		1838/39
		H		1839/40

TM	T	DL	SH	
		J		1840/41
		K		1841/42
		L		1842/43
		M		1843/44
		N		1844/45
		O		1845/46
		P		1846/47
		Q		1847/48
		R		1848/49
		S		1849/50
		T		1850/51
		U		1851/52
		V		1852/53
		W		1853/54
		X		1854/55
		Y		1855/56
		Z		1856/57

TM	T	DL	SH	
		I		1865/66
		K		1866/67
		L		1867/68
		M		1868/69
		N		1869/70
		O		1870/71
		P		1871/72
		Q		1872/73
		R		1873/74
		S		1874/75
		T		1875/76
		U		1876/77
		V		1877/78
		W		1878/79
		X		1879/80
		Y		1880/81
		Z		1881/82

1857–1882

TM	T	DL	SH	
		A		1857/58
		B		1858/59
		C		1859/60
		D		1860/61
		E		1861/62
		F		1862/63
		G		1863/64
		H		1864/65

1882–1906

TM	T	DL	SH	
		a		1882/83
		b		1883/84
		c		1884/85
		d		1885/86
		e		1886/87
		f		1887/88
		g		1888/89
		h		1889/90

TM	T	DL	SH		TM	T	DL	
🔲	🔲	i	🔲	1890/91	🔲	🔲	I	1914/15
		k		1891/92			K	1915/16
		l		1892/93			L	1916/17
		m		1893/94			M	1917/18
		n		1894/95			N	1918/19
		o		1895/96			O	1919/20
		p		1896/97			P	1920/21
		q		1897/98			U	1921/22
		r		1898/99			R	1922/23
		s		1899/1900			S	1923/24
		t		1900/1			T	1924/25
		v		1901/2			U	1925/26
		w		1902/3			V	1926/27
		x		1903/4			W	1927/28
		y		1904/5			X	1928/29
		z		1905/6			Y	1929/30
							Z	1930/31

1906–1931

TM	T	DL					
🔲	🔲	A	1906/7				
		B	1907/8				
		C	1908/9				
		D	1909/10				
		E	1910/11				
		F	1911/12				
		G	1912/13				
		H	1913/14				

1931–1956

TM	T	DL	SH	
🔲	🔲	A		1931/32
		B		1932/33
		C	🔲	1933/34
		D		1934/35
		E		1935/36
		F		1936/37
		G		1937/38
		H		1938/39

TM	T	DL	SH	
		I		1939/40
		K		1940/41
		L		1941/42
		M		1942/43
		N		1943/44
		O		1944/45
		P		1945/46
		Q		1946/47
		R		1947/48
		S		1948/49
		T		1949/50
		U		1950/51
		V		1951/52
		W		1952/53
		X		1953/54
		Y		1954/55
		Z		1955/56

1956–1974

TM	T	DL	
		A	1956/57
		B	1957/58
		C	1958/59
		D	1959/60
		E	1960/61
		F	1961/62
		G	1962/63
		H	1963/64
		I	1964/65
		K	1965/66
		L	1966/67
		M	1967/68
		N	1968/69
		O	1969/70
		P	1970/71
		Q	1971/72
		R	1972/73
		S	Oct 73–Dec 1974

1975–

TM	LR	DL	
		A	1975
		B	1976
		C	1977
		D	1978
		E	1979
		F	1980
		G	1981
		H	1982
		I	1983
		K	1984
		L	1985
		M	1986
		N	1987
		O	1988
		P	1989
		Q	1990
		R	1991
		S	1992

As from January 1975 the lion rampant (LR) replaces the thistle (T) as the standard mark.

Exeter

Assay office apparently not legally existing here before 1701, though making of wrought silver recorded in Middle Ages; office closed 1883. Marks: **Roman capital letter "X"** as "town" mark, 16th and 17th centuries; sometimes found crowned; **three-towered turreted castle**, as "town" mark, from 1700/1; **leopard's head**, up to 1776; **Britannia**, and **lion's head erased**, to 1719; **Sovereign's head**, as duty mark, 1784–1890; **date letter**, begun November 1701, then changed annually in August from 1702; **maker's mark**.

1570	1590	1635	1640/50	1646/98	1680

TM	B	LHE	DL		TM	B	LHE	DL	
			A	1701/2				S	1718/19
			B	1702/3				T	1719/20
			C	1703/4		LHC	LP	V	1720/21
			D	1704/5				W	1721/22
			E	1705/6				X	1722/23
			F	1706/7				Y	1723/24
			G	1707/8				Z	1724/25
			H	1708/9					
			I	1709/10					
			K	1710/11			**1725–1749**		
			L	1711/12	TM	LHC	LP	DL	
			M	1712/13				a	1725/26
			N	1713/14				b	1726/27
			O	1714/15				c	1727/28
			P	1715/16				d	1728/29
			Q	1716/17				e	1729/30
			R	1717/18				f	1730/31
								g	1731/32

TM	LHC	LP	DL		TM	LHC	LP	DL	
🛡	🛡	🦁	h	1732/33	🛡	🛡	🦁	H	1756/57
			i	1733/34				I	1757/58
			k	1734/35				K	1758/59
			l	1735/36				L	1759/60
			m	1736/37				M	1760/61
			n	1737/38				N	1761/62
			o	1738/39				O	1762/63
			p	1739/40				P	1763/64
			q	1740/41				Q	1764/65
			r	1741/42				R	1765/66
			s	1742/43				S	1766/67
			t	1743/44				T	1767/68
			u	1744/45				U	1768/69
			w	1745/46				W	1769/70
			x	1746/47				X	1770/71
			y	1747/48				Y	1771/72
			z	1748/49				Z	1772/73

		1749–1773					1773–1797		
TM	LHC	LP	DL		TM	LHC	LP	DL	
🛡	🛡	🦁	A	1749/50	🛡	🛡	🦁	A	1773/74
			B	1750/51				B	1774/75
			C	1751/52				C	1775/76
			D	1752/53				D	1776/77
			E	1753/54				E	1777/78
			F	1754/55				F	1778/79
			G	1755/56				G	1779/80

TM	LP	DL	LHC	
🛡	🛡	H	🛡	1780/81
		I		1781/82/83
		K	SH	1783/84
		L	🛡	1784/85
		M		1785/86
		N	🛡	1786/87
		O		1787/88
		P		1788/89
		q		1789/90
		r		1790/91
		f		1791/92
		t		1792/93
		u		1793/94
		w		1794/95
		x		1795/96
		y		1796/97

TM	LP	DL	
🛡	🛡	I	1805/6
		K	1806/7
		L	1807/8
		M	1808/9
		N	1809/10
		O	1810/11
		P	1811/12
		Q	1812/13
		R	1813/14
		S	1814/15
		T	1815/16
		U	1816/17

1797–1817

TM	LP	DL	SH	
🛡	🛡	A	🛡	1797/98
		B		1798/99
		C		1799/1800
		D		1800/1
		E		1801/2
		F		1802/3
		G		1803/4
		H		1804/5

1817–1837

TM	LP	DL	SH	
🛡	🛡	a	🛡	1817/18
		b		1818/19
		c		1819/20
		d		1820/21
		e		1821/22
		f	🛡	1822/23
		g		1823/24
		h		1824/25
		i		1825/26
		k		1826/27
		l		1827/28
		m		1828/29

TM	LP	DL	SH	
𝕹	🦁	𝖓		1829/30
		𝖔		1830/31
		𝖕	◐	1831/32
		𝖖		1832/33
		𝖗		1833/34
		𝖘	◯	1834/35
		𝖙		1835/36
		𝖚		1836/37

1837–1857

TM	LP	DL	SH	
🛡	🦁	𝕬	◯	1837/38
		𝕭	◯	1838/39
		𝕮		1839/40
		𝕯		1840/41
		𝕰		1841/42
		𝕱		1842/43
		𝕲		1843/44
		𝕳		1844/45
		𝕴		1845/46
		𝕶		1846/47
		𝕷		1847/48
		𝕸		1848/49
		𝕹		1849/50
		𝕺		1850/51
		𝕻		1851/52
		𝕼		1852/53
		𝕽		1853/54

TM	LP	DL	
🛡	🦁	𝕾	1854/55
		𝕿	1855/56
		𝖀	1856/57

1857–1877

TM	LP	DL	SH	
🛡	🦁	𝗔	◉	1857/58
		𝗕		1858/59
		𝗖		1859/60
		𝗗		1860/61
		𝗘		1861/62
		𝗙		1862/63
		𝗚		1863/64
		𝗛		1864/65
		𝗜		1865/66
		𝗞		1866/67
		𝗟		1867/68
		𝗠		1868/69
		𝗡		1869/70
		𝗢		1870/71
		𝗣		1871/72
		𝗤		1872/73
		𝗥		1873/74
		𝗦		1874/75
		𝗧		1875/76
		𝗨		1876/77

		1877–1883								
TM	LP	DL	SII		TM	I.P	DL		
🖼	🦁	**A**	👤	1877/78	🖼	🦁	**D**	1880/81
		B		1878/79			**E**	1881/82
		C		1879/80			**F**	1882/83

Glasgow

Assay office established here in 1819. Marks: **lion rampant**, as "standard" mark; **Tree, fish**, and **bell** (city arms), as "town" mark; **Sovereign's head**, as duty mark, until 1890; **thistle mark**, added 1914; **date letter**, changed annually in July; **maker's mark**. N.B. A date letter was used on Glasgow wrought silver, 1681–1710; discontinued until 1819. Finally closed March 1964.

TM	DL		TM	DL	
🛡	𝖆	1681/82	🛡	𝖙	1699/1700
	𝖇	1682/83		𝖚	1700/1
	𝖈	1683/84		𝖛	1701/2
	𝖉	1684/85		𝖜	1702/3
	𝖊	1685/86		𝖝	1703/4
	𝖋	1686/87		𝖞	1704/5
	𝖌	1687/88		𝖟	1705/6
	𝖍	1688/89			
	𝖎	1689/90		**1706–1765**	
	𝖐	1690/91	🛡	𝐀	1706/7
	𝖑	1691/92		𝐁	1707/8
	𝖒	1692/93		𝐃	1709/10
	𝖓	1693/94		𝐒	1728/31
	𝖔	1694/95		𝐒	1725/35
	𝖕	1695/96		𝐒	1743/52
	𝖖	1696/97		𝐒	1747/60
	𝖗	1697/98		𝐒	1756/76
	𝖘	1698/99			

TM	DL	
Z		1756/76
		1757/80
		1757/80
		1757/80
	S	1758/65

TM	LR	DL	SH	
		K		1829/30
		L		1830/31
		M		1831/32
		N		1832/33
		O		1833/34
		P		1834/35
		Q		1835/36
		R		1836/37
		S		1837/38
		T		1838/39
		U		1839/40
		V		1840/41
		W		1841/42
		X		1842/43
		Y		1843/44
		Z		1844/45

1763–1800

TM	DL	
	E	1763/70
	F	1763/70
	S	1773/80
	O	1776/80
	O	1785/95
	S	1785/95
	S	1781/1800

1819–1845

TM	LR	DL	SH	
		A		1819/20
		B		1820/21
		C		1821/22
		D		1822/23
		E		1823/24
		F		1824/25
		G		1825/26
		H		1826/27
		I		1827/28
		J		1828/29

1845–1871

TM	LR	DL	SH	
		A		1845/46
		B		1846/47
		C		1847/48
		D		1848/49
		E		1849/50
		F		1850/51
		G		1851/52
		H		1852/53
		I		1853/54

TM	LR	DL	SH	
🛡	🦁	I	👤	1854/55
		K		1855/56
		L		1856/57
		M		1857/58
		N		1858/59
		O		1859/60
		P		1860/61
		Q		1861/62
		R		1862/63
		S		1863/64
		T		1864/65
		U		1865/66
		V		1866/67
		W		1867/68
		X		1868/69
		Y		1869/70
		Z		1870/71

TM	LR	DL	SH	
🛡	🦁	I	👤	1879/80
		I		1880/81
		K		1881/82
		L		1882/83
		M		1883/84
		N		1884/85
		O		1885/86
		P		1886/87
		Q		1387/88
		R		1888/89
		S		1889/90
		T		1890/91
		U		1891/92
		V		1892/93
		W		1893/94
		X		1894/95
		Y		1895/96
		Z		1896/97

1871–1897

TM	LR	DL	SH	
🛡	🦁	A	👤	1871/72
		B		1872/73
		C		1873/74
		D		1874/75
		E		1875/76
		F		1876/77
		G		1877/78
		H		1878/79

1897–1923

TM	LR	DL	
🛡	🦁	A	1897/98
		B	1898/99
		C	1899/1900
		D	1900/1
		E	1901/2
		F	1902/3
		G	1903/4

TM	LR	DL	T		Year
🛡	🦁	ℋ			1904/5
		𝒥			1905/6
		𝒥			1906/7
		𝒦			1907/8
		ℒ			1908/9
		ℳ			1909/10
		𝒩			1910/11
		𝒪			1911/12
		𝒫			1912/13
		𝒬			1913/14
		ℛ	🌹		1914/15
		𝒮			1915/16
		𝒯			1916/17
		𝒰			1917/18
		𝒱			1918/19
		𝒲			1919/20
		𝒳			1920/21
		𝒴			1921/22
		𝒵			1922/23

TM	LR	T	DL	SH	Year
🦁	🦁	🏰	f		1928/29
			g		1929/30
			h		1930/31
			i		1931/32
			j		1932/33
			k	🌹	1933/34
			l		1934/35
			m		1935/36
			n		1936/37
			o		1937/38
			p		1938/39
			q		1939/40
			r		1940/41
			s		1941/42
			t		1942/43
			u		1943/44
			v		1944/45
			w		1945/46
			x		1946/47
			y		1947/48
			z		1948/49

1923–1949

TM	LR	T	DL	Year
🛡	🦁	🏰	a	1923/24
			b	1924/25
			c	1925/26
			d	1926/27
			e	1927/28

1949– 1964

TM	LR	T	DL	Year
🛡	🦁	🏰	𝕬	1949/50
			𝕭	1950/51
			𝕮	1951/52

TM	LR	T	DL	SH	
🛡	🦁	🌳	𝕯	🐟	1952/53
			𝕰		1953/54
			𝕱		1954/55
			𝕲		1955/56
			𝕳		1956/57
			𝕴		1957/58

TM	LR	T	DL	
🛡	🦁	🌳	𝕷	1958/59
			𝕸	1959/60
			𝕹	1960/61
			𝕺	1961/62
			𝕻	1962/63
			𝕽	1963/64

83

Newcastle

Goldsmiths recorded working here from mid-13th century; some examples (later 17th century) have marks including a single castle ("town" mark), and a lion passant. Assay office re-established 1702, closed down 1884. Marks: **three** distinct **castles**, as "town" mark (from city arms), from *c.* 1670; **lion's head erased** and **Britannia**, 1702–19; **lion passant**, recorded 1721–28, facing right; **Sovereign's head**, as duty mark, 1784 to closure; **date letter**, changed annually with some regularity at first, later not consistently carried on; **maker's mark**.

1658

1702–1721

TM	B	LHE	DL	
				1702/3
				1703/4
				1704/5
				1705/6
				1706/7
				1707/8
				1708/9
				1709/10
				1710/11
				1711/12
				1712/13
				1713/14
				1714/15
				1715/16
				1716/17
				1717/18

TM	B	LHE	DL	
				1718/19
				1719/20
				1720/21

1721–1740

LP	LHC	DL	
			1721/22
			1722/23
			1723/24
			1724/25
			1725/26
			1726/27
			1727/28
			1728/29
			1729/30
			1730/31

TM	LP	LHC	DL	
🛡	🦁	🛡	L	1731/32
			O	1732/33
			N	1733/34
			O	1734/35
			P	1735/36
			Q	1736/37
			R	1737/38
			S	1738/39
			T	1739/40

1740–1759

TM	LP	LHC	DL	
🛡	🦁	🛡	A	1740/41
			B	1741/42
			C	1742/43
			D	1743/44
			E	1744/45
			F	1745/46
			G	1746/47
			H	1747/48
			I	1748/49
			K	1749/50
			L	1750/51
			M	1751/52
			N	1752/53
			O	1753/54

TM	LP	LHC	DL	
🛡	🦁	🛡	P	1754/55
			Q	1755/56
			R	1756/57
			S	1757/58
			T	1758/59

1759–1791

TM	LP	LHC	DL		
🛡	🦁	👑	A		1759/60
			B		1760/68
			C		1769/70
			D		1770/71
			E		1771/72
			F		1772/73
			G		1773/74
			H		1774/75
			I		1775/76
			K		1776/77
			L		1777/78
			M		1778/79
			N		1779/80
			O		1780/81
			P		1781/82
			Q		1782/83
			R	SH	1783/84
			S	👤	1784/85

TM	LP	LHC	DL	SH	
🛡	🦁	👑	T	👤	1785/86
			U	👤	1786/87
			W		1787/88
			X		1788/89
			Y		1789/90
			Z		1790/91

1791–1815

TM	LP	LHC	DL	SH	
🛡	🦁	👑	A	👤	1791/92
			B		1792/93
			C		1793/94
			D		1794/95
			E		1795/96
			F		1796/97
			G	👤	1797/98
			H		1798/99
			I		1799/1800
			K	👤	1800/1
			L		1801/2
			M		1802/3
			N	👤	1803/4
			O		1804/5
			P		1805/6
			Q		1806/7
			R		1807/8
			S		1808/9
			T	👤	1809/10

TM	LP	LHC	DL	SH	
🛡	🦁	👑	U	👤	1810/11
			W		1811/12
			X		1812/13
			Y		1813/14
			Z		1814/15

1815–1839

TM	LP	LHC	DL	SH	
🛡	🦁	👑	A	👤	1815/16
			B		1816/17
			C		1817/18
			D		1818/19
			E		1819/20
			F		1820/21
			G	👤	1821/22
			H		1822/23
			I		1823/24
			K		1824/25
			L		1825/26
			M		1826/27
			N		1827/28
			O		1828/29
			P		1829/30
			Q		1830/31
			R		1831/32
			S	👤	1832/33
			T		1833/34
			U		1834/35

TM	LP	LHC	DL	SH	
🛡	🦁	🦁	W	◯	1835/36
			X		1836/37
			Y		1837/38
			Z		1838/39

1839–1864

TM	LP	LHC	DL	SH	
🛡	🦁	🦁	A	◯	1839/40
			B		1840/41
			C	🗿	1841/42
			D		1842/43
			E		1843/44
			F		1844/45
	LH		G		1845/46
	🦁		H		1846/47
			I		1847/48
			J		1848/49
			K		1849/50
			L		1850/51
			M		1851/52
			N		1852/53
			O		1853/54
			P		1854/55
			Q		1855/56
			R		1856/57
			S		1857/58
			T		1858/59
			U		1859/60

TM.	LP	LH	DL	SH	
🛡	🦁	🦁	W	🗿	1860/61
			X		1861/62
			Y		1862/63
			Z		1863/64

1864–1884

TM.	LP	LH	DL	SH	
🛡	🦁	🦁	a	🗿	1864/65
			b		1865/66
			c		1866/67
			d		1867/68
			e		1868/69
			f		1869/70
			g		1870/71
			h		1871/72
			i		1872/73
			k		1873/74
			l		1874/75
			m		1875/76
			n		1876/77
			o		1877/78
			p		1878/79
			q		1879/80
			r		1880/81
			s		1881/82
			t		1882/83
			u		1883/84

Norwich

Assay marks recorded here from mid-16th century until end 17th century. Marks: **castle** over a **lion passant**; **date letter**, changed annually in September, 1565–85, and from 1624–43, again 1688; **crowned rose**, recorded 1610/11, perhaps used as a standard mark; **crown** as separate mark, 1642–88; **rose sprig**, 1643–88; **maker's mark**.

1565–1585

TM	DL				
	A	1565/66	S		1582/83
	B	1566/67	T		1583/84
	C	1567/68	V		1584/85
	D	1568/69			
	E	1569/70	**1600–1610**		
	F	1570/71			1600/10
	G	1571/72			
	H	1572/73	**1624–1644**		
	I	1573/74	TM	RC	DL
	K	1574/75			A	1624/25
	L	1575/76			B	1625/26
	M	1576/77			C	1626/27
	N	1577/78			D	1627/28
	O	1578/79			E	1628/29
	P	1579/80			F	1629/30
RC	Q	1580/81			G	1630/31
	R	1581/82			H	1631/32

TM	RC	DL		TM	RC	DL	
					1688–1702		
			1632/33				
			1633/34	TM	RC	DL	
			1634/35				1688
			1635/36				1689
			1636/37				1690
			1637/38				1691
			1638/39				1692
			1639/40				1693
			1640/41				1694
			1641/42				1695
			1642/43				1696
			1643/44				1697

TM		DL		TM	LHE	B	DL	
			1660					1701/2
			1670					
			1675					
			1680					

Sheffield

Assay office for silver (not 'Sheffield plate') established here 1773; continues. Marks: **crown** as "hall" mark of company (1773–1974); N.B. stamped upside down 1815 to 1819; **Tudor rose** as "hall" mark 1975 onwards; **lion passant** (11 oz. 10 dwts) and **Britannia** (11 oz. 10 dwts) as standard marks; **Sovereign's head**, as duty mark (1784–1890); **date letter** formerly changed annually in July, from 1975 changed 1 January; **maker's mark**.

1773–1799

TM	LP	DL	SH	
👑	🦁	C		1773/74
		F		1774/75
		N		1775/76
		R		1776/77
		H		1777/78
		S		1778/79
		A		1779/80
		⊕		1780/81
		D		1781/82
		G		1782/83
		B		1783/84
		I	●	1784/85
		⊕		1785/86
		K	●	1786/87
		T		1787/88
		U		1788/89
		X		1789/90
		L		1790/91
		⊕		1791/92

TM	LP	DL	SH	
👑	🦁	U	●	1792/93
		O		1793/94
		m		1794/95
		q		1795/96
		Z		1796/97
		X		1797/98
		V		1798/99

1799–1824

TM	LP	DL	SH	
👑	🦁	E	●	1799/1800
		N		1800/1
		H		1801/2
		M		1802/3
		F		1803/4
		G		1804/5
		B		1805/6
		A		1806/7
		S		1807/8
		P		1808/9

TM	LP	DL	SH	
👑	🦁	K		1809/10
		L		1810/11
		C		1811/12
		D		1812/13
		R		1813/14
		W		1814/15
		O		1815/16
		T		1816/17
		X		1817/18
		I		1818/19
		V		1819/20
		V		1819/20
		Q		1820/21
		Y		1821/22
		Z		1822/23
		U		1823/24

TM	LP	DL	SH	
👑	🦁	k		1832/33
		l		1833/34
		m		1834/35
		p		1835/36
		q		1836/37
		r		1837/38
		s		1838/39
		t		1839/40
		u		1840/41
		v		1841/42
		x		1842/43
		Z		1843/44

1824–1844

TM	LP	DL	SH	
👑	🦁	a		1824/25
		b		1825/26
		c		1826/27
		d		1827/28
		e		1828/29
		f		1829/30
		g		1830/31
		h		1831/32

1844–1868

TM	LP	DL	SH	
👑	🦁	A		1844/45
		B		1845/46
		C		1846/47
		D		1847/48
		E		1848/49
		F		1849/50
		G		1850/51
		H		1851/52
		I		1852/53
		K		1853/54
		L		1854/55
		M		1855/56

TM	LP	DL	SH	
👑	🦁	N	👤	1856/57
		O		1857/58
		P		1858/59
		R		1859/60
		S		1860/61
		T		1861/62
		U		1862/63
		V		1863/64
		W		1864/65
		X		1865/66
		Y		1866/67
		Z		1867/68

TM	LP	DL	SH	
👑	🦁	O	👤	1881/82
		P		1882/83
		Q		1883/84
		R		1884/85
		S		1885/86
		T		1886/87
		U		1887/88
		V		1888/89
		W		1889/90
		X		1890/91
		Y		1891/92
		Z		1892/93

1868–1893

TM	LP	DL	SH	
👑	🦁	A	👤	1868/69
		B		1869/70
		C		1870/71
		D		1871/72
		E		1872/73
		F		1873/74
		G		1874/75
		H		1875/76
		J		1876/77
		K		1877/78
		L		1878/79
		M		1879/80
		N		1880/81

1893–1918

TM	LP	DL	
👑	🦁	a	1893/94
		b	1894/95
		c	1895/96
		d	1896/97
		e	1897/98
		f	1898/99
		g	1899/1900
		h	1900/1
		i	1901/2
		k	1902/3
		l	1903/4
		m	1904/5
		n	1905/6

TM	LP	DL		TM	LP	DL	SH	
👑	🦁	o	1906/7	👑	🦁	O		1931/32
		p	1907/8			P		1932/33
		q	1908/9			Q	⬤	1933/34
		r	1909/10			R		1934/35
		s	1910/11			S		1935/36
		t	1911/12			T		1936/37
		u	1912/13			U		1937/38
		v	1913/14			V		1938/39
		w	1914/15			W		1939/40
		x	1915/16			X		1940/41
		y	1916/17			Y		1941/42
		z	1917/18			Z		1942/43

1918–1943

TM	LP	DL	
👑	🦁	a	1918/19
		b	1919/20
		c	1920/21
		d	1921/22
		e	1922/23
		f	1923/24
		g	1924/25
		h	1925/26
		i	1926/27
		k	1927/28
		l	1928/29
		m	1929/30
		n	1930/31

1943–1968

TM	LP	DL	SH	
👑	🦁	A		1943/44
		B		1944/45
		C		1945/46
		D		1946/47
		E		1947/48
		F		1948/49
		G		1949/50
		H		1950/51
		I		1951/52
		K	⬤	1952/53
		L		1953/54
		M		1954/55
		N		1955/56

TM	LP	DL	
		O	1956/57
		P	1957/58
		Q	1958/59
		R	1959/60
		S	1960/61
		T	1961/62
		U	1962/63
		V	1963/64
		W	1964/65
		X	1965/66
		Y	1966/67
		Z	1967/68

1968–1974

TM	LP	DL	
		A	1968/69
		B	1969/70
		C	1970/71
		D	1971/72
		E	1972/73
		F	1973/74
		G	July–Dec 1974

1975–

TM	LP	DL	
		A	1975
		B	1976
		C	1977
		D	1978
		E	1979
		F	1980
		G	1981
		H	1982
		J	1983
		K	1984
		L	1985
		M	1986
		N	1987
		O	1988
		P	1989
		Q	1990
		R	1991
		S	1992

The 1773 form of the date letter F was used to mark the
Sheffield Assay office bicentary in 1973/74.

York

Assay mark used here from mid-16th century; office closed 1717, re-opened *c.* 1774/5, closed finally 1856. Marks: **half leopard's head/half fleur-de-lis**, as "town" mark (1562–1631); **half rose crowned/half fleur-de-lis**, as "town" mark (1632–98); **cross with five lions passant** on it, as "town" mark (from 1700); **Sovereign's head**, as duty mark (1784–1856); **date letter; maker's mark**. N.B. Very few pieces assayed and marked during period *c.* 1716 to 1776.

	1559–1583			TM	DL		
TM	DL			⊕	V		1578/79
⊕	A	1559/60			W		1579/80
	B	1560/61			X		1580/81
	C	1561/62			Y		1581/82
	D	1562/63			Z		1582/83
	E	1563/64					
	F	1564/65			1583–1607		
	G	1565/66		TM	DL		
	H	1566/67		⊕	a		1583/84
	I	1567/68		⊕	b		1584/85
	K	1568/69			c		1585/86
	L	1569/70			d		1586/87
	M	1570/71			e		1587/88
	N	1571/72			f		1588/89
	O	1572/73			g		1589/90
	P	1573/74			h		1590/91
	Q	1574/75			i		1591/92
	R	1575/76			k		1592/93
	S	1576/77					
	T	1577/78					

TM	DL		TM	DL	
🛡	I	1593/94	🛡	J	1615/16
	m	1594/95		K	1616/17
	n	1595/96		L	1617/18
	o	1596/97		M	1618/19
	p	1597/98		N	1619/20
	q	1598/99		O	1620/21
	r	1599/1600		P	1621/22
	s	1600/1		Q	1622/23
	t	1601/2		R	1623/24
	u	1602/3		S	1624/25
	w	1603/4		T	1625/26
	x	1604/5		U	1626/27
	v	1605/6		W	1627/28
	z	1606/7		X	1628/29
				Y	1629/30
				Z	1630/31

1607–1631

TM	DL	
🛡	A	1607/8
	B	1608/9
	C	1609/10
	D	1610/11
	E	1611/12
	F	1612/13
	G	1613/14
	H	1614/15

1631–1657

TM	DL	
🛡	a	1631/32
	b	1632/33
	c	1633/34
	d	1634/35
	e	1635/36
	f	1636/37

TM	DL		TM	DL	
🔵	*g*	1637/38	🔵	*C*	1659/60
	h	1638/39		*D*	1660/61
	i	1639/40		*E*	1661/62
	j	1640/41		*F*	1662/63
	k	1641/42		*G*	1663/64
	l	1642/43		*H*	1664/65
	m	1643/44		*I*	1665/66
	n	1644/45		*K*	1666/67
	o	1645/46		*L*	1667/68
	p	1646/47		*M*	1668/69
	q	1647/48		*N*	1669/70
	r	1648/49		*O*	1670/71
	ſ	1649/50		*P*	1671/72
	t	1650/51		*Q*	1672/73
	u	1651/52		*R*	1673/74
	v	1652/53		*S*	1674/75
	w	1653/54		*T*	1675/76
	x	1654/55		*U*	1676/77
	y	1655/56		*V*	1677/78
	z	1656/57		*W*	1678/79
				X	1679/80
				Y	1680/81
				Z	1681/82

1657–1682

TM	DL	
🔵	*A*	1657/58
	B	1658/59

1682–1700

TM	DL	
	A	1682/83
	B	1683/84
	C	1684/85
	D	1685/86
	E	1686/87
	F	1687/88
	G	1688/89
	H	1689/90
	I	1690/91
	K	1691/92
	L	1692/93
	M	1693/94
	N	1694/95
	O	1695/96
	P	1696/97
	Q	1697/98
	R	1698/99
	S	1699/1700

1700–1717

TM	B	LHE	DL	
			A	1700/1
			B	1701/2
			C	1702/3
			D	1703/4
				1704/5
			F	1705/6
			G	1706/7
				1707/8
			I	1708/9
				1709/10
				1710/11
			M	1711/12
				1712/13
			O	1713/14

1776–1787

TM	LHC	LP	DL	SH	
			A		1776/77
			B		1777/78
			C		1778/79
			D		1779/80
			E		1780/81
			F		1781/82
			G		1782/83
			H		1783/84
			J		1784/85

1787–1812

TM	LHC	LP	DL	SH	
			A		1787/88
			b		1788/89
			c		1789/90
			d		1790/91

TM	LHC	LP	DL	SH		TM	LHC	LP	DL	SH	
⊕	🅔	🐆	e	◉	1791/92	⊕	🅥	🐆	f	◉	1817/18
			f		1792/93				g		1818/19
			g		1793/94				h		1819/20
			h		1794/95				i		1820/21
			i		1795/96				k		1821/22
			k		1796/97				l		1822/23
			l		1797/98				m		1823/24
			M		1798/99				n		1824/25
			N		1799/1800				o		1825/26
			O		1800/1				p		1826/27
			P		1801/2				q		1827/28
			Q		1802/3				r		1828/29
			R		1803/4				s		1829/30
			S		1804/5				t	◉	1830/31
			T		1805/6				u		1831/32
			U		1806/7				v		1832/33
			V		1807/8				w		1833/34
			W		1808/9				x		1834/35
			X		1809/10				y		1835/36
			Y		1810/11				z		1836/37
			Z		1811/12						

1812–1837

TM	LHC	LP	DL	SH	
⊕	🅥	🐆	a	◉	1812/13
			b		1813/14
			c		1814/15
			d		1815/16
			e		1816/17

1837–1857

TM	LHC	LP	DL	SH	
⊕	🅥	🐆	A	◉	1837/38
			B		1838/39
			C		1839/40
			D		1840/41
			E		1841/42
			F		1842/43

TM	LHC	LP	DL	SH		TM	LHC	LP	DL	SH	
⊕	⬦	🦁	G	👤	1843/44	⊕	⬦	🦁	O	👤	1850/51
			H		1844/45				P		1851/52
			I		1845/46				Q		1852/53
			K		1846/47				R		1853/54
			L		1847/48				S		1854/55
			M		1848/49				T		1855/56
			N		1849/50				V		1856/57

Marks on English Gold Plate

At the London Assay Office up to 1798 gold was marked first with the leopard's head crowned, later with the lion passant. In 1798 the 18-carat standard was established, the mark being a crown and the figure 18; the 22-carat mark continued to be the lion passant (1798–1843). From 1844 only the crown was used, with the appropriate figures, 22 or 18. In Scotland the thistle was used with the figures 18 or 22. Lower standard marks (from 1854) carried the relevant figures only. In addition, town mark, maker's mark, and date letter were used (as on silver). Foreign gold and silver wares imported into England received (from 1876–1904) the mark of the assay office concerned and an "F" in an oval or rectangle. From 1904 onwards individual assay offices received distinctive marks to use. For changes made since the Hallmarking Act 1973, *see* p. 14.

Higher Standard Marks		**Lower Standard Marks**	
	19·20 carat (1300–1476)		15 carat (1854–1931)
	18 carat (1477–1544)		12 carat (1854–1931)
	18 carat (1544–1574)		9 carat (1854–1931)
	22 carat (1575–1843)		14 carat (1932–1974)
	18 carat (1798–1974)		9 carat (1932–1974)
	22 carat (1844–1974)		

Assay Office Marks on Imported Gold Plate

	Birmingham (1904–)		Glasgow	(1904–1906)
	Chester (1904–1961)			(1906–1964)
	Dublin (1904–1906)		London	(1904–1906)
	(1906–)			(1906–)
	Edinburgh (1904–)		Sheffield	(1904–1906)
				(1906–)

Irish Silver

Dublin

Company established 1637; Assay Office continues. Marks: **harp crowned**, introduced 1637 as "fineness" mark; **Hibernia figure** adopted March 1730, at first used as duty mark; from 1807 onward may be considered as special mark of Dublin Goldsmiths Company (*cf.* town marks in England); **Sovereign's head** as duty mark (1807–90); **date letter** changed during May up to 1932; from 1932 changed January; **maker's mark**.

1638–1658

HC	DL	
	A	1638/39
	B	1639/40
	C	1640/41
	D	1641/42
	E	1642/43
	F	1643/44
	G	1644/45
	H	1645/46
	I	1646/47
	K	1647/48
	L	1648/49
	M	1649/50
	N	1650/51
	O	1651/52
	P	1652/53
	Q	1653/54
	R	1654/55

HC	DL	
	S	1655/56
	T	1656/57
	U	1657/58

1658–1678

HC	DL	
	a	1658/59
	b	1659/60
	c	1660/61
	d	1661/62
	e	1662/63
	f	1663/64
	g	1664/65
	h	1665/66
	j	1666/67
	k	1667/68
	l	1668/69
	m	1669/70

HC	DL		HC	DL	
	n	1670/71		P	1702/3
	o	1671/72		Q	1703/4
	p	1672/73		R	1704/5/6
	q	1673/74		S	1706/7/8
	r	1674/75		T	1708/9/10
	s	1675/76		U	1710/11/12
	t	1676/77		W	1712/13/14
	u	1677/78		X	1714/15
				Y	1715/16
				Z	1716/17

1678–1717

HC	DL	
	A	1678/79
	B	1679/80
	C	1680/81
	D	1681/82
	E	1682/83
	F	1683/84
	G	1685/86/87
	H	1688/92
	I	1688/92
	K	1693/94/95
	L	1696/99
	M	1699/1700
	N	1700/1
	O	1701/2

1717–1731

HC	DL	
	A	1717/18
	B	1718/19
	C	1719/20
	C	1719/20
	A	1720/21
	B	1721/22
	C	1722/23
	D	1723/24
	E	1724/25
	F	1725/26
	G	1726/27

HC	DL	
		1727/28
		1728/29
		1729/30
		1730/31

1731–1746

HC	H	DL	
			1731/32
			1732/33
			1733/34
			1734/35
			1735/36
			1736/37
			1737/38
			1738/39
			1739/40
			1740/41
			1741/42/43
			1743/44
			1745
			1746

1747–1772

HC	H	DL	
			1747

HC	H	DL	
			1748
			1749
			1750
			1751/52
			1752/53
			1753/54
			1754/55
			1757
			1758
			1759
			1760
			1761
			1762
			1763
			1764
			1765
			1766
			1767
			1768
			1769
			1770
			1771
			1772

1773–1796

HC	H	DL		
		A	1773	
		B	1774	
		C	1775	
		D	1776	
		E	1777	
		F	1778	
		G	1779	
		H	1780	
		I	1781	
		K	1782	
		L	1783	
		M	1784	
		N	1785	
		O	1786	
		P	1787	
		Q	1788	
		R	1789	
		S	1790	
		T	1791	
		U	1792	
		W	1793	
		X	1794	
		Y	1795	
		Z	1796	

1797–1820

HC	H	DL	SH	
		A		1797
		B		1798
		C		1799
		D		1800
		E		1801
		F		1802
		G		1803
		H		1804
		I		1805
		K		1806
		L		1807
		M		1808
		N		1809
		O		1810
		P		1811
		Q		1812
		R		1813
		S		1814
				1815
		T		1816
		U		1817
		W		1818
		X		1819
		Y		1820
		Z		

1821–1846

HC	H	DL	SH	
		A		1821
		B		1822
		C		1823
		D		1824
		E		1825/26
		F		1826/27
		G		1827/28
		H		1828/29
		I	I	1829/30
		K		1830/31
		L		1831/32
		M		1832/33
		N	N	1833/34
		O	O	1834/35
		P	P	1835/36
		Q	Q	1836/37
		R	R	1837/38
		S		1838/39
		T		1839/40
		U	U	1840/41
		V		1841/42
		W		1842/43
		X		1843/44
		Y		1844/45
		Z		1845/46

1846–1871

HC	H	DL	SH	
		a		1846/47
		b		1847/48
		c		1848/49
		d		1849/50
		e		1850/51
		f	f	1851/52
		g	g	1852/53
		h	h	1853/54
		j		1854/55
		k		1855/56
		l		1856/57
		m		1857/58
		n		1858/59
		o		1859/60
		p		1860/61
		q		1861/62
		r		1862/63
		s		1863/64
		t		1864/65
		u		1865/66
		v		1866/67
		w		1867/68
		x		1868/69
		y		1869/70
		z		1870/71

1871–1896

HC	H	DL	SH	
		A		1871/72
		B		1872/73
		C		1873/74
		D		1874/75
		E		1875/76
		F		1876/77
		G		1877/78
		H		1878/79
		I		1879/80
		K		1880/81
		L		1881/82
		M		1882/83
		N		1883/84
		O		1884/85
		P		1885/86
		Q		1886/87
		R		1887/88
		S		1888/89
		T		1889/90
		U		1890/91
		V		1891/92
		W		1892/93
		X		1893/94
		Y		1894/95
		Z		1895/96

1896–1916

HC	H	DL	
		A	1896/97
		B	1897/98
		C	1898/99
		D	1899/1900
		E	1900/1
		F	1901/2
		G	1902/3
		H	1903/4
		I	1904/5
		K	1905/6
		L	1906/7
		M	1907/8
		N	1908/9
		O	1909/10
		P	1910/11
		Q	1911/12
		R	1912/13
		S	1913/14
		T	1914/15
		U	1915/16

1916–1941

HC	H	DL	
		A	1916/17
		B	1917/18
		C	1918/19
		D	1919/20

HC	H	DL	
		e	1920/21
		f	1921/22
		g	1922/23
		h	1923/24
		i	1924/25
		k	1925/26
		l	1926/27
		m	1927/28
		n	1928/29
		o	1929/30
		p	1930/31
		q	1932
		r	1933
		s	1934
		t	1935
		u	1936
		v	1937
		w	1938
		x	1939
		y	1940
		z	1941

HC	H	DL	JM	
		E		1946
		F		1947
		G		1948
		H		1949
		I		1950
		J		1951
		K		1952
		L		1953
		M		1954
		N		1955
		O		1956
		P		1957
		Q		1958
		R		1959
		S		1960
		T		1961
		U		1962
		V		1963
		W		1964
		X		1965
		Y	(Sword of Light mark)	1966
		Z		1967

1942–1967

HC	H	DL	
		A	1942
		B	1943
		C	1944
		D	1945

Jubilee Mark ("the Sword of Light") for 1966, commemorated the golden jubilee of the rising of 1916; used on Irish gold and silver on all items except jewellery and watch cases, in addition to the normal hallmarks during the year 1966.

	1968—							
HC	H	DL	EEC		HC	H	DL	
				1968				1974
				1969				1975
				1970				1976
				1971				
				1972				
				1973				

EEC mark for 1973, used in addition to the normal hallmark for 1973, and called the "EEC Commemorative Mark". It consists of a miniature representation of the prehistoric (c. 700 BC) Gleninsheen gold collar enclosing the date 1973 in the centre and without a surrounding border.

Marks on Irish Gold Plate

There are five standards prescribed for the manufacture of gold in Ireland, expressed in terms of carats, i.e. 22, 20, 18, 14 and 9. The first three each have a symbol, e.g. **Harp Crowned,** plus maker's mark with the appropriate numeral. The others are expressed in numerals only, which are not included with the maker's mark.

22 carat

 fineness mark from 1637, plus numeral 22 and maker's mark

20 carat

 fineness mark from 1784, plus numeral 20 and maker's mark

18 carat

fineness mark from 1784, plus numeral 18 and maker's mark

14 carat

 fineness mark from 1935

9 carat

 fineness mark from 1854

AR   **Abel Ram**
(letters conjoined: with ram below in shield-shaped punch, 1663; with
(?) animal below, in bordered oval punch, 1664; with (?) bird below
in oval punch, 1665)

CL   **Charles Leslie**
(with thistle above in trefoil-shaped punch, 1734)

CT   **Charles Townsend**
(in rectangular punch, 1776)

DE   **Daniel Egan**
(in rectangular punch, 1804)

DK   **David King**
(in oval punch, 1701; D enclosing K, in shaped punch, 1703)

ID   **Isaac D'Olier**
(in oval punch, 1758)

I.H   **John Hamilton**
(with crown over, 1739)

I.K.   **James Keating**
(in rectangular punch, 1799)

IL   **John Laughlin**
(with crown over and star between, in shaped rectangular punch,
1768)

I.L.B   **James Le Bass**
(in rectangular punch, 1842)

I.S   **Joseph Stoker** or **John Slicer**
(with pellet above and below, in oval bordered punch, 1663)

J.P   **John Pittar**
(in rectangular punch, 1787)

J.R.N   **J. R. Neill**
(in rectangular punch, 1858)

JJ   **John Tuite**
(with ewer between in rectangular punch, 1751)

JW   **Joseph Walker**
(italic letters in shield-shaped punch, 1696)

LAW   **William Law**
(punched into metal, 1814)

M.K   **Michael Keating**
(in rectangular punch, 1779; without pellet, in rectangular punch,
1793)

MW   **Matthew Walker**
(monogram in rectangular punch, 1725)

MW   **Matthew Walsh**
(in flattened shield-shaped punch)

M.W   **Michael Walsh**
(with crown over in shaped rectangular punch, 1780)

MW&S   **M. West & Sons** (retailers)
(in rectangular punch, 1821)

NEILL   **J. R. Neill** (retailers)
(in rectangular punch, 1858)

RC   **Robert Calderwood**
(in oval punch, 1727; with mullet between in shaped oval punch, 1741 and 1760)

TB   **Thomas Bolton**
(monogram in shield-shaped punch, 1694)

TW   **Thomas Walker**
(with crown over in shaped rectangular punch, c.1755)

W&Co.   **Alderman West & Co.** (retailers)
(in rectangular punch, 1826).

W&S   **West & Son** (retailers)
(in rectangular punch; in shield-shaped punch; in clover-leaf, 1879)

W.B   **William Bond**
(italic letters in rectangular punch, early 18th century)

WEST   **Alderman West** (retailer)
(in rectangular punch, late 18th-early 19th century)

WL   **William Law**
(in rectangular punch, 1789)

W.T   **William Townsend**
(in rectangular punch; without pellet in nipped oval punch, 1734)

WW   **William Williamson**
(with rosette above in trefoil-shaped punch, 1733)

Marks on Sheffield Plate

No date letters are to be found, since none were in use. Makers of Sheffield plate marked their wares (*c.* 1750–*c.* 1785) with their initials, following the practice of the London goldsmiths and silversmiths. From 1784 makers of Sheffield plate were permitted by law to use an emblem or device with their names. By the early 19th century, the emblem may be found alone, a practice fairly general during that period. Makers often used in addition the mark of a crown to indicate quality, but in 1896 this practice was forbidden.

ALL GOOD	Allgood, John	(*c.* 1812)	Birmingham
ASHFORTH & CO	Ashforth & Co	(*c.* 1784)	Sheffield
ASH LEY	Ashley	(*c.* 1816)	Birmingham
BANI STER	Banister, William	(*c.* 1808)	Birmingham
BARNET T	Barnet		
BEL DON	Beldon, George	(*c.* 1809)	Sheffield
BELDON HOYLAND & CO	Beldon, Hoyland & Co	(*c.* 1785)	Sheffield
BEST	Best, Henry	(*c.* 1814)	Birmingham

BEST	Best & Wastidge	(*c.* 1816)	Sheffield
W. BINGLEY	Bingley, William	(*c.* 1787)	Birmingham
BOULTON	Boulton	(*c.* 1784)	Birmingham
BRAD SHAW	Bradshaw, Joseph	(*c.* 1822)	Birmingham
BRITTAIN.WILKIN SON & BROWNILL	Brittain, Wilkinson & Brownill	(*c.* 1785)	Sheffield
BUTTS	Butts, T.	(*c.* 1807)	Birmingham

CAUSER	Causer, John Fletcher	(*c.* 1824)	Birmingham
Ches-ton	Cheston, Thomas	(*c.* 1809)	Birmingham
CHILD	Child, Thomas	(*c.* 1821)	Birmingham
W. COLDWELL	Coldwell, William	(*c.* 1806)	Sheffield
COPE	Cope, Charles Gretter	(*c.* 1817)	Birmingham
CORN & Cọ.	Corn, James, & Sheppard, John	(*c.* 1819)	Birmingham

CRACK NALL	Cracknall, John	(*c.* 1814)	Birmingham
CRESWICKS	Creswick, Thomas, & James	(*c.* 1811)	Sheffield

DAVIS	Davis, John	(*c.* 1816)	Birmingham
DEAKIN SMITH & Cº	Deakin, Smith & Co	(*c.* 1785)	Sheffield
J DIXON	Dixon, James, & Son	(*c.* 1835)	Sheffield
DIXON & Cº	Dixon & Co	(*c.* 1784)	Birmingham
I·DRABBLE & Cº	Drabble, James, & Co	(*c.* 1805)	Sheffield
DUNN	Dunn, George Bott	(*c.* 1810)	Birmingham
S·EVANS	Evans, Samuel	(*c.* 1816)	Birmingham

FOX·PROCTOR PASMORE·& Cº	Fox, Proctor Pasmore & Co	(*c.* 1784)	Sheffield
FREETH	Freeth, Henry	(*c.* 1816)	Birmingham
FROGGATT COLDWELL & LEAN	Froggatt, Coldwell & Lean	(*c.* 1797)	Sheffield

---

GAINSFORD	Gainsford, Robert	(*c.* 1808)	Sheffield

Garnett, William	(c. 1803)	Sheffield
Gibbs, Joseph	(c. 1808)	Birmingham
Gilbert, John	(c. 1812)	Birmingham
Goodman, Alexander & Co	(c. 1800)	Sheffield
Goodwin, Edward	(c. 1794)	Sheffield
Green, John, & Co	(c. 1799)	Sheffield
Green, Joseph	(c. 1807)	Birmingham
Green, W. & Co	(c. 1784)	Sheffield
Hall, William	(c. 1820)	Birmingham
Hanson, Matthias	(c. 1810)	Birmingham
Harrison, Joseph	(c. 1809)	Birmingham
Hatfield, Aaron	(c. 1808)	Sheffield

Hatfield, Aaron	(c. 1810)	Sheffield
Hill, Daniel & Co	(c. 1806)	Birmingham
Hinks, Joseph	(c. 1812)	Birmingham
Hipkiss, J.	(c. 1808)	Birmingham
Hipwood, William	(c. 1809)	Birmingham
Holland & Co	(c. 1784)	Birmingham
Holy, Daniel, Parker & Co	(c. 1804)	Sheffield
Holy, Daniel, Wilkinson & Co	(c. 1784)	Sheffield
Horton, David	(c. 1808)	Birmingham
Horton, John	(c. 1809)	Birmingham
Howard, Stanley & Thomas	(c. 1809)	London
Hutton, William	(c. 1807)	Birmingham
Jervis, William	(c. 1789)	Sheffield
Johnson, James	(c. 1812)	Birmingham

Jones	(c. 1824)	Birmingham
Jordan, Thomas	(c. 1814)	Birmingham
Kirkby, Samuel	(c. 1812)	Sheffield
Law, John, & Son	(c. 1807)	Sheffield
Law, John	(c. 1810)	Sheffield
Law, Richard	(c. 1807)	Birmingham
Law, Thomas, & Co	(c. 1784)	Sheffield
Lea, Abner Cowel	(c. 1808)	Birmingham
Lees, George	(c. 1811)	Birmingham
,,	,,	,,
Linwood, John	(c. 1807)	Birmingham
,,	,,	,,
Linwood, William	,,	,,

Linwood, Matthew, & Son	(*c.* 1808)	Birmingham
Love, John & Co	(*c.* 1785)	Sheffield
Love, Silverside, Darby & Co	(*c.* 1785)	Sheffield
Lilly, John	(*c.* 1815)	Birmingham
Lilly, Joseph	(*c.* 1816)	Birmingham

Madin, P., & Co	(*c.* 1788)	Sheffield
Markland, William	(*c.* 1818)	Birmingham
Meredith, Henry	(*c.* 1807)	Birmingham
Moore, Frederick	(*c.* 1820)	Birmingham
Moore, J.	(*c.* 1784)	Birmingham
Morton, Richard, & Co	(*c.* 1785)	Sheffield

Newbould, William, & Sons   (*c.* 1804)   Sheffield

J·NICHOLDS	Nicholds, James	(c. 1808)	Birmingham
IOHN·PARSONS&Cº	Parsons, John, & Co	(c. 1784)	Sheffield
PEAKE✶C	Peake	(c. 1807)	Birmingham
PEAR SON	Pearson, Richard	(c. 1811)	Birmingham
PEAR SON	Pearson, Richard	(c. 1813)	Birmingham
PEMBERTON	Pemberton & Mitchell	(c. 1817)	Birmingham
Pim ley	Pimley, Samuel	(c. 1810)	Birmingham
ROBERTS &CADMAN	Roberts & Cadman	(c. 1785)	Sheffield
I & S. ROBERTS.	Roberts, Samuel, & Co	(c. 1786)	Sheffield
ROGERS	Rogers, John	(c. 1819)	Birmingham
ROD GERS	Rodgers, Joseph, & Sons	(c. 1822)	Sheffield
RYLAND	Ryland, William, & Sons	(c. 1807)	Birmingham
RYLAND	,, ,,	,, ,,

119

	Sansom, Thomas, & Sons	(c. 1821)	Sheffield
	Scott, William	(c. 1807)	Birmingham
	Shephard, Joseph	(c. 1817)	Birmingham
	Silk, Robert	(c. 1809)	Birmingham
	Silkirk, William	(c. 1807)	Birmingham
	Small, Thomas	(c. 1812)	Birmingham
	Smith & Co	(c. 1784)	Birmingham
	Smith, Isaac	(c. 1821)	Birmingham
	Smith, N. & Co	(c. 1784)	Sheffield
	Smith, Nicholson, Tate and Hoult	(c. 1810)	Sheffield
	Smith, William	(c. 1812)	Birmingham
	Staniforth, Parkin & Co	(c. 1784)	Sheffield

Stot, Benjamin	(*c.* 1811)	Sheffield
Sutcliff, Robert, & Co	(*c.* 1786)	Sheffield
Sykes & Co	(*c.* 1784)	Sheffield
Thomas, Stephen	(*c.* 1813)	Birmingham
Thomason, Edward, & Dowler	(*c.* 1807)	Birmingham
,,	,,	,,
Tonks, Samuel	(*c.* 1807)	Birmingham
Tonks & Co.	(*c.* 1824)	Birmingham
Tudor & Co	(*c.* 1784)	Sheffield
,,	,,	,,
Turley, Samuel	(*c.* 1816)	Birmingham
Turton, John	(*c.* 1820)	Birmingham

Tyndall, Joseph	(*c.* 1813)	Birmingham

Waterhouse & Co	(*c.* 1807)	Birmingham
Waterhouse, J. & Co	(*c.* 1833)	Sheffield
Waterhouse, John, Hatfield, Edward, & Co	(*c.* 1836)	Sheffield
Watson, Fenton & Bradbury	(*c.* 1795)	Sheffield
Watson, Pass & Co	(*c.* 1811)	Sheffield
White, John	(*c.* 1811)	Birmingham
Wilkinson, Henry, & Co	(*c.* 1836)	Sheffield
Willmore, Joseph	(*c.* 1807)	Birmingham
Woodward, William	(*c.* 1814)	Birmingham
Worton, Samuel	(*c.* 1821)	Birmingham
Wright, John, & Fairbairn, George	(*c.* 1809)	Sheffield

Younge, S. & C., & Co	(*c.* 1813)	Sheffield

British Pewterers' Marks, or "Touches"

It was laid down by law *c.* 1503 that each pewterer should have his own individual mark, which was to be officially recorded on "touch plates". Marks recorded up to the year of the Great Fire of London were unfortunately destroyed in the conflagration. After the rebuilding of the Pewterers' Hall, recording of touches was resumed, and a vast quantity (at least 1,000) accumulated over the years. Individual touches were at first small, but from the early 18th century were more elaborate. The mark of the crowned rose, which previously was supposed to be reserved for use by members of the company only, was from *c.* 1671 intended for use on exported pewter exclusively. By the end of the 17th century it was considerably used as an extra touch by the majority of the London pewterers, and the custom copied by a number of provincial makers also. A series of small marks in shield outlines were also frequently used. Labels with such words as "superfine metal" etc., with or without the maker's name, formed additional touches.

A Selective List

Adams, Henry: (*fl.* 1692–1724) London Mark used: representation of The Fall, with HEN:ADAMS in curve above, and PICKADILLY below, in shaped outline.

Adkinson, William: (recorded 1671) London Mark used: Cupid with bow, between palm leaves, with W:ADKINSON over, curved.

Alder, William: (*fl.* early 18th century) Sunderland, Co. Durham Mark used: sailing ship between two columns, with WILLIAM curved over, and ALDER below, supported on SUNDERLAND in semicircle, all in shaped outline.

Alderson, George: (*fl.* first half 18th century) London Marks used: griffin over a coronet, with GEORGE over and ALDERSON below in cartouche outline; similar Cartouche with CARNABY/STREET/LONDON within, in three lines.

Alderson, Sir George: (*fl.* 1817–1826) London Marks included: lion (?) arising from a coronet, with GEORGE above and ALDERSON below, in cartouche; also ALDERSON forming circle, in circular outline.

Alderson, John: (*fl.* 1764–1792) London Marks used: lion arising from a coronet with JOHN and ALDERSON under, in rounded outline; crowned rose with LONDON over and palm leaves under, following broad oval outline; small marks, consecutively: WS; Britannia; lion's head erased; a coffeepot.

Angel, Philemon: (*fl. c.* 1685–1700) London Marks included: figure of an angel over LONDON with a wreath under, in round outline; four small marks, i.e. shields, containing, consecutively: P (italic); A (italic); angel figure; lion rampant.

Annison, William Glover: (recorded 1742) London Marks used: shield per pale, with an animal, and two stars over an open book, with Wᴹ GLOVER over, and ANNISON under, in rounded cartouche; label, ANNISON / CROOKED LANE / LONDON in three lines, in wavy outline.

Bache, Richard: (*fl.* 1779–1805) London
Mark used: figure of standing angel between columns, with RICHARD above and BACHE below, in near rectangular outline.

Bacon, George: (*fl. c.* 1745–1771) London
Marks used: a pig in a circle, with GEORGE curving above, and BACON below, in oval outline; a rectangular label IN THE STRAND/LONDON in two lines.

Bacon, Thomas: (*fl. c.* 1725 onward) London
Marks used: pig with FECIT over, in oval, with THOMAS above and BACON below, in broad oval outline; crowned rose over LONDON in circular outline.

Bancks, James: (*fl.* first half 18th century) Wigan, Lancashire
Marks included: label with ·IAMES·/ BANCKS in two lines, curved; crowned rose between palm leaves, in oval outline; four small marks, consecutively: IB; bird; fleur-de-lis; lion rampant; in block outline.

Barber, Nathaniel: (*fl. c.* 1777–1788) London
Marks used include: shield divided per pale, with NATHANIEL over and BARBER below, in broad oval outline; four small marks, consecutively: SS; Britannia; crowned rose; griffin's head (?) erased; curved label with LONDON/ SUPERFINE in two lines; SNOW-HILL/LONDON in two lines in cartouche outline.

Barlow, John: (*fl.* end 17th century) London
Marks included: lily rising from ploughshare (?) with JOHN above and BARLOW under, in curved outline; crowned rose with palm leaves under LONDON in circular outline; four small marks, i.e. shields, which include: lion rampant; griffin's head erased; and IB.

Barton, Daniel: (*fl. c.* 1670–1699) London
Marks included: helmet between palm leaves, with DA·BARTON over, in rounded triangular outline; four small marks: D.B in shield; helmet in lozenge; lion passant in rectangle; fleur-de-lis in lozenge.

Belson, John: (*fl. c.* 1745–1783) London
Marks included: bell over sun in splendour, between columns, with LONDON in curve over, and BELSON below, in rectangular outline with curved top; crowned rose between columns, with FISH curved over, and STREET HILL under, in similar outline; a bell in a circle, with LONDON in outer ring, and JOHN BELSON above outside, in circular scalloped outline; small marks, consecutively, in shields: TB; a bell; lion's head.

Benson, John: (*fl.* mid 18th century) London
Marks included: two-headed eagle displayed, with IOHN over and BENSON below, in broad oval outline; small marks (rectangular) with, consecutively: lion passant; crown; I; and B (the initials as Gothic caps); as a label, I·BENSON/ IN LONDON in two lines, in plain rectangle.

Bentley, C.: (*fl.* 1840s) London
Marks used: circle surrounded by C·BENTLEY WOODSTOCK Sᵀ in circular outline; small marks included in small rectangles: CB; lion rampant; rosette.

Blackwell, Benjamin: (*fl.* 1740s) London
Marks included: a bell, with BENIAMIN over, and BLACKWELL under, in curved outline; crowned rose with leaf sprays under, and LONDON over, in curved outline; small marks, four rectangles, each with lion passant, to right.

Bonvile, John: (*fl.* 1679–1686) London
Marks included: crown over five stars between palm leaves, with IOHN over and BONVILE below, in shaped outline; crowned rose between palm leaves, with LONDON over, in rounded triangular outline; four small marks: I·B; globe; three stars; lion passant.

Bridges, Stephen: (recorded 1692) London
Marks included: full name in oval outline, dotted; crowned rose between palm leaves; large X between initials SB in wreath-bordered circular outline; small shield marks include: lion passant; lion's head; label with S·BRIDGES in rectangle with wavy edges.

Broadhurst, Jonathan: (*fl. c.* 1719–1738) London

Mark used: stag between columns, with IONATHAN curved above, and BRODHVRST under, in shaped outline.

Brooker, Joseph: (*fl.* later 18th century) London
Mark used: demi-unicorn between palm leaves, with IOSEPH above and BROOKER below, in curved outline.

Brown(e), A.: (*fl.* early 18th century) Edinburgh, Midlothian
Mark used: thee-towered castle between initials A B, found over a date, all in triangular outline.

Browne & Swanson: (*fl.* 1760s) London
Mark used: an animal (? dog) with BROWNE over and & SWANSON in shaped outline.

Bryce, David: (recorded 1660) Edinburgh, Midlothian
Mark used: castle between initials D B found over a date (e.g. 1654) in rectangle of cross form.

Burford & Green: (*fl. c.* 1748–1780) London
Marks included: two shields (one with three stags on it) with BURFORD over and & GREEN under, in shaped outline; crowned rose, with MADE IN over, and LONDON under, in shaped outline; four small marks, i.e. shields, with consecutively: B & G; lion passant; figure of Britannia; crowned lion's head; curved label with IN·Y·POULTRY over LONDON.

Butcher, James, Jr: (before *c.* 1720) Bridgewater, Somerset
Marks included: rose and crown over with IAMES·BUTCHER around, in broad oval outline; four small marks, consecutively: IB; lion rampant; harp; rose and crown.

Carpenter, John: (*fl. c.* 1710–1747) London
Marks included: compasses enclosing globe between scrolled outline with IOHN over and CARPENTER below, in shaped outline; four small marks, i.e. rectangles with, consecutively, IC; lion passant; globe.

Carpenter & Hamberger: (*fl. c.* 1798–1805) London

Marks included: compasses enclosing globe, with CARPENTER over and HAMBERGER under, in shaped outline; crowned rose over LONDON.

Carter, A.: (*fl.* mid 18th century) London
Marks included: two lions rampant affronté with small crescent over, with crest above, and Latin motto under, in shaped outline; crowned rose, over LONDON, in broad oval outline.

Cartwright, Thomas: (*fl. c.* 1712–1743) London
Marks included: a bird (sometimes resembling a hoopoe) with THOMAS over and CARTWRIGHT under, in broad oval or circular outline; curved label with SUPERFINE over HARD METAL.

Chamberlain, Johnson: (*fl. c.* 1734) London
Marks included: crown over Prince-of-Wales feathers, with IOHNSON over and CHAMBERLAIN under; rectangular label with CHAMBERLAIN.

Chamberlain, Thomas: (*fl.* 1730s–1806) London
Mark used: crown over Prince-of-Wales feathers, with THOMAS over and CHAMBERLAIN under

Cleeve, Alexander: (*fl.* 1688–1739) London
Marks included: hand holding a rose between initials A C in a dotted circle; crowned rose over LONDON in shaped outline; small marks (shield or rectangle) with e.g. lion's head; or AC; curved label with MADE·IN over LONDON.

Cleeve, Alexander: (*fl. c.* 1715–1748) London
Marks included: hand holding Tudor rose with buds, with ALEX over, and CLEEVE under, in broad oval outline; shield, quartered, with ALEX CLEEVE running round over, in dotted circle; LONDON over crowned rose between palm leaves, in dotted oval; hand holding Tudor rose, between columns, with ALEX and CLEEVE; crowned rose between columns, with MADE IN over, and LONDON under; four small marks, shield-shaped, with e.g. lion's head; lion rampant; RW.

Cleeve, Bourchier: (*fl. c.* 1736–1757) London
Marks included: large Tudor rose in hand, between columns, with BOUR-CHIER over and CLEEVE under, in rectangular outline with curved top; crowned rose between columns, with MADE IN over in curve, and LONDON under, in similar outline.

Cleeve, Bourchier & Richard: (*c.* 1754) London
Marks included: hand holding Tudor rose, between columns, with BOURR & RICHD over, and CLEEVE; crowned rose between columns, with MADE IN over and LONDON below.

Coats, Archibald and William: (recorded 1799) Glasgow, Lanarkshire
Marks included: sailing ship with ARCHD/ WILLM/ COATS/ LONDON on four sides of square outline containing the touch; crown and rose between I F in oval outline.

Cocks, Samuel: (*fl.* early 19th century) London
Marks included: two cocks facing, with COCKS over and LONDON under, in wide oval outline; crowned Tudor rose with MADE IN over and LONDON under, in shaped outline.

Compton, Thomas: (*fl.* 1775–1817) London
Marks included: COMPTON, with or without LONDON under, in oval outline; crowned Tudor rose with MADE IN over and LONDON under; rectangular label with COMPTON/LONDON in two lines; shaped label with SUPERFINE/HARD METAL in two lines.

Compton, Thomas & Townsend: (*fl.* 1810–1815) London
Marks included: dove flying over animal (? a horse) surrounded by the three names following the oval outline; crowned Tudor rose with MADE IN over and LONDON below; four small marks (rectangular) with a chevron, lion passant, T & C.

Cotton, Jonathan: (*fl.* 1704–1740) London
Mark used: bird with rose and crescent, circled by IONATHAN COTTON in large oval outline.

Cotton, Jonathan: (*fl.* 1735–1760) London
Mark used: eagle and stalked rose over bird in oval, surrounded by IONATHAN COTTON in broad oval outline.

Cotton, Jonathan & Thomas: (*fl. c.* 1750) London
Marks included: eagle, flowers, and bird, with IONATHAN/& THOMAS in two curving lines over, and COTTON curving below, in shaped outline; small marks included: eagle; lion's head crowned; X; bird; label with LONDON/BRIDGE in two lines in rectangle with wavy edge.

Cutlove, Thomas: (*fl.* before 1680) London
Mark used: three fleur-de-lis among three stars, between palm leaves, with T·CUTLOVE curved over, all in oval outline.

Donne, John: (*fl.* 1692–1730) London
Marks included: hand with a bell (?) between two palm leaves, with IOHN over, and DONNE under, in shaped outline; crowned Tudor rose between palm leaves, with LONDON over and the date MDCXCII under, in rounded outline; label MADE IN/LONDON in two curving lines.

Durand, Jonas: (*fl. c.* 1692–1735) London
Mark used: E SONNANT over 1699 over a rose, between palm leaves, with IONAS over, and DURAND below.

Durand, Jonas: (*fl.* 1732–1775) London
Mark used similar to that of earlier Jonas Durand.

Dyer, Lawrence: (*fl. c.* 1645–1675) London
Marks included: shield bearing three anchors, with palms below, and LONDON over L. DYER above; crowned Tudor rose and palm leaves, with LONDON over; initials L D among three anchors in rounded shield outline; small marks in shields: lion passant; lion's head; three anchors; LD.

Dyer, Lawrence: (*fl.* early 18th century) London
Mark used: three anchors on a shield between palm leaves, with LAW over and DYER below, in shaped outline.

Eddon, William: (*fl. c.* 1689–1737) London
Marks included: emblem between initials W E in dotted circular outline; small marks of oval outline with lion's head; circle; lion passant; WE.

Edwards, J.: (*fl. c.* 1800) London
Mark used: crescent surrounded by EDWARDS WILDERNESS ROAD in circle with wavy edge.

Elderton, John: (*fl. c.* 1693–*c.* 1731) London
Marks included: three tuns, with IOHN over and ELDERTON below, in cartouche outline; small marks, shield shape, with, consecutively: three tuns; IE; lion passant; crowned leopard's head.

Elliott, Bartholomew: (*fl.* 1738–1746) London
Mark used: fancy figure, surrounded by BARTHOLOMEW ELLIOTT in wide oval.

Ellis, Samuel: (*fl. c.* 1720–1773) London
Marks included: fleece, with SAMUEL over and ELLIS below, in broad oval outline; crowned Tudor rose between palms, with LONDON over; small marks in rough ovals: fleece; lion's head erased, Britannia; SE; curving label with S:ELLIS/LONDON in two lines.

Fleming, William: (recorded 1717) Edinburgh, Midlothian
Marks included: bust (man in wig) with MAY TRADE FLOURISH arranged around it, in cartouche; crown over rose with FLEMING curved under, all in shaped outline.

Fletcher, Richard: (*fl. c.* 1678–1701) London
Marks included: windmill between the initials R F; crowned Tudor rose date 169–; small marks: lion passant; barred circle; lion's head; RI.

Fly, Martha: (*fl.* later 17th century) London
Mark used: fly between palm leaves, and MARTHA·FLY curving above, in shaped outline.

Fly, Timothy: (*fl. c.* 1710–1739) London
Marks included: a fly with TIM FLY curving over, in cartouche outline; crowned rose with palm leaves, and LONDON above, in similar outline; small marks: lion passant; lion's head crowned; fly; TF; labels, TIM·FLY/ IN LONDON in two curving lines; MADE·IN/·LONDON in two lines in rectangle.

Fly, William: (*fl. c.* 1680–1700) London
Marks included: a fly between palm leaves, with WILL FLY over in shaped outline; crowned rose with LONDON cutting across horizontally, in shaped outline; small marks: lion passant; lion's head crowned; fly; WF over fly (?).

Fly & Thompson: (*fl.* 1730s) London
Mark used: a fly surrounded by FLY AND THOMPSON in rounded outline.

Foster, Benjamin: (*fl.* 1730s onward) London
Marks included: oval "shield" with label over chevron and three emblems,, with BEN.·FOSTER curving above, and LONDON below, in cartouche outline; labels with SUPERFINE/HARD METTLE in two curving lines, or LONDON in rectangle with beaded border.

Gerardin & Watson: (*fl.* early 19th century) London
Marks included: GERARDIN with WATSON in circle round & in circular outline; WATSON * GERARDIN around numeral (2) in circular outline.

Giffin, Thomas: (*fl.* 1713–1764) London
Mark used: heart under coronet, with THOMAS · GIFFIN around, in broad oval outline.

Giffin, Thomas: (*fl. c.* 1760–1777) London
Marks included: crown over heart over spear, between columns, with THOMAS above and GIFFIN below, in shaped outline; crowned Tudor rose between columns, with MADE IN above and LONDON below; small marks: lion rampant; lion's head erased; coronet over sword; TG with two pellets over; all in small shields; label with THO GIFFIN/IN LONDON in two curving lines.

Gisburne, James: (*fl.* early 18th century) London

Mark used: lion rampant against a shield, in oval, with IAMES curving above and ·GISBURNE below, in shaped outline.

Gray & King: (recorded 1718) London
Marks included: pelican in her piety, with IO·GRAY over, and IA·KING below, in shaped outline; crowned Tudor rose, in shaped outline; label with MADE IN/LONDON in two lines in rectangle with scalloped edges.

Green, William Sandys: (*fl. c.* 1725–1737) London
Marks included: a griffin crest, with Wᴹ SANDYS over and GREEN below, in cartouche outline; crowned Tudor rose between two flowers, with Wᴹ SANDYS over and GREEN below.

Gregory, Edward: (recorded between 1705 and not later than 1733) Bristol, Somerset
Marks included: double-headed eagle displayed, between columns, with ED-WARD GREGORY in two curves above, in shaped outline; four small marks, consecutively: EG; Britannia; griffin's head erased; double-headed eagle.

Hammerton, Henry: (*fl. c.* 1705–1741) London
Marks included: crown over tun, between initials H H; crown over tun between palm leaves, with HENRY HAMMERTON curving round above, and date 1707 below; crowned Tudor rose with palm leaves, in shaped outline.

Harton & Sons: (*fl. c.* 1860–1890) London
Marks included: sword between TRADE MARK with H&S over, and LONDON below; crowned X; small marks: crown; H; sword; S; rose; SUPERFINE HARD METAL in two lines.

Hitchman, James: (*fl.* early 18th century) London
Marks included: lion holding key, with ·I·HITCHMAN curving over, in dotted oval outline; IH alongside lion with key, in round outline; crowned rose over LONDON in dotted broad oval outline; small marks (shields): IH; anchor; fleur-de-lis (?); and lion's head; labels with HITCHMAN over LONDON forming semicircle, in semicircular out-line; or I·HITCHMAN/MADE·IN·LONDON in two lines, in shaped rect-angular outline.

Hitchman, Robert: (*fl.* 1737–1761) London
Marks included: animal between columns, with R·HITCHMAN below, or similar with ROBERT above and HITCHMAN below, in shaped out-line; small marks (shields): RH; lion passant; Britannia; and anchor; label with R·HITCHMAN/IN LONDON in two curving lines.

Holmes, George: (recorded 1742) London
Marks included: four fleur-de-lis with GEORGE above and HOLMES be-low; labels with LONDON or SUPER-FINE/HARD METAL in two curved lines.

Home, John: (*fl. c.* 1749–1771) London
Marks included: shield device with six partlets on one side, with IOHN above and HOME below, in shaped outline; labels with SNOWHILL/LONDON in two curving lines, or LONDON/SUPERFINE the same; small marks: S·S; Britannia; crowned lion's head; lion's head erased.

Howard, William: (*fl.* late 17th century) London
Marks included: crown over shield bear-ing fleur-de-lis, between palm leaves, with WILLIAM over and HOWARD be-low; crowned rose between palm leaves, with DRURY LANE over and LON-DON below, both touches in similar broad oval outline; crowned rose between palms, over LONDON in rounded shaped outline; small marks: WH; lion's head crowned; fleur-de-lis; lion passant; also: lion passant; lion's head; FF in italics; WH with two pellets above and one below.

Hulls, John: (*fl. c.* 1676–1709) London
Mark used: Prince of Wales feathers be-tween palm leaves, with IOHN·HVLLS curved over, and LONDINI (or LONDON) below.

Hulls, Ralph: (*fl. c.* 1660–1682) London
Marks included: initials RH over a grasshopper, in dotted circular outline.

Hunton, Nicholas: (*fl. c.* 1660–1670) London

Marks included: initials NH over a talbot (dog) with a date between its legs (1662), in dotted circular outline; half-animal holding a stag's head, between palm leaves, with crown over NICH·HUNTON above, the whole in a shaped outline.

Iles, Robert: (*fl.* 1691–1735) London
Marks included: acorn sprig between initials RI in beaded circular outline; crown over rose between palm leaves with LONDON curved over, in near-oval outline; small marks: four lozenges each with lion rampant; four with, consecutively' R; I (both italics); lion passant; acorn sprig; each in small rectangle.

Ingles, Jonathan: (*fl.* 1669–1702) London
Marks included: initials II over clasped hands over date (1670) all in beaded circular outline; clasped hands under date (1671) with star below, between palm leaves, with IO·INGLES curving over, in dotted oval outline; small marks: oval with initials II.

Jackman, Nicholas: (*fl.* 1699–1736) London
Marks included: figure with stand (?) surrounded by NICHOLAS IACKMAN in dotted round outline; small marks, consecutively: NI; anchor; eagle; and lion passant; label MADE·IN/ LONDON in two curved lines.

Jackson, John: (*fl.* 1689–1716) London
Marks included: leaf (?) between palm leaves with I·IACKSON above; crown and rose between palm leaves, with LONDON over; four small marks, consecutively: NI; anchor; bird; lion passant; label LONDON in rectangle with serrated edges.

de Jersey, William: (*fl.* 1732–1785) London
Marks included: eagle surrounded by WILLIAM DE·IERSEY, in shaped outline; crowned rose in circle.

Jones, Charles: (*fl.* 1786–1795) London
Marks included: Paschal lamb between columns with C·JONES curved above and LONDON below, in shaped rectangular outline; paschal lamb with MADE IN above and LONDON below, in square outline; label with C·JONES.

Jones, John: (*fl.* 1727–1750) London
Marks included: bull with open book over, with IOHN above and IONES below, in shaped outline; crown and rose between palm leaves with LONDON over, in shaped outline; open book between initials II over bull with date (1700) below, in dotted circular outline; label with IN LONDON in curved line.

Joseph, Henry: (*fl.* 1736–1771) London
Marks included: escallop shell with HENRY over and IOSEPH curved below, in cartouche outline; labels with various inscriptions, e.g. NEW·STREET/ ST BRIDES/LONDON in three lines; MADE·IN / LONDON in two lines in rectangular outline; and SUPER· FINE/ HARD·METAL in two lines in rectangular outline.

Joseph, Henry and Richard: (*fl. c.* 1780) London
Marks included: escallop shell with H^Y & R^D over and IOSEPH below, in cartouche outline; escallop shell with HENRY &/RICHARD curved over in two lines, and IOSEPH below, in cartouche outline.

Jupe, John: (*fl.* 1735–1781) London
Marks included: fleur-de-lis and rose with IOHN over and IUPE below, in cartouche outline; crown and rose with MADE IN over and LONDON below, in cartouche outline; small marks with consecutively: lion rampant; lion's head; bird; I·I; labels with: SUPERFINE/ FRENCH/METAL; SUPERFINE/ HARD METAL in decorative outline; QUEEN/STREET/LONDON in three lines in shaped outline.

Jupe, Robert: (*fl.* 1697–1738) London
Marks included: fleur-de-lis over rose, with ROBERT over, and IUPE below, in cartouche outline; crown and rose with LONDON over and date below (1698); label MADE·IN/LONDON in shaped rectangular outline with wavy bottom edge.

Jupe, Robert: (recorded 1776) London
Marks included: fleur-de-lis over rose between palm leaves, with ROBERT over and JUPE below, in cartouche outline; label with R·IUPE·IN/LONDON in shaped outline.

Kelk, Nicholas: (*fl. c.* 1640–1687) London
Marks included: hand holding flower
spray between initials N K in dotted circular outline; crown over rose in shield.

Kenton, John: (*fl.* 1677–1717) London
Marks included: initials I K with star
above and below, with IOHN·KEN-
TON curved above, and palm leaves
around below, in shaped outline; crown
over rose between palm leaves with
LONDON above in shaped outline;
four small marks: IH; star; lion's head;
lion passant.

King, Richard: (*fl. c.* 1745–1798) London
Marks included: bird between columns
with KING below, or with RICHARD
over in addition; crown and rose between
columns, with GRACIOUS/STREET
below, or with GRACIOUS above and
STREET below; labels with: RD·
KING/IN:LONDON in rectangle;
SUPERFINE/HARD·METAL in
dotted rectangle; and LONDON in
plain rectangle.

Langford, John: (*fl. c.* 1719–1757) London
Marks included: a tun with a hand over
holding a hammer, between leaf sprays,
with JOHN over and LANGFORD
below, in broad oval outline; crown over
rose in shaped outline.

Langford, John: (recorded 1780) London
Marks included: hand with hammer held
near the horizontal over a tun, with
JOHN over, and LANGFORD under
in cartouche outline; labels with LON-
DON in scalloped rectangle, or SUPER·
FINE/HARD·METAL in two curved
lines; four small marks: I·L; hand holding hammer; tun; lion rampant (to R).

Lawrence, Stephen: (*fl. c.* 1667–1689)
London
Marks included: crown over initials SL
with double quatrefoil between palm
leaves, in oval outline; the same, but
without the crown or leaves, in dotted
circular outline; LAWRENCE with
crown above and SL below between palm
leaves, in broad oval outline; small shield
marks: SL.; lion passant; globe.

Lawrence, Stephen: (recorded 1708)
London
Marks included: trefoil between SL
under a crown, between palm leaves, with
STEPHEN over and LAWRENCE

below, in cartouche outline; crowned rose
between palm leaves, with LONDON
below, in shaped outline; small marks in
shield form: lion passant; globe; S:L.

Leach, Jonathan: (*fl. c.* 1740–1769)
London
Marks included: shield quartered with
swords, rose, etc., with IONATHAN
above and LEACH below, in cartouche
outline; small marks in shield form: I·L;
rider (?); lion passant; lion's head.

Leapidge, Edward: (*fl. c.* 1699–1724)
London
Marks included: unicorn (on right) facing a wheatsheaf, between palm leaves,
with EDW·LEAPIDGE/LONDON
curving above, in oval outline; crown and
rose between palm leaves with LON-
DON in curve over, in shaped outline;
small marks: EL; wheatsheaf; lion's
head, globe.

Leapidge, Edward: (recorded 1728)
London
Marks included: small animal emblem
between columns with EDWARD over
and LEAPIDGE below, in square
panel; crown and rose between columns
with MADE·IN above and LONDON
below, also in square panel; small marks
in shield form: EL; wheatsheaf (?); lion's
head; globe.

Leapidge, Thomas: (recorded 1691)
London
Marks included: animal facing wheatsheaf (?), between palm leaves, with
THO·LEAPIDGE/LONDON curv-
ing over, in broad oval outline; crown
and rose between palm leaves, in oval
outline.

Little, Henry: (*fl.* 1734–1764) London
Marks included: crown over cock, between columns, with HENRY curving
over, and LITTLE below, in shaped
outline; crown over rose, over LON-
DON in shaped outline; small marks in
shield form: lion rampant (?); lion's head
crowned; lion passant; H·L; label with
·H·LITTLE·/IN·LONDON· in two
curved lines.

Lovell, John: (*fl.* 1725–1742) Bristol,
Somerset
Marks included: crowned rose between
initials IL, in cartouche with dotted
border; small marks, in shield form: I·L;

crowned X; lion rampant; lion's head; label of wavy outline with IOHN· LOVELL.

Marten, Robert: (*fl. c.* 1645–1674) London
Marks included: R M over a bird (marten) in beaded circular outline; small marks: lion's head; globe; S A; also lion passant, and R H over a bird.

Maxwell, Stephen: (*fl.* 1780s) Glasgow, Lanarkshire
Marks included: sailing ship surrounded by SUCCESS · TO / Y · BRITISH / COLONIES and S MAXWELL to side of square outline with serrated edges; sailing ship surrounded by MAY · Y · UNITED / STATES · OF / AMERICA FLOURISH, arranged around sides of rectangular shape.

Moir, Alexander: (recorded 1675) Edinburgh, Midlothian
Mark used: castle between initials A M over a date (1672).

Munday, Thomas: (*fl.* 1754–1774) London
Marks included: bust of man in wig, with THOMAS curved above, and MUNDAY below, in cartouche outline; small marks with: T·M; bust; lion's head; Britannia.

Munden & Grove: (*fl.* 1760–1773) London
Mark used: stalk with rose on left and thistle (?) on right, with W M above and EG below, the initials arranged in the corners of the square outline (the corners being canted).

Nash, Edward: (*fl.* 1717–1738) London
Marks included: three fleurs-de-lis with EDWARD curved above and NASH below, in shaped outline; crown over rose between palms, in shaped outline; labels with: ED·NASH / IN LONDON in two curved lines, and LONDON in rectangle with serrated edges.

Newham, John: (*fl.* 1699–1731) London
Marks included: globe between palm leaves with lion passant over, surmounted by IOH·NEWHAM in oval outline; globe between I N with lion passant over, in circular outline; small marks: lion passant; Britannia; globe; I. N.

Newman, Richard: (recorded 1747; d. 1789) London
Mark used: mitre between two columns, with RICHARD curved over, and NEWMAN below, in rectangle with curved top.

Nicholson, Robert: (*fl.* 1690–1731) London
Marks included; goose (?) flying on a globe, with ROBERT over and NICHOLSON below; crown and rose over LONDON in cartouche outline; label, NICHOLSON.

Norfolk, Richard: (*fl. c.* 1735–1783) London
Marks included: three fleurs-de-lis with lion, with RᴰNORFOLK curved above, and IN·LONDON below, in shaped outline; LONDON over crown and rose; small marks: crown over R·N; Britannia; lion passant; lion's head crowned; labels with: MADE·IN / LONDON in two curved lines, or SUPERFINE / HARD METTLE in two curved lines.

Oliver, John: (*fl.* later 17th century) London
Mark used: seven-branched candlestick, surrounded by IOHN·OLIVER· LONDON in dotted oval outline.

Parr, Norton: (*fl. c.* 1742; d. 1773) Cork, Ireland
Mark used: swan between columns, with NORTON curved above, and PARR below.

Parr, Robert: (recorded *c.* 1681) London
Marks included: bust of man in ruff, with OLD THO PARR curved over, and AGED 152 below, in cartouche outline; label with: ROBᵀ PARR in curved line.

Patience, Robert: (*fl. c.* 1735–1777) London
Marks included: draped figure with ROBERT curved over, and PATIENCE below, in cartouche outline; crown and rose between palm leaves, with LONDON curved over, in broad oval outline.

Pedder, Joseph: (*fl. c.* 1727) London
Mark used: cock over crossed keys, with IOSEPH curved above and PEDDER below, in oval outline.

Perchard, Hellier: (*fl. c.* 1710–1740) London
Marks included: anchor with date (1709) about it, and HELLARY curved over, and PERCHARD below, in cartouche outline; small marks: bird (?); lion passant; JW; also: lion passant; lion's head crowned; fleur-de-lis; I·H.

Pettitt, John: (*fl. c.* 1685–1713) London
Marks included: unicorn passant, with IOHN curved above, and PETTIT below, in cartouche outline; crown and rose with initials I P in shaped outline small marks: lion passant; B; lion's head crowned; I·P; label, FREE·OF·LONDON.

Piggott, Francis: (*fl. c.* 1736–1760) London
Marks included: crescent over flower spray with FRANCIS curved over, and PIGGOTT under, in cartouche outline; crown and rose with MADE IN over and LONDON below, in cartouche outline; small marks: Britannia; lion's head erased; others indecipherable; label with NEWGATE/STREET/LONDON.

Pitt & Dadley: (recorded *c.* 1781) London
Marks included: hare passant with PITT over and & DADLEY below, in oval cartouche outline; PITT and DADLEY forming circle about & in circular outline; small marks: lion passant; lion's head; cross (?); R·P.

Pitt & Floyd: (recorded *c.* 1769) London
Mark used: hare passant, with PITT over, and & FLOYD below, in cartouche outline.

Pitts, Richard: (*fl. c.* 1747–1792) London
Marks included: hare passant with RICHARD over and PITTS below, in flattened oval outline, or cartouche outline; small marks: lion passant; lion's head; cross (?) R·P.

Porteus, Robert: (*fl. c.* 1760–1790)
Marks included: ostrich with ROBERT over and PORTEUS below, in shaped outline; crown and rose with MADE IN curved over, and LONDON below, in shaped outline; label with GRACE-CHURCH/STREET·LONDON in decorative panel.

Porteus, Robert and Thomas: (recorded 1762) London

Marks included: ostrich with ROB:& THO curved over, and PORTEUS below, in shaped outline; crown and rose with SUCCESSORS·TO above and RICHᴰ·KING below, in shaped outline; label with: GRACECHURCH/STREET·LONDON in decorative outline.

Priddle, Samuel: (*fl. c.* 1773–1800)
Mark used: crescent over flower spray with SAMUEL curved over, and PRIDDLE below, in cartouche outline.

Raper, Christopher: (*fl. c.* 1670–1694) London
Mark used: sword among three castles, between palm leaves, with CHRIS* RAPER over, in broad oval outline.

Rawlinson, John: (*fl. c.* 1674) London
Mark used: mitre between palm leaves, with IOHN/LONDINI curved over, and RAWLINSON below, in cartouche outline.

Rhodes, Thomas: (*fl. c.* 1721–1746) London
Marks included: dove under sunrays, between columns, with THOMAS over and RHODES below, in square-shaped outline; dove between initials TR in circular outline; crowned X over rose, in shaped outline.

Ridding, Thomas: (*fl. c.* 1674–1697) London
Mark used: pelican in her piety on a shield, between palm leaves, with THOMAS/RIDDING curved over, in broad oval outline.

Ridding, Thomas: (recorded 1699) London
Marks included: pelican in her piety between palm leaves, with THOMAS over and RIDDING below, in shaped outline; small marks: TR; sun (?); globe; lion rampant.

Righton, Samuel: (*fl. c.* 1732–1743) London
Marks included: cock over olive branches, with SAMUEL·RIGHTON curving over, in oval outline; small marks: lion passant; Britannia; cock; S·R.

Rudsby, Andrew: (*fl. c.* 1712–1730) London

132

Marks included: dove flying over wheatsheaf (?), between columns, with ANDREW in semicircle above, and RUDSBY below, in shaped outline; small marks: A·R; wheatsheaf; lion rampant.

de St Croix, John: (*fl. c.* 1730) London
Marks included: three lions passant, surrounded by IOHN DE ST CROIX in shaped outline; initials IDSX with six-point star above and below, in rough circle; the initials XSID arranged as a cross, in a circle; small marks include: IW; Britannia; lion's head erased; label with MADE IN/LONDON in two lines, curving.

Sandys, William: (*fl. c.* 1692–1703) London
Marks included: griffin rampant, with WILLIAM curved over and SANDYS below, in cartouche outline; griffin rampant, among six fleurs-de-lis, with WILLIAM over and SANDYS below, in cartouche outline.

Scattergood, Thomas: (*fl. c.* 1700–1732) London
Mark used: rosette over two hands holding mallets, between palms, with THOMAS over and SCATTERGOOD below, in circular outline.

Scattergood, Thomas: (*fl. c.* 1736–1775) London
Mark used; hand over rounded shield with three hands (?) upon it, with THOMAS over and SCATTERGOOD below, in cartouche outline.

Shorey, John, Jr: (*fl. c.* 1708–1725) London
Marks included: bird on rose, between palm leaves, with IOH SHOREY curving over, in oval outline; crown and rose between palm leaves, with LONDON over, in cartouche outline; crown and rose with LONDON over, and GOD PROTECT under, in cartouche outline; small marks: lion passant; lion's head; wheatsheaf (?); IS; also lion passant; cock; lion's head crowned; IS in italic caps; labels with I·SHOREY/LONDON in two curved lines, or LONDON plain.

Smith, Richard: (*fl. c.* 1677–1705) London
Marks included: name running round inside beaded circle; with date (1677); small marks: lion passant; lion's head crowned; rose; RS.

Smith, Samuel: (recorded 1728) London
Marks included: paschal lamb between columns, with SAMUEL curved above, and SMITH below; in shaped outline; hare and wheatsheaf (?) between columns, with SAMUEL over, and SMITH below, in rectangular outline; crown and rose between columns, with MADE·IN over, and LONDON below, in rectangular outline; labels with: MADE·ON / SNOW HILL / LONDON in three curved lines, or MADE·IN·/ ·LONDON.

Smith & Leapidge: (*fl. c.* 1728) London
Mark used: hare and wheatsheaf between columns, with SMITH & over, and LEAPIDGE below, in rectangular outline.

Spackman, James: (*fl. c.* 1704–1758) London
Mark used: fleur-de-lis between Maltese crosses over coronet and palm leaves, with IAMES curving over, and SPACKMAN under, in cartouche outline.

Spackman, Joseph: (*fl. c.* 1749–*c.* 1764) Marks included: fleur-de-lis and stars (?) over coronet and palm leaves, with IOSEPH curved over, and SPACKMAN below, in cartouche outline; crown and rose, with MADE IN over and LONDON below, in shaped outline; small marks: fleur-de-lis; lion's head crowned; labels with: SPACKMAN/ FENCHURCH / STREET / LONDON or CORNHILL/LONDON in curved lines.

Spackman, Joseph, & Co: (*fl. c.* 1785) London
Marks included: Royal coat-of-arms, surrounded by: HIS·MAJESTY'S· PATENT, in flattened oval outline; fleur-de-lis, coronet, palm leaves, with IOSEPH curved over, and SPACKMAN & CO under, in shaped outline; labels with: SPACKMAN/CORNHILL / LONDON, or PATENT/ OVAL, each in flattened oval outline.

Spackman, Joseph & James: (*fl. c.* 1782) London
Marks included: fleur-de-lis and coronet among crosses, over palm leaves, with

JOSH & JAS curved over, and SPACK-MAN below, in cartouche outline; crown and rose, with MADE·IN curved over, and LONDON below, in cartouche outline; label with CORNHILL/LONDON in curved lines.

Spackman & Grant: (*fl. c.* 1709) London
Marks included: fleur-de-lis over coronet with crosses, between palm leaves, and SPACKMAN curved over and & GRANT below, in cartouche outline; crown and rose between palm leaves, with LONDON over, in dotted oval outline; crown and rose over LONDON in shaped outline; small marks: lion passant; lion's head crowned; globe; IS; label: MADE IN/LONDON in rectangle with wavy edges.

Stanton, James: (*fl. c.* 1815–1835) London
Marks included: escallop with STANTON curved over and SHOE LANE below, in broken oval outline; escallop with STANTON over, and LITTLE/BRITAIN under, in near-oval outline; small marks: lion passant; Britannia; lion's head erased; three escallops.

Stanton, Robert: (*fl. c.* 1810–1842) London
Marks included: Royal standard, with R STANTON 97 BLACKMAN ST BORO round it, in beaded upright broad oval outline; small marks: RS; lion passant; three fleurs-de-lis (?); Britannia.

Swanson, Thomas: (*fl. c.* 1753–1783) London
Marks included: a talbot (dog) with THOMAS curving above, and SWANSON below, in shaped outline; a fleece with THOMAS above and SWANSON below, in broad oval outline; crown and rose with MADE IN curving above and LONDON below; small marks: fleece; lion's head erased; Britannia; SE; label with SUCCESSOR/TO·S·ELLIS/LONDON in curved lines.

Templeman, Thomas: (*fl. c.* 1670–1697) London
Marks included: crown over temple between columns, with T·TEMPLEMAN over and LONDON below, in oval outline; crown and rose between palm leaves; temple over palm leaves, with

THOMAS TEMPLEMAN around above, in broad oval outline; label: TEMPLEMAN.

Tisoe, James: (*fl. c.* 1733–1771) London·
Marks included: portcullis, with IAMES above and TISOE below, in cartouche outline; crown and rose, with WESTMINSTER above and LONDON below, in cartouche outline; small marks: I·T; lion's head; two mullets with sword (?); lion passant.

Townsend, John: (*fl. c.* 1748–1801) London
Marks included: dove and lamb, with JOHN over, and TOWNSEND below, in cartouche outline; dove and lamb with TOWNSEND below in oval outline; hand holding flower spray, between columns, with MADE IN curving over, and LONDON below, in shaped outline; small marks: lamb and dove; lion's head; Britannia; IT; labels with: MADE IN/LONDON, or FENCHURCH/STREET LONDON, in shaped rectangles, or SUPERFINE/HARD METAL in two curved lines.

Townsend & Compton: (*fl. c.* 1785–1805) London
Marks included: dove and lamb, with TOWNSEND & COMPTON around, in cartouche outline; crown and rose with MADE·IN over and LONDON below, in shaped outline; small marks: lion rampant; sword: T&C; labels with: SUPER FINE / HARD METAL or FEN CHURCH / STREET LONDON in decorative rectangles.

Vaughan, John: (*fl. c.* 1753–1807) London
Marks included: Paschal lamb on a field, between columns, with IOHN curving above, and VAUGHAN below, in shaped outline; Paschal lamb with MADE IN above and LONDON below; small marks: I·V; lion's head crowned; lion passant; lion's head; label with: I·VAUGHAN.

Walmsley, John: (*fl.* early 18th century) Gainsborough, Lincs.
Mark used: crown over heart, between palm leaves, with IOHN over and WALMSLEY under, in cartouche outline.

Watts, John: (*fl. c.* 1725–1760) London
Marks included: globe on stand, resting on INO WATTS, in shaped outline; crown and rose on LONDON, in shaped outline; small marks recorded include: I V; globe on stand; lion passant to right; lion's head; also I V; globe on stand; Britannia; lion passant to right; and lion rampant; lion's head; bird: LR.

Whittle, Francis: (*fl. c.* 1715–1738) London
Marks included: dove on tree, with FRANCIS above and WHITTLE below, in cartouche outline; small marks: FW; Britannia; lion or griffin's head erased; dove; label with SUPER FINE/HARD METAL in two curved lines.

Withers, Benjamin: (*fl. c.* 1719–1730) London
Marks included: crown over a cock, with BENIAMIN curving over, and WITHERS below, in cartouche outline; crown and rose between palms, over LONDON; small marks: cock; lion's head crowned; lion passant; BW; labels with: LONDON in rectangle with serrated edges, or B·WITHERS/IN· LONDON in decorative rectangle.

MODERN PEWTER: QUALITY MARK

In 1970 the pewter manufacturers, with the blessing of the Worshipful Company of Pewterers, London, formed the Association of British Pewter Craftsmen. This body has introduced a quality mark, first used in late 1971.

Conditions for its use include: the piece so marked must contain at least 90% tin, the balance being copper/antimony/bismuth, with not more than 0.5% of lead and 0.1% of trace elements; that the standard of craftsmanship, finish and design of the marked piece should not be such as to bring British pewterware into disrepute. In addition, the user should be a full member of the Association of British Pewter Craftsmen; further, besides the quality mark, the maker should also mark his pieces with his own individual mark.

American Silversmiths' Marks

From the beginning, the American government laid down no laws regarding marking. American silversmiths at first followed English usage; by the 18th century, they employed either initials, or the surname in full, in a square or oblong panel with plain or serrated edges; this was the normal custom. The use of the surname differs from the English custom, for in England, by decree, the use of initials only was allowed.

AB	**Adrien Bancker** (1703–1772) New York, N.Y. (oval punch)
AB	**Abel Buel** (1742–1825) New Haven, Conn. (elongated oval punch)
AB	**A. Billing** (recorded 1780) Troy, N.Y. (square punch)
AC	**Alexander Camman** (*fl.* early 19th century) Albany, N.Y. (oblong punch)
AC	**Aaron Cleveland** (recorded 1820) Norwich, Conn. (oblong punch with canted corners)
AC	**Arnold Collins** (*fl.* late 17th century) Newport, R.I. (scutcheon, heart-shape, or small oblong punch)
AC	**Albert Cole** (*fl.* early 19th century) New York, N.Y. (A over C, in diamond-shape punch)
AC	**Abraham Carlisle** (*fl.* 1790s) Philadelphia, Pa. (square punch)
AD	**Amos Doolittle** (1754–1832) New Haven, Conn. (oval punch)
AD	**Abraham Dubois** (*fl. c.* 1778) Philadelphia, Pa. (oval punch, letters sometimes conjoined)
A·E·W	**Andrew E. Warner** (1786–1870) Baltimore, Maryland. (oblong punch with serrated ends; also AEW in interlaced italic caps, in plain oblong punch)
A.F or **A.F.** or **AGF**	**Abraham G. Forbes** (*fl. c.* 1770) New York, N.Y. (oblong punch)
A & G.W.	**A. & G. Welles** (*fl.* early 19th century) Boston, Mass. (oblong punch)
AH	**Ahasuerus Hendricks** (*fl. c.* 1675) New York, N.Y. (oval punch, letters conjoined)
A·J·&·C°.	**A. Jacobs & Co** (*fl. c.* 1820) Philadelphia, Pa. (oblong punch)

AL   **Aaron Lane** (*fl. c.* 1780) Elizabeth, N.J.
(oblong punch)

AL   **Adam Lynn** (*fl.* late 18th century) D.C.
(oblong punch)

AP   **Abraham Poutreau** (*fl. c.* 1725) New York, N.Y.
(heart-shape punch)

A&R   **Andras & Richard** (*fl.* 1790s) New York, N.Y.
(oblong punch)

A.S.   **Anthony Simmons** (*fl.* late 18th century) Philadelphia, Pa.
(oblong punch)

AT   **Andrew Tyler** (1692–1741) Boston, Mass.
(oblong or heart-shape punch; also AT sometimes
crowned, in shaped punch)

AU   **Andrew Underhill** (*fl.* 1780s) New York, N.Y.
(oblong punch)

AW   **Antipas Woodward** (*fl.* 1790s) Middletown, Conn.
(oblong punch)

BB   **Benjamin Bussey** (1757–1842) Dedham, Mass.
(oblong punch)

BB   **Benjamin Brenton** (1695 1749) Newport, R.I.
(oblong punch)

BB   **Benjamin Benjamin** (*fl. c.* 1825) New York, N.Y.
(incised, or in oblong punch with canted corners)

B&D   **Barrington & Davenport** (*fl. c.* 1805) Philadelphia, Pa.
(oblong punch with serrated edges)

B.G   **Baldwin Gardiner** (*fl. c.* 1814) Philadelphia, Pa.
(oblong punch)

B.G.&CO   **B. Gardiner & Co** (*fl. c.* 1836) New York, N.Y.
(oblong punch)

BH   **Benjamin Hurd** (1739–1781) Boston, Mass.
(oblong punch)

BH   **Benjamin Hiller** (b. 1687) Boston, Mass.
(shield shaped or oblong punch with waved top and bottom edges)

B&I *or* **B&J**   **Boyce & Jones** (*fl. c.* 1825) New York, N.Y.
(each in oblong punch)

BL   **Benjamin Lamar** (*fl. c.* 1785) Philadelphia, Pa.
(oval punch)

B&M   **Bradley & Merriman** (*fl. c.* 1825) New Haven, Conn.
(oblong punch, or shaped to include star)

B.P   **Benjamin Pierpont** (1730–1797) Boston, Mass.
(square or heart-shape punch)

BR   **Bartholomew Le Roux** (recorded 1688) New York, N.Y.
(oblong punch with curved ends)

BR   **Bartholomew Le Roux** (recorded 1713) New York, N.Y.
(shaped punch)

B&R   **Brower & Rusher** (recorded 1834) New York, N.Y.
(oblong punch)

B&R   **Burnet & Ryder** (*fl.* late 18th century) Philadelphia, Pa.
(cursive letters, oblong punch)

BS   **Benjamin Sanderson** (1649–1678) Boston, Mass.
(oblong, or near-oblong punch)

BS   **Bartholomew Schaats** (1683–1758) New York, N.Y.
(heart-shape or oblong punch)

B&S   **Beach & Sanford** (1785–1788) Hartford, Conn.
(oblong punch)

BT&B   **Ball, Tompkins & Black** (*fl. c.* 1839) New York, N.Y.
(oblong punch)

BW   **Barnard Wenman** (recorded 1789) New York, N.Y.
(oblong punch)

BW   **Billious Ward** (1729–1777) Guilford, Conn.
(shaped or oval punch)

B.W   **Bancroft Woodcock** (recorded 1754) Wilmington, Delaware.
(oval punch)

BW&C⁰   **Butler, Wise & Co** (recorded 1845) Philadelphia, Pa.
(oblong with rounded end)

B&W   **Beach & Ward** (1789–1795) Hartford, Conn.
(oblong punch with rounded ends)

C.A.B.   **Charles A. Burnett** (recorded 1793) Alexandria, Va.
(oblong punch)

C.B   **C. Brigden** (recorded 1770) Boston, Mass.
(oblong punch)

CB   **Clement Beecher** (1778–1869), Berlin, Conn.
(oblong or rounded punch, both serrated)

CC   **Charles Candell** (recorded 1795) New York, N.Y.
(oblong punch)

CC   **Christian Cornelius** (recorded 1810) Philadelphia, Pa.
(oblong punch)

CC&D   **Charters, Cann & Dunn** (recorded 1850) New York, N.Y.
(oblong punch)

C.C.&S.   **Curtis, Candee & Stiles** (recorded 1840) Woodbury, Conn.
(oblong punch)

CG   **Cesar Ghiselin** (recorded 1695) Philadelphia, Pa.
(oblong or inverted heart-shape punch)

C.H   **Charles Hequembourg, Jr.** (1760–1851) New Haven, Conn.
(shaped punch)

C.H   **Christopher Hughes** (1744–1824) Baltimore, Maryland.
(oblong punch flanked by striations)

CK   **Cornelius Kierstede** (1675–1757) New Haven, Conn.
(oblong or oval punch)

CL   **Charles Leach** (1765–1814) Boston, Mass.
(oblong punch with waved edges)

C.L.B   **Charles L. Boehme** (1774–1868) Baltimore, Maryland.
(oblong punch)·

C&M   **Coit & Mansfield** (recorded 1816) Norwich, Conn.
(oblong punch, sometimes with rounded corners)

C.O.B.   **Charles Oliver Bruff** (*fl. c.* 1763) New York, N.Y.
(oblong punch)

C&P   **Cleveland & Post** (*fl. c.* 1815) Norwich, Conn.
(oblong punch, sometimes with serrated edges)

C&P   **Curry & Preston** (recorded 1831) Philadelphia, Pa.
(oblong punch)

CR   **Charles Le Roux** (1689–1745) New York, N.Y.
(oval punch)

CR   **Christopher Robert** (1708–1783) New York, N.Y.
(oval punch)

C.S.   **Caleb Shields** (recorded 1773) Baltimore, Maryland.
(oval or oblong punch)

CVB   **Cornelius Vanderburgh** (1653–1699) New York, N.Y.
(CV over B in heart-shape punch)

CVGF
or C.V.G.F.   **Collins V. G. Forbes** (recorded 1816) New York, N.Y.
(oblong punch)

CW   **Charles Whiting** (1725–1765) Norwich, Conn.
(oval or shaped punch)

C.W   **Christian Wiltberger** (1770–1851) Philadelphia, Pa.
(oblong punch)

DB   **Daniel Boyer** (1726–1779) Boston, Mass.
(oblong punch or nipped oval punch)

DB&AD   **Bayley & Douglas** (recorded 1789) New York, N.Y.
(oblong punch)

D.C   **Daniel B. Coan** (recorded 1789) New York, N.Y.
(oblong punch)

DCF **Daniel C. Fueter** (recorded 1756) New York, N.Y.
(oblong punch with rounded ends)

DD **Daniel Deshon** (1697–1781) New London, Conn.
(shaped punch)

D:D *or* **DD** **Daniel Dupuy** (1719–1807) Philadelphia, Pa.
(shaped, oval, or oblong punch)

DDD **Dupuy & Sons** (recorded 1784) Philadelphia, Pa.
(shaped punch)

DF **Daniel C. Fueter** (recorded 1756) New York, N.Y.
(oblong punch)

DH **Daniel Henchman** (1730–1775) Boston, Mass.
(oblong punch)

DH **David Hall** (1760–1779) Philadelphia, Pa.
(shaped punch)

D.I **David Jesse** (1670–1705) Boston, Mass.
(oval punch)

DI **David Jackson** (*fl. c.* 1782) New York, N.Y.
(shaped punches)

DM **David Mygatt** (1777–1822) Danbury, Conn.
(oblong punch)

DM **David Moseley** (1753–1812) Boston, Mass.
(oblong punch)

DN **David I. Northee** (d. 1788) Salem, Mass.
(oblong punch)

D&P **Downing & Phelps** (recorded 1810) New York, N.Y.
(oblong punch)

D.R *or* **DR** **Daniel Rogers** (d. 1792) Newport, R.I.
(oblong punch)

DR **Daniel Russel** (*fl. c.* 1720) Newport, R.I.
(shaped oval punch)

DS **David Smith** (*fl.* later 18th century) Philadelphia, Pa.
(oblong punch)

DT **David Tyler** (1760–1804) Boston, Mass.
(flattened oval punch)

D.T.G. **D. T. Goodhue** (*fl.* 1840s) Boston, Mass.
(oblong punch)

D.V **Daniel Vinton** (*fl. c.* 1790) Providence, R.I.
(oblong punch)

DV *or* **D.V.**
or **DVV** **Daniel Van Voorhis** (*fl. c.* 1770) New York, N.Y.
(oblong punch)

D&W	**Davis & Watson** (*fl. c.* 1815) Boston, Mass. (italic caps in oblong punch)
DY	**Daniel You** (*fl.* 1740s) Charleston, South Carolina. (rounded oval punch)
EA	**Ebenezer Austin** (*fl.* 1780s) Hartford, Conn. (oblong punch)
EB	**E.Baker** (1740 1790) New York, N.Y. (oblong punch)
EB	**Elias Boudinot** (1706–1770) Philadelphia, Pa. (oblong or close oval punch)
EB	**Everardus Bogardus** (*fl.* late 17th century) New York, N.Y. (oblong punch)
EB	**Ezekiel Burr** (1764–1846) Providence, R.I. (oblong punch; also EB in italic caps, in shaped or oval punch)
EB	**Ephraim Brasher** (recorded 1760s) New York, N.Y. (oblong or tight oval punch)
EB&CO	**Erastus Barton & Co** (*fl.* 1820s) New York, N.Y. (oblong punch)
E·C	**Elias Camp** (recorded 1825) Bridgeport, Conn. (oblong punch with serrated edges)
EC	**Ebenezer Chittenden** (1726–1812) New Haven, Conn. (oblong or oval punch)
ED	**E. Davis** (recorded 1775) Newburyport, Mass. (oblong punch with rounded corners)
EH *or* **E·H**	**Eliakim Hitchcock** (1726–1788) New Haven, Conn. (oblong punch)
EH	**Eliphaz Hart** (1789–1866) Norwich, Conn. (oblong punch)
EL	**Edward Lang** (1742–1830) Salem, Mass. (oblong punch)
EM	**Edmund Milne** (recorded 1757) Philadelphia, Pa. (oblong punch)
EME	**Edgar M. Eoff** (1785–1858) New York, N.Y. (oblong punch)
EP.	**Edward Pear** (*fl.* 1830s) Boston, Mass. (oblong punch with serrated edges)
EP	**Elias Pelletreau** (1726–1810) Southampton, N.Y. (oblong punch)
EPL	**Edward P. Lescure** (*fl.* 1820s) Philadelphia, Pa. (italic caps in oblong punch)

E&P **Eoff & Phyfe** (recorded 1844) New York, N.Y.
(oblong punch, rounded end at P)

E&S **Easton & Sanford** (recorded 1816) Nantucket, Mass.
(oblong punch)

EW **Edward Webb** (early 18th century) Boston, Mass.
(oblong punch)

EW **Edward Winslow** (1669–1753) Boston, Mass.
(oblong or shaped punch)

F.&G. **Fletcher & Gardiner** (recorded 1812) Philadelphia, Pa.
(oblong punch)

F&H **Farrington & Hunnewell** (*fl.* 1830s) Boston, Mass.
(oblong punch)

F.M **Frederick Marquand** (*fl.* 1820s) New York, N.Y.
(oblong punch; also F·M)

F&M **Frost & Munford** (recorded 1810) Providence, R.I.
(oblong punch with serrated edges)

FR **Francis Richardson** (d. 1729) Philadelphia, Pa.
(heart-shape punch; also FR crowned, in closely-shaped punch)

FW **Freeman Woods** (*fl.* late 18th century) New York, N.Y.
(italic caps in oblong punch)

F.W.C **Francis W. Cooper** (*fl.* 1840s) New York, N.Y.
(FWC over NY in tight oblong punch)

G.B **George Bardick** (recorded 1790) Philadelphia, Pa.
(oblong punch)

GB
or G.B **Geradus Boyce** (recorded 1814) New York, N.Y.
(oblong punch)

B
GO **Gerrit Onkelbag** (1670–1732) New York, N.Y.
(close-shaped trefoil punch)

GC **George Canon** (early 19th century) Warwick, R.I.
(oblong punch)

GD **George Drewry** (*fl.* 1760s) Philadelphia, Pa.
(oval punch, indented upper edge, between G and D)

GD **George Dowig** (*fl.* 1770s) Philadelphia, Pa.
(oblong or oval punch; also G·D in oval punch)

G&D **Goodwin & Dodd** (*fl. c.* 1813) Hartford, Conn.
(oblong punch)

GF **George Fielding** (*fl.* 1730s) New York, N.Y.
(oval punch)

GH   **George Hutton** (recorded 1799) Albany, N.Y.
(oval punch)

G.H   **George Hanners** (1697–1740) Boston, Mass.
(oblong punch; also crowned G.H in scutcheon-shape punch)

G&H   **Gale & Hayden** (*fl.* 1840s) New York, N.Y.
(oblong punch with canted corners)

GL   **Gabriel Lewin** (recorded 1771) Baltimore, Maryland.
(oblong punch)

G&M   **Gale & Moseley** (recorded 1830) New York, N.Y.
(oblong punch, plain or with serrated edges)

GR   **George Ridout** (recorded 1745) New York, N.Y.
(oblong punch with canted corners)

GRD   **G. R. Downing** (*fl. c.* 1810) New York, N.Y.
(oblong punch)

GS   **George Stephens** (recorded 1790) New York, N.Y.
(flattened oval punch; also G.S. in concave oblong punch with serrated end)

G&S   **Gale & Stickler** (*fl.* 1820s) New York, N.Y.
(oblong punch)

GT   **George Tyler** (1740–1785) Boston, Mass.
(oblong punch)

G.W.&H   **Gale, Wood & Hughes** (recorded 1835) New York, N.Y.

H.B   **Henry Bailey** (recorded 1780) Boston, Mass.
(oblong punch)

HB   **Henricus Boelen** (1684–1755) New York, N.Y.
(apparently crowned HB in close-shaped oval punch)

H&B   **Hart & Brewer** (first years 19th century) Middletown, Conn.
(oblong punch)

HH   **Henry Hurst** (1665–1717) Boston, Mass.
(oblong or flattened scutcheon punch)

H&H   **Hall & Hewson** (recorded 1819) Albany, N.Y.
(oblong punch)

H&I   **Heydorn & Imlay** (*fl. c.* 1810) Hartford, Conn.
(oblong punch with waved edges)

H.L   **Harvey Lewis** (recorded 1811) Philadelphia, Pa.
(oblong punch)

H.L.W. & CO   **Henry L. Webster & Co** (*fl.* 1840s) Providence, R.I.
(oblong punch)

H&M   **Hays & Myers** (*fl.* 1770s) New York, N.Y.
(oblong punch)

H&M   **Hall & Merriman** (recorded *c.* 1826) New Haven, Conn.
(incised)

H&N   **Hyde & Nevins** (recorded *c.* 1798) New York, N.Y.
(oblong punch)

·HP   **Henry Pitkin** (*fl.* 1830s) East Hartford, Conn.
(flattened octagonal punch)

HRT   **Henry R. Truax** (recorded 1815) Albany, N.Y.
(italic caps in oblong punch with serrated edges; also plain HRT
in plain oblong punch)

HS   **Hezekiah Silliman** (1739–1804) New Haven, Conn.
(oblong punch)

H&S   **Hart & Smith** (recorded *c.* 1815) Baltimore, Maryland.
(oblong punch; also H&S incised)

H&S   **Hotchkiss & Shreuder** (mid 19th century) Syracuse, N.Y.
(H in round punch, & in diamond-shape punch, S in round punch)

H&W   **Hart & Wilcox** (early 19th century) Norwich, Conn.
(oblong punch)

IA   **I. Adam** (*fl. c.* 1800) Alexandria, Va.
(italic caps in oval punch)

IA   **John Allen** (1691–1760) Boston, Mass.
(quatrefoil, oval, or knobbed oval punch)

IA   **Isaac Anthony** (*fl.* early 18th century) Newport, R.I.
(oval punch)

IA   **Joseph Anthony** (recorded 1783) Philadelphia, Pa.
(italic caps in oblong punch)

IA   **John Avery** (1732–1794) Preston, Conn.
(oblong punch)

I.A   **Josiah Austin** (1718–1780) Charlestown, Mass.
(oblong punch)

I.A   **Minott & Austin** (*fl.* 1765–1769) Boston, Mass.
(oblong punch, with "Minott" in separate oblong punch)

**IA
IE**   **Allen & Edwards** (early 18th century) Boston, Mass.
(in two separate shaped punches)

I·B   **John Benjamin** (1731–1796) Stratford, Conn.
(oblong punch)

IB
or **I·B**   **Jacob Boelen** (recorded 1773) New York, N.Y.
(oval or oblong punch)

I·B   **John Burger** (recorded 1786) New York, N.Y.
(oblong punch)

IB   **Jacob Boelen** (1659–1729) New York, N.Y.
(rounded scutcheon punch, with shaped top)

IB   **John Burt** (1691–1745) Boston, Mass.
(with crown above and dot below, in shaped punch; also
I:B in oblong punch; also crowned I:B in shaped scutcheon punch)

IBL   **John Burt Lyng** (recorded 1761) New York, N.Y.
(oblong punch)

IBV   **John Brevoort** (1715–1775) New York, N.Y.
(flattened oval, or trefoil punch)

IC   **John Carman** (recorded 1771) Philadelphia, Pa.
(oblong punch with canted corners)

I·C   **John Champlin** (1745–1800) New London, Conn.
(oblong punch)

I.C   **Jonathan Clarke** (recorded 1734) Newport, R.I.
(also IC, in oblong punch; also IC in oval punch)

I·C   **Joseph Carpenter** (1747–1804) Norwich, Conn.
(oblong punch)

I.C   **John Coburn** (1725–1803) Boston, Mass.
or IC   (square punch)

IC   **John Coddington** (1690–1743) Newport, R.I.
(oval punch, with top and tail resembling a turnip)

IC   **John Coney** (1655–1722) Boston, Mass.
(oval or oblong punch; also IC over four-point star, in
cartouche-shape punch; also crowned IC over animal in scutcheon)

ID   **Jeremiah Dummer** (1645–1718) Boston, Mass.
(oblong punch; also ID over star in scutcheon or cartouche punch)

ID   **John David** (1736–1794) Philadelphia, Pa.
(oval punch)

ID   **John Dixwell** (1680–1725)
(almost circular punch)

IE   **John Edwards** (recorded 1700) Boston, Mass.
(crowned, with star under, in scutcheon punch)

IE   **Joseph Edwards** (1707–1777) Boston, Mass.
or I·E   (oblong punch)

IG   **John Gardiner** (1734–1776) New London, Conn.
(rounded oblong punch)

IG   **Joseph Goldthwaite** (1706–1780) Boston, Mass.
(crowned, in plain scutcheon punch)

IG   **John Gray** (1692–1720) New London, Conn.
(flattened oval punch)

I.G   **John D. Germon** (recorded 1782) Philadelphia, Pa.
(oblong punch)

IGL   **Jacob G. Lansing** (*fl.* 1730s) Albany, N.Y.
(oblong punch, the G being a very small letter)

IH *or* I·H	**John Hastier** (recorded 1726) New York, N.Y. (oblong, oval, scutcheon, or heart-shaped punch)
IH	**John Hull** (1624–1683) Boston, Mass. (in heart-shaped punch; also IH with star above, in shaped oblong punch)
I·H	**Jacob Hurd** (1702–1758) Boston, Mass. (shaped oval punch)
I.H *or* IH	**John Hutton** (*fl. c.* 1721) New York, N.Y. (oblong punch; also as I·H)
IH *with* RS	**Hull & Sanderson** (recorded *c.* 1652) Boston, Mass. (RS with star above, in shaped punch; IH as for John Hull)
IHL	**Josiah H. Lownes** (d. 1822) Philadelphia, Pa. (oblong punch; also JHL in oblong punch)
IHM	**John H. Merkler** (recorded *c.* 1780) New York, N.Y. (oblong punch)
IHR	**John H. Russell** (*fl.* 1790s) New York, N.Y. (oblong punch with serrated edges)
I·I	**Jacob Jennings** (1739–1817) Norwalk, Conn. (oblong punch)
I·J	**John Jenkins** (recorded 1777) Philadelphia, Pa. (square punch)
IK	**Joseph Keeler** (1786–1824) Norwalk, Conn. (oblong punch, with plain, or serrated, edges)
I·L	**Jeffery Lang** (1708–1758) Salem, Mass. (oblong punch)
IL	**John Leacock** (recorded 1751) Philadelphia, Pa. (oval or square punch; also I·L in oblong punch)
IL *or* I·L	**John Lynch** (1761–1848) Baltimore, Maryland. (square punch)
I·L·T	**John Le Telier** (recorded 1770) Philadelphia, Pa. (oblong punch)
I·M	**John McMullin** (recorded *c.* 1790) Philadelphia, Pa. (oblong punch; also IM incised)
IM	**Jacob Marius Groen** (*fl.* early 18th century) New York, N.Y. (oblong punch)
I:M *or* I·M	**John Moulinar** (recorded 1744) New York, N.Y. (oblong punch)
I.M.	**James Murdock** (*fl. c.* 1779) Philadelphia, Pa. (oblong punch)
IN	**Joseph Noyes** (d. 1719) Philadelphia, Pa. (flattened oval punch)

IN   **Johannis Nys** (*fl.* late 17th century) Philadelphia, Pa.
(heart-shape punch; also IN in oblong punch)

I·NR   **Joseph & Nathaniel Richardson** (*fl.* 1785) Philadelphia, Pa.
(oblong punch, or incised)

I·O   **Jonathan Otis** (1723–1791) Newport, R.I.
(oblong punch)

IP   **Job Prince** (1680–1704) Milford, Conn.
(rough oval punch)

I·P   **Jacob Perkins** (1766–1849) Newburyport, Mass.
(shaped punch; also crowned IP in shaped scutcheon punch)

IP   **John Pearson** (*fl.* 1790s) New York, N.Y.
(oblong punch)

I·P   **John Potwine** (recorded 1737) Boston, Mass.
(oblong punch)

I.P.T. & SON   **John P. Trott & Son** (*fl.* 1820s) New London, Conn.
(oblong punch)

I&PT   **John & Peter Targee** (*fl.* early 19th century) New York, N.Y.
(oblong punch)

IR   **John Le Roux** (recorded 1723) New York, N.Y.
(oval punch)

I.R   **Joseph Richardson** (1711–1784) Philadelphia, Pa.
(oblong punch)

I·R   **Joseph Rogers** (recorded 1808) Newport, R.I.
(flattened oval punch)

I.R   **Joseph Richardson, Jr.** (recorded 1786) Philadelphia, Pa.
(oblong punch with softened corners)

IR&S   **Isaac Reed & Son** (*fl. c.* 1810) Stamford, Conn.
(oblong punch)

I&R   **Johnson & Riley** (*fl.* 1780s) Baltimore, Maryland.
(italic caps in oblong punch with rounded ends)

I·S   **John Stuart** (d. 1737) Providence, R.I.
(square punch; also IS in square punch)

I·S   **I. Smith** (1742–1789) Boston, Mass.
(oblong punch)

IT   **John Tanner** (*fl. c.* 1740) Newport, R.I.
(oval heart-shaped punch)

I.T.   **John Targee** (recorded 1799) New York, N.Y.
(oblong punch)

IT   **John Touzell** (recorded 1756) Salem, Mass.
(square punch)

I.T   **James Turner** (d. 1759) Boston, Mass.
(oval punch)

ITE   **Jacob Ten·Eyck** (1704–1793) Albany, N.Y.
(the TE conjoined; in oblong or shaped punch)

IV   **J. Vanderhan** (*fl. c.* 1740) Philadelphia, Pa.
(italic caps in shaped punch)

I·V   **John Vernon** (*fl.* 1790s) New York, N.Y.
(oblong or shaped oval punch)

I·V   **Underhill & Vernon** (recorded 1787) New York, N.Y.
with TU   (IV in shaped oval punch, with TU in square punch)

S   **Jacobus Van de Spiegel** (1668–1708) New York, N.Y.
I V   (in trefoil punch; also IVS in oblong punch with serrated edges;
also IVS in flattened oval or rough oblong)

IVK   **John Van Newkirke** (recorded *c.* 1716) New York, N.Y.
(the IV conjoined; oblong punch)

IW   **Joshua Weaver** (*fl. c.* 1815) West Chester, Pa.
(shaped oval punch)

IW   **John Waite** (*fl. c.* 1770) Kingstown, R.I.
or I·W   (oblong punch)

IWF   **John W. Forbes** (recorded 1805) New York, N.Y.
(found over NY in oblong punch)

I.W.G   **John Ward Gilman** (recorded 1792) New York, N.Y.
(incised)

JA   **Jeromimus Alstyne** (*fl. c.* 1766) New York, N.Y.
or J.A   (oblong punch, plain or with serrated edges)

J&A.S   **J. & A. Simmons** (*fl.* early 19th century) New York, N.Y.
(oblong punch)

J.B   **John Boyce** (recorded *c.* 1800) New York, N.Y.
(oblong punch; found accompanied by NY in separate oblong punch)

J.B   **James Black** (recorded 1811) Philadelphia, Pa.
(oblong punch)

J.B   **James Butler** (recorded 1734) Boston, Mass.
(oval punch)

JC   **Joseph Clark** (recorded 1791) Danbury, Conn.
(oblong punch)

JC   **Jonathan Crosby** (1743–1769) Boston, Mass.
(rounded oval punch)

J.C.M   **John C. Moore** (*fl.* 1840s) New York, N.Y.
(oblong punch)

JD   **John Denise** (recorded *c.* 1797) New York, N.Y.
or J:D   (oblong punch)

JD   **John David, Jr.** (recorded 1792) Philadelphia, Pa.
or **J.D**   (oblong, oval, or flattened oval punch)

J.F   **Foster & Richards** (recorded *c.* 1815) New York, N.Y.
(oblong punch)

JG   **John Gardiner** (1734–1776) New London, Conn.
(dented circle punch)

J.G   **John Gibbs** (recorded 1798) Providence, R.I.
(shaped punch)

JG   **James Gough** (*fl.* later 18th century) New York, N.Y.
(oblong punch)

J.H.C   **John H. Connor** (*fl.* 1830s) New York, N.Y.
(oblong punch)

J.J.S.   **John J. Staples, Jr.** (*fl.* 1780s) New York, N.Y.
(oblong punch)

JL   **John Lynch** (*fl.* late 18th century) Baltimore, Maryland.
(oblong punch)

J.L   **Joseph Loring** (recorded 1788) Boston, Mass.
(rounded oblong punch)

J.L.W   **John L. Westervell** (recorded 1845) Newburgh, N.Y.
(oblong punch)

J.M   **Joseph Moulton** (*fl.* early 18th century) Newburyport, Mass.
(oblong punch)

JM   **J. Merchant** (*fl.* late 19th century) New York, N.Y.
(oval punch)

J.M'F.   **John McFarlane** (recorded *c.* 1796) Boston, Mass.
(oblong punch)

J.P.T   **John Proctor Trott** (recorded 1799) New London, Conn.
(oblong punch)

J.P.W   **Joseph P. Warner** (1811–1862) Baltimore, Maryland.
(oblong punch)

JR   **Joseph Richardson, Jr.** (*fl.* 1770s) Philadelphia, Pa.
(oblong punch; also JR incised)

J.R   **Joseph Richardson** (1711–1784) Philadelphia, Pa.
(oblong punch)

J.S   **Joseph Shoemaker** (recorded 1798) Philadelphia, Pa.
(oval punch)

JS   **Joel Sayre** (1778–1818) New York, N.Y.
(oblong punch)

J.S.B   **John Starr Blackman** (1777–1851) Danbury, Conn.
(oblong or flattened oval punch)

J.&T.D   **John & Tunis Denise** (*fl.* 1770s) South Kingston, R.I.
(oblong punch)

J.W   **John Waite** (recorded *c.* 1798) New York, N.Y.
(shaped punch)

J.W   **John Wendover** (*fl. c.* 1695) New York, N.Y.
(shaped oblong punch)

J.W   **Joseph Wyatt** (recorded 1797) Philadelphia, Pa.
(oblong punch)

JW   **James Ward** (1768–1856) Hartford, Conn.
(oval punch)

J.W.B   **Joseph W. Boyd** (*fl. c.* 1820) New York, N.Y.
(oblong punch)

J.W.F.   **John W. Faulkner** (*fl. c.* 1835) New York, N.Y.
(oblong punch)

J&W   **Jones & Ward** (mid 19th century) Boston, Mass.
(oval punch)

K.C.&J.   **Kidney, Cann & Johnson** (mid 19th century) New York, N.Y.
(oblong punch)

K&D   **Kidney & Dunn** (*fl.* 1840s) New York, N.Y.
(oblong punch, plain or with serrated edges)

KL   **Knight Leverett** (recorded 1736) Boston, Mass.
(flattened oval, or shaped oval punch)

K.&S.   **Kirk & Smith** (*fl. c.* 1815) Baltimore, Maryland.
(oblong punch)

KE   **Koenraet Ten Eyck** (1678–1753) New York, N.Y.
(oblong punch)

L.B   **Luther Bradley** (1772–1830) New Haven, Conn.
(oblong punch)

L.B   **Loring Bailey** (recorded 1780) Hingham, Mass.
(oblong punch)

LF   **Lewis Fueter** (*fl.* 1770s) New York, N.Y.
(italic caps in oblong punch)

L&G   **Lincoln & Green** (recorded *c.* 1810) Boston, Mass.
(oblong punch)

LH   **Ludwig Heck** (*fl. c.* 1760) Lancaster, Pa.
(oblong punch)

LH   **Littleton Holland** (1770–1847) Baltimore, Maryland.
(italic caps in oblong punch)

LW   **Lemuel Wells** (recorded 1791) New York, N.Y.
(oblong punch)

L.W.&Co   **Lemuel Wells & Co** (recorded 1790s) New York, N.Y.
(oblong punch)

L&W   **Leonard & Wilson** (recorded 1847) Philadelphia, Pa.
(oblong punch with serrated edges)

MB   **Miles Beach** (1743–1828) Litchfield, Conn.
(rounded oval punch; also M·B in oblong punch)

M&B   **Merriman & Bradley** (recorded 1817) New Haven, Conn.
(oblong punch, plain or with serrated edges)

M.G
or **MG**   **Miles Gorham** (1757–1847) New Haven, Conn.
(oblong punch)

MH   **Marquette Hastier** (*fl. c.* 1770) New York, N.Y.
(oblong punch)

M.J
or **MJ**   **Munson Jarvis** (1742–1824) Stamford, Conn.
(oblong punch)

MM   **Marcus Merriman** (1762–1850) New Haven, Conn.
(oblong punch with serrated edges; also M in square punch;
also M·M in oblong punch; also MM in segmental punch)

MM   **Myers Myers** (1723–1795) New York, N.Y.
(oblong punch; also italic caps in oval punch)

M.M&Co   **Marcus Merriman & Co** (recorded 1817) New Haven, Conn.
(oblong punch with serrated edges)

MP
or **M·P**   **Matthew Petit** (recorded 1811) New York, N.Y.
(oblong punch)

MR   **Moody Russel** (recorded 1694) Barnstable, Mass.
(oval or shaped oblong punch)

M&R   **McFee & Reeder** (recorded 1796) Philadelphia, Pa.
(oblong punch)

N·A   **Nathaniel Austin** (1734–1818) Boston, Mass.
(oblong punch)

NB   **Nathaniel Burr** (1698–1784) Fairfield, Conn.
(oblong punch)

N·B   **Nathaniel Bartlett** (recorded 1760) Concord, Mass.
(oblong punch)

NC   **Nathaniel Coleman** (*fl. c.* 1775) Burlington, New Jersey.
(oval punch)

NH   **Nathaniel Helme** (1761–1789) South Kingston, R.I.
(oblong punch)

NH   **Nicholas Hutchins** (1777–1845) Baltimore, Maryland.
(flattened oval punch)

N.H&CO N. Harding & Co (*fl. c.* 1830) Boston, Mass.
(oblong punch)

NM Nathaniel Morse (*fl.* early 18th century) Boston, Mass.
(oblong punch; also crowned NM in shaped punch)

NN Nehemiah Norcross (recorded *c.* 1796) Boston, Mass.
(oblong punch)

N·R Nicholas Roosevelt (1715–1769) New York, N.Y.
(oblong or flattened oval punch)

NS Nathaniel Shipman (1764–1853) Norwich, Conn.
(oblong punch)

NV Nathaniel Vernon (1777–1843) Charleston, South Carolina.
(oblong punch)

OP Otto Paul De Parisien (*fl.* 1760s) New York, N.Y.
(oval punch: also OPDP in oblong punch with rounded ends)

O&S Oakes & Spencer (*fl. c.* 1814) Hartford, Conn.
(oblong punch)

PA Pygan Adams (1712–1776) New London, Conn.
(oblong punch, sometimes with slightly rounded corners)

PB Phineas Bradley (1745–1797) New Haven, Conn.
(oblong punch)

P.D Phillip Dally (recorded *c.* 1779) New York, N.Y.
(oblong punch)

PD Peter David (1707–1755) Philadelphia, Pa.
(oval punch)

PDR Peter De Riemer (1736–1814) Philadelphia, Pa.
(oblong punch, sometimes with rounded ends)

PG Philip Goelet (recorded 1731) New York, N.Y.
(oblong or oval punch)

PH Philip Hurlbeart (recorded *c.* 1761) Philadelphia, Pa.
(irregular shaped punch)

PH Philip Huntington (recorded 1796) Norwich, Conn.
(oblong punch)

P.L Peter Lupp (1797–1827) New Brunswick, New Jersey.
(oval punch)

P.L.K Peter L. Krider (mid 19th century) Philadelphia, Pa.
(oblong punch)

P.M P. Mood (recorded 1806) Charleston, South Carolina.
(oblong punch)

P&M Parry & Musgrave (recorded 1793) Philadelphia, Pa.
(oblong punch)

PO   **Peter Oliver** *(fl. c.* 1710*)* Boston, Mass.
(heart-shape punch)

P.O   **Peter Olivier** (recorded 1797) Philadelphia, Pa.
(oblong punch with serrated edges)

PP   **Peter Perreau** (recorded 1797) Philadelphia, Pa.
(oblong punch; also P·P in shaped punch)

P.Q   **Peter Quintard** (1699–1762) New York, N.Y.
(oblong punch; also PQ in rounded punch, and PQ in oblong punch)

PR   **Paul Revere** (1702–1754) Boston, Mass.
(in crowned scutcheon punch)

PR   **Paul Revere II** (1735–1818) Boston, Mass.
(oblong punch; also PR in italic caps in circle or oblong punch)

PS   **Philip Syng** (1676–1739) Philadelphia, Pa.
(oblong punch)

P.S   **Philip Sadtler** (1771–1860) Baltimore, Maryland.
(shaped oblong punch)

PS   **Philip Syng II** (1702–1789) Philadelphia, Pa.
(oblong or heart-shape punch)

P&U   **Pelletreau & Upson** (recorded 1818) New York, N.Y.
(oblong punch)

PV   **Peter Vergereau** (1700–1755) New York, N.Y.
(oblong punch with rounded end; also P.V in shaped oblong punch)

PVB   **Peter Van Beuren** (recorded 1798) New York, N.Y.
(italic caps in plain oblong punch or shaped punch)

P.VB   **Peter Van Inburgh** (1689–1740) New York, N.Y.
(oblong punch, the VB as monogram)

PVD
or P.V.D   **Peter Van Dyke** (1684–1750) New York, N.Y.
(flattened oval punch; also shaped punch)

R.&A.C.   **R. & A. Campbell** (recorded 1853) Baltimore, Maryland.
(oblong punch)

RB   **Roswell Bartholomew** (1781–1830) Hartford, Conn.
(oblong punch with serrated edges)

RB   **Robert Brookhouse** (mid 18th century) Salem, Mass.
(italic caps in rounded oblong punch)

RC   **Robert Campbell** (recorded 1834) Baltimore, Maryland.
(oblong punch)

RD   **Robert Douglas** (recorded 1776) New London, Conn.
(oblong punch)

RD   **Richard Van Dyke** (1717–1770) New York, N.Y.
(rounded oval punch)

RE *or* **R·E**	**Robert Evans** (d. 1812) Boston, Mass. (oblong punch)
RF	**Rufus Farnam** (recorded 1796) Boston, Mass. (oblong punch)
RF	**Robert Fairchild** (1703–1794) Durham, Conn. (oval or shaped oval punch)
R·G	**Rufus Greene** (1707–1777) Boston, Mass. (oblong punch with serrated edges or shaped round punch; also RG in plain oblong punch)
RG	**Rene Grignon** (d. 1715) Norwich, Conn. (in crowned curved punch)
R&G	**Riggs & Griffith** (recorded 1816) Baltimore, Maryland. (oblong punch)
RH	**Richard Humphreys** (*fl.* 1770s) Philadelphia, Pa. (oblong punch; also R·H in flattened oval punch; also RH in italic caps, rounded punch)
R&L	**Roberts & Lee** (recorded 1775) Boston, Mass. (oblong punch with serrated edges)
R·M	**Reuben Merriman** (1783–1866) Litchfield, Conn. (oblong punch with serrated edges)
RR	**Richard Riggs** (d. 1819) Philadelphia, Pa. (shaped oval oblong punch)
RS	**Robert Sanderson** (d. 1693) Boston, Mass. (with star over RS in trefoil-shape punch)
RVD	**Richard Van Dyke** (1717–1770) New York, N.Y. (oblong punch with rounded ends; also RD in heart-shape punch)
RW *or* **R·W**	**Robert Wilson** (recorded 1816) New York, N.Y. (oval punch)
R&WW	**R. & W. Wilson** (*fl.* 1820s) Philadelphia, Pa. (oblong punch)
SA	**Samuel Avery** (1760–1836) Preston, Conn. (oblong punch; also found with SA in italic caps)
S·A	**Samuel Alexander** (*fl.* early 19th century) Philadelphia, Pa. (oblong punch)
SB *or* **S·B**	**Samuel Burt** (1724–1754) Boston, Mass. (oblong punch)
SB *or* **S·B**	**Stephen Bourdett** (recorded 1730) New York, N.Y. (rounded oblong punch)
SB	**Standish Barry** ((1763–1844) Baltimore, Maryland. (oblong punch)

SB   **Samuel Buel** (1742–1819) Middletown, Conn.
(rounded oval punch; also S·B in oblong punch)

SB   **Samuel Burill** (recorded 1733) Boston, Mass.
(flattened oval punch; also "sb" over a star in heart-shape punch)

S&B   **Shepherd & Boyd** (recorded 1810) Albany, N.Y.
(oblong punch)

S·C   **Samuel Casey** (1724–1773) South Kingston, R.I.
(rounded oval punch)

SC&Co   **Simon Chaudrons & Co** (recorded 1807) Philadelphia, Pa.
(oblong punch)

S&C   **Storrs & Cooley** (*fl. c.* 1830) New York, N.Y.
(shaped punch)

S*D   **Samuel Drowne** (1749–1815) Portsmouth, New Hampshire.
(flattened oval punch)

SE   **Samuel Edwards** (1705–1762) Boston, Mass.
(crowned SE over small star, in scutcheon punch)

S.E   **Stephen Emery** (1725–1801) Boston, Mass.
(oblong punch with rounded ends; also SE in rounded punch)

SF   **Samuel Ford** (recorded 1797) Philadelphia, Pa.
(oblong punch)

SG   **Samuel Gilbert** (*fl. c.* 1798) Hebron, Conn.
(oblong punch)

SG   **Samuel Gray** (1684–1713) New London, Conn.
(heart-shape punch)

S:H   **Stephen Hopkins** (1721–1796) Waterbury, Conn.
(oblong punch)

SH
or S·H   **Stephen Hardy** (1781–1843) Portsmouth, New Hampshire.
(oblong punch)

SH   **Samuel Haugh** (1675–1717) Boston, Mass.
(squat letters in oblong punch)

S.J   **Samuel Johnson** (*fl. c.* 1780) New York, N.Y.
(oblong punch)

S.K   **Samuel Kirk** (1792–1872) Baltimore, Maryland.
(oblong punch, plain, or with serrated edges)

S.L
or S·L   **Samuel Leach** (*fl.* 1740s) Philadelphia, Pa.
(oblong punch)

S·M   **Samuel Merriman** (1769–1805) New Haven, Conn.
(oblong punch)

SM   **Sylvester Morris** (1709–1783) New York, N.Y.
(flattened oval punch)

S&M   **Sibley & Marble** (*fl.* 1801–1806) New Haven, Conn.
(oblong punch)

SP   **Samuel Parmelee** (1737–1803) Guilford, Conn.
(oblong or oval punch)

SR   **Samuel R. Richards, Jr.** (recorded 1793) Philadelphia, Pa.
(flattened oval punch)

S&R   **Sayre & Richards** (recorded 1802) New York, N.Y.
(oblong or flattened oval punch)

SS   **Simeon Soumain** (1685–1750) New York, N.Y.
(oblong punch)

SS   **Silas Sawin** (recorded 1823) Boston, Mass.
(square punch)

SS   **Samuel Soumaien** (*fl. c.* 1754) Philadelphia, Pa.
(square or oval punch)

ST   **Samuel Tingley** (*fl. c.* 1767) New York, N.Y.
(oblong punch; also italic caps in shaped or square punch)

SV   **Samuel Vernon** (1683–1735) Newport, R.I.
(over star, in heart-shape punch)

SW   **Samuel Warner** (*fl.* late 18th century) Philadelphia, Pa.
(oblong punch)

S·W   **Samuel Waters** (recorded 1790) Philadelphia, Pa.
(oblong punch)

S·W   **Samuel Williamson** (recorded 1794) Philadelphia, Pa.
(oblong punch; also SW in flattened oval punch)

S W   **Silas White** (recorded 1792) New York, N.Y.
(each initial in separate, square punch; also SW in oblong punch)

SWL   **S. W. Lee** (*fl.* early 18th century) Providence, R.I.
(oblong punch)

TA   **Thomas Arnold** (1739–1828) Newport, R.I.
(Roman or italic caps in oblong punch)

TB   **Thauvet Besley** (recorded 1727) New York, N.Y.
(crowned monogram, incised)

TB   **Timothy Brigden** (recorded 1813) Albany, N.Y.
(oblong punch with serrated edges)

T·B   **Thomas Burger** (*fl. c.* 1805) New York, N.Y.
(oblong punch)

TB.   **Timothy Bontecou** (1693–1784) New Haven, Conn.
(incised)

T·B   **Timothy Bontecou, Jr.** (1723–1789) New Haven, Conn.
(soft oblong punch; also TB in oval punch)

T&B   **Trott & Brooks** (recorded 1798) New London, Conn.
(oblong punch)

TC   **Thomas Carson** (*fl. c.* 1815) Albany, N.Y.
(shaped punch)

T.C.C.   **Thomas Chester Coit** (*fl. c.* 1812) Norwich, Conn.
(oblong punch)

T.C&H   **Thomas Carson & Hall** (recorded 1818) Albany, N.Y.
(oblong punch)

T&C   **Trott & Cleveland** (*fl.* 1790s) New London, Conn.
(oblong punch)

TD   **Timothy Dwight** (1645–1691) Boston, Mass.
(heart-shape punch)

T·D·D   **Tunis D. Dubois** (recorded 1799) New York, N.Y.
(oblong punch)

T.E   **Thomas Knox Emery** (1781–1815) Boston, Mass.
(oblong punch)

TE   **Thomas Edwards** (1701–1755) Boston, Mass.
(crowned, in shaped square punch; also T.E. in oblong punch)

T.E.S   **T. E. Stebbins** (recorded 1810) New York, N.Y.
(oblong punch)

TH   **Thomas Hammersley** (1722–1781) New York, N.Y.
or T·H   (oblong punch with rounded ends, or shaped punch; also TH in
italic caps in square punch)

T&H   **Taylor & Hinsdale** (recorded 1801) New York, N.Y.
(oblong punch)

T·K   **Thomas Kinne** (1786–1824) Norwich, Conn.
(oblong punch with serrated edges; also TK and T.K. in
oblong punches)

T.K   **Thaddeus Keeler** (recorded 1805) New York, N.Y.
(oblong punch)

TM   **Thomas Millner** (1690–1745) Boston, Mass.
or T·M   (flattened oval punch)

TN   **Thomas Norton** (recorded 1796–1806) Farmington, Conn.
(oblong punch)

TR   **Thomas Revere** (recorded 1789) Boston, Mass.
(oval punch)

TS   **Thomas Savage** (recorded 1689) Boston, Mass.
(heart-shape punch)

T·S   **Thomas Shields** (*fl. c.* 1771) Philadelphia, Pa.
(also TS, in oblong punch)

TS   **Thomas Skinner** (1712–1761) New York, N.Y.
(flattened oval punch)

TSB   **Tobias Stoutenburgh** (1700–1759) New York, N.Y.
(flattened oval punch)

T·T   **Thomas Trott** (1701–1777) Boston, Mass.
(oblong punch; also T.T in shaped punch)

T.U   **Thomas Underhill** (recorded 1779) New York, N.Y.
(oblong punch)

T.W   **Thomas H. Warner** (1780–1828) Baltimore, Maryland.
(shaped oval punch)

T·U
with I·V   **Underhill and Vernon** (recorded 1787) New York, N.Y.
(the TU in oblong punch, the IV in shaped oval punch)

T·W   **Thomas Whartenby** (recorded 1811) Philadelphia, Pa.
(oblong punch)

T·Y   **Thomas You** (*fl. c.* 1756) Charleston, South Carolina.
(oval punch)

U&B   **Ufford & Burdick** (*fl. c.* 1814) New Haven, Conn.
(oblong punch)

V&C   **Van Voorhis & Cooley** (recorded 1786) New York, N.Y.
(oblong punch)

V.V&S   **Van Voorhis & Schanck** (recorded 1791) New York, N.Y.
(oblong punch)

V&W   **Van Ness & Waterman** (recorded 1835) New York, N.Y.
(oblong punch)

WA   **William Anderson** (recorded 1746) New York, N.Y.
(oblong punch)

W&B   **Ward & Bartholomew** (recorded 1804) Hartford, Conn.
(oblong punch)

WB   **William Ball** (*fl. c.* 1752) Philadelphia, Pa.
(oblong punch with rounded ends; also W.B in italic caps
in shaped punch)

WB   **William Breed** (*fl. c.* 1750) Boston, Mass.
(oval punch; also WB as monogram in near heart-shape punch)

W.B.N   **William B. North** (1787–1838) New York, N.Y.
(oblong punch)

W&B   **Ward & Bartholomew** (recorded 1804) Hartford, Conn.
(oblong punch, plain, or with serrated edges)

WC   **William Clark** (*fl. c.* 1774) New Milford, Conn.
(oval punch)

WC   **William Cross** (*fl. c.* 1712) Boston, Mass.
(rough oblong punch)

W·C   **William Cleveland** (1770–1837) New London, Conn.
(oblong punch; also WC in oblong punch with serrated edges)

WC   **William Cowell** (1682–1736) Boston, Mass.
(scutcheon, flattened oval, or shaped punch; also W.C in shaped punch)

W·F   **William Forbes** (recorded 1830) New York, N.Y.
(oblong punch)

WG   **William Gale** (recorded 1816) New York, N.Y.
(oblong punch)

WG   **William Ghiselin** (*fl. c.* 1751) Philadelphia, Pa.
(in almost square punch)

WG   **William Grant, Jr.** (recorded 1785) Philadelphia, Pa.
(oval punch)

W.G   **William Gurley** (*fl.* early 19th century) Norwich, Conn.
(oblong punch)

W&G   **Woodward & Grosjean** (recorded 1847) Boston, Mass.
(oblong punch with rounded ends)

W.G&S   **William Gale & Son** (recorded 1823) New York, N.Y.
(oblong punch)

WH   **William Haverstick** (*fl. c.* 1781) Philadelphia, Pa.
(oblong punch)

W·H   **William Hollingshead** (recorded 1770) Philadelphia, Pa.
(oblong punch; also WH in italic caps in shaped punch)

WH   **William Heurtin** (recorded 1731) New York, N.Y.
(oblong punch)

W.H   **William Homes, Jr.** (1742–1835) New York, N.Y.
(oblong punch; also WH)

W.H   **William Homes** (recorded 1733) Boston, Mass.
(oblong punch; also WH in oblong or oval punch)

W&H   **Wood & Hughes** (recorded 1846) New York, N.Y.
(oblong punch)

W·I   **William Jones** (1694–1730) Marblehead, Mass.
(oblong punch)

WJ   **William B. Johonnot** (1766–1849) Middletown, Conn.
(oblong punch)

WK   **William Kimberly** (*fl. c.* 1795) New York, N.Y.
(oblong punch)

W.K
B   **Benjamin Wynkoop** (1675–1751) New York, N.Y.
(initials arranged thus in heart-shape punch)

WK
B   **Cornelius Wynkoop** (recorded 1724) New York, N.Y.
(WK over B in heart-shape punch)

WL   **William Little** (*fl. c.* 1775) Newburyport, Mass.
(oblong punch)

WM   **William Moulton** (*fl. c.* 1807) Newburyport, Mass.
(oblong punch)

W.P   **William Pollard** (*fl.* early 18th century) Boston, Mass.
(flattened oval punch)

W·R   **William Roe** (*fl.* early 19th century) Kingston, N.Y.
(oblong punch)

WR   **William Rouse** (1639–1705) Boston, Mass.
(oval punch; also WR with star above and below, in shaped punch)

W·S   **William Simes** (1773–1824) Portsmouth, New Hampshire.
(oblong punch with rounded ends)

W·S
with **Minott**   **Minott & Simpkins** (*fl.* 1770s) Boston, Mass.
(each in oblong punch)

W·S·N   **William S. Nichol** (1785–1871) Newport, R.I.
(oblong punch)

W.S.P.
with **TR**   **Pelletreau & Richards** (*fl. c.* 1825) New York, N.Y.
(in separate oblong punches)

W.S.P.   **William Smith Pelletreau** (1786–1842) Southampton, Long
Island, N.Y.
(oblong punch with serrated edges)

WT   **Walter Thomas** (recorded 1769)
(shaped punch)

WV   **William Vilant** (*fl. c.* 1725) Philadelphia, Pa.
(heart-shape punch)

W.V.B   **William Van Beuren** (recorded 1790) New York, N.Y.
(shaped oval punch)

W.W   **William Whetcroft** (1735–1799) Baltimore, Maryland.
(oblong punch)

W.W   **William Ward** (1742–1828) Litchfield, Conn.
(oblong punch)

WWG   **W. W. Gaskins** (*fl.* 1830s) Providence, R.I.
(oblong punch)

ZB
or **Z·B**   **Zachariah Brigden** (1734–1787) Boston, Mass.
(nearly square punch)

ZS   **Zebulon Smith** (1786–1865) Maine.

American Pewterers' Marks

Early makers of pewter in the U.S.A. used "touches" (the correct term for a mark on pewter) that could be easily recognised by means of the distinction of the device employed. Unfortunately today such marks are all too often somewhat unrecognisable due to wear, or indeed by having been somewhat hastily applied in the first instance. Three periods of fashion in marking may be distinguished. At first (pre-Revolutionary) English customs strongly influenced American usage. The rose and crown, and the lion rampant, were favourite devices, very often found associated with a number of other marks (in square or shield punches) of no real significance. The middle period (during or after the War of Independence) the American eagle was commonly used, sometimes with more or less stars in allusion to the current number of States in the Union. The later period (from *c.* 1825 onward) displays the common practice of using the individual pewterer's name with place of origin, either enclosed in a rectangular label, or merely incised.

Archer, Ellis S.: (*fl. c.* 1845) Philadelphia.
Mark recorded:
ARCHER'S PATENT PHILADᴬ
in three lines, over JUNE 18th 1842,
arranged in large flattened oval.

Archer & Janney: (*fl. c.* 1847) St Louis, Mo.
Mark recorded:
ARCHER & N. E. JANNEY. ST. LOUIS in a long narrow panel.

Armitages & Standish: (*fl. c.* 1840)
Mark recorded:
ARMITAGES
& STANDISH

Austin, Nathaniel: (1741–1816) Charlestown, Mass.
Marks recorded include:
Lion rampant enclosed between two columns with NATHL (above) and AUSTIN (below); N. AUSTIN in a circle, or in a label with CHARLESTOWN; the American eagle between columns.

Austin, Richard: (*fl.* 1792–1817) Boston, Mass.
Marks recorded include:
R.A. BOSTON plain, or in an oblong panel; RICHARD AUSTIN as curved oval panel, associated with emblems of a bird and animal.

Babbitt, Crossman & Co.: (*fl.* 1826/28) Taunton, Mass.
Mark recorded: full name in oblong panel.

Babbitt & Crossman: (1814–1826) Taunton, Mass.
Mark recorded: name in oblong panel.

Badger, Thomas, Jr: (1764–1826) Boston, Mass.
Mark recorded: American eagle with THOMAS (above) and BADGER (below), in square panel with curved top edge.

Bailey & Putnam: (*c.* 1830–1835) Malden, Mass.
Mark recorded: BAILEY in punch with serrated edges, over & in round punch, over PUTNAM in punch with serrated edges.

Barns, Blakeslee: (*fl. c.* 1805–1810) Berlin, Conn. Also at Philadelphia. Pa. (1812–1817).
Marks recorded include: B. BARNS over PHILADA in a square panel; B. BARNES over PHILADIA in a square panel; BB under a bird, in a round or oval punch with a serrated edge; B BARNS over an eagle, in a round punch.

Barns, Stephen: (*fl. c.* 1795) Conn.

161

Mark recorded: American eagle with stars above in upright oval panel, with STEPHEN (above) and BARNS (below) outside.

Bartholdt, William: (*fl.* 1850–1854) Williamsburg, N.Y.
Mark recorded: WM BARTHOLDT incised.

Bassett, Francis, II: (*fl.* 1754, d. 1800) New York, N.Y.
Marks recorded include: FB with a star over, in an oval punch; animal over FB, in round punch; cartouche enclosing F. BASSETT over a fleur-de-lys between two stars, a coronet and palm leaves under.

Bassett, Frederick: (*fl.* 1761–1780, and 1785–1800) New York, N.Y. Also at Hartford, Conn. (1781–1785).
Marks recorded include: FB with a fleur-de-lys above and below, in an oval; also FREDERICK BASSET surrounding a crown over NY over a rose, in a cartouche.

Bassett, John: (*fl.* 1720–1761) New York, N.Y.
Mark recorded: I.B with fleur-de-lys above and below, in oval punch.

Belcher, Joseph, Jr: (*fl.* 1776–1784) Newport, R.I. Also at New London, Conn. (after 1784).
Mark recorded; J:B in an oval; the name BELCHER apparently part of a cartouche, may be his.

Billings, William: (*fl.* 1791–1806) Providence, R.I.
Marks recorded include: anchor between W.B in upright oval panel; W. BILLINGS in curved label.

Boardman, Henry S.: (recorded 1841) Hartford, Conn. Also at Philadelphia, Pa. (*c.* 1844–1861).
Mark recorded: BOARDMAN over PHILADᴬ.

Boardman, Luther: (recorded 1836) South Reading, Mass. Also at Chester, Conn. (*fl.* 1837–*c.* 1842).
Marks recorded include: L.B in oblong panel; eagle with stars, surrounded by L. BOARDMAN WARRANTED, in circular panel.

Boardman, Thomas D.: (*fl.* 1804–1850) Hartford, Conn.
Marks recorded include: cartouche enclosing name and American eagle; T.D.B. in oblong with serrated edges; T. D. BOARDMAN in long oblong label, over HARTFORD in oblong serrated panel.

Boardman, T. D. & S.: (*fl. c.* 1810–1850) Hartford, Conn.
Mark recorded: eagle, facing left, in circle, surrounded by BOARDMAN WARRANTED, circular punch; TD & SB in oblong panel; imputed marks include: American eagle in wide oval; American eagle, facing right, in cartouche; also BOARDMAN with animal over, in shaped cartouche.

Boardman, Timothy, & Co: (*fl.* 1822–1825) New York, N.Y. Merchant trading for T. D. & S. Boardman.
Used the mark TB & Cº in oblong panel with serrated edges.

Boardman & Co: (*fl.* 1825–1837) New York, N.Y.
Said to have traded for T. Boardman & Co.
Mark recorded: American eagle surrounded by BOARDMAN & CO NEW YORK in upright or horizontal oval panel.

Boardman & Hall: (*fl. c.* 1845) Philadelphia, Pa.
Connected with Boardman & Co (above).
Mark recorded: BOARDMAN over & HALL in shaped rectangle with PHILADA in oblong panel.

Boardman & Hart: (*fl.* 1827–1850) New York, N.Y.
Connected with Boardman & Co (above).
Marks recorded include: BOARDMAN over & HART in shaped rectangle, associated with N. YORK in oblong punch; also N. YORK surrounded by BOARDMAN & HART in large oval with serrated edges.

Boyd, Parks: (*fl.* 1797–1819) Philadelphia, Pa.
Marks recorded include the words P. BOYD. PHILA with or without an eagle in the punch.

Boyle, Robert: (*fl.* 1753–1758) New York, N.Y.

Mark recorded: a device between two columns, with ROBERT (above) and BOYLE (below); NEW-YORK in oblong.

Bradford, Cornelius: (*fl.* 1752) New York, N.Y. Also (*fl.* 1758–1770) at Philadelphia, Pa.; New York again until 1785,
Marks recorded include: crowned rose between columns with CORNELIUS (above) and BRADFORD (below); also C. BRADFORD with PHILADELPHIA.

Brook Farm: (*c.* 1845) West Roxbury, Mass.
Mark recorded: BROOK FARM in curved panel.

Brunstrom, John A.: (*fl.* 1783–1793) Philadelphia, Pa.
Mark recorded: IAB in rectangular punch.

Buckley, Townsend M.: (*fl. c.* 1855) Troy, N.Y.
Mark recorded: T. M. BUCKLEY incised.

Byles, Thomas: (*fl.* 1738–1771) Philadelphia, Pa.
Mark recorded: crowned rose between columns over T. BY (incomplete).

Cahill, J. W. & Co: (*fl. c.* 1835)
Provenance not determined.
Mark recorded: J. W. CAHILL & CO in curved label with serrated edges.

Calder, William: (*fl. c.* 1817–1856) Providence, R. I.
Mark recorded: American eagle with CALDER (above) and PROVIDENCE (below) in cartouche; also CALDER in oblong panel with serrated edges.

Capen, Ephraim: (*fl. c.* 1848) New York, N.Y.
Mark recorded: E· CAPEN· incised.

Capen & Molineux: (*fl.* 1848–1854) New York, N.Y.
Mark recorded: NY in oblong panel with CAPEN & in curved label (above) and MOLINEUX in curved label (below).

Carnes, John: (1698–1760) Boston, Mass.
Mark ascribed: crowned shield between BOSTON on left and (presumably) own name on right, in cartouche.

Coldwell, George: (*fl. c.* 1789–1810) New York, N.Y.
Mark recorded: G. COLDWELL in oblong panel with wavy edges.

Colton, Oren: (*fl. c.* 1835) Philadelphia, Pa.
Mark recorded: O. COLTON incised.

Copeland, Joseph: (*fl. c.* 1675–1691) Chuckatuck and Jamestown, Va.
Mark recorded: heart surrounded by CHUCKATUCK in a circle, with 1675. JOSEPH·COPELAND· forming outer circle in circular punch.

Cox, William: (*fl.* 1715–1721) Philadelphia, Pa.
Mark recorded: animal head with WILLIAM over and COX under, forming oval design.

Crossman, West & Leonard: (*fl.* 1828–1830) Taunton, Mass.
Mark recorded CROSSMAN over WEST & LEONARD incised.

Curtis, Lemuel J.: (*fl.* 1836–1849) Meriden, Conn.
Mark recorded: L. J. CURTISS in oblong panel.

Curtiss, Daniel: (*fl.* 1822–1850) Albany, N.Y.
Marks recorded include: D CURTISS in swirling label; D. CURTISS over an urn in an (incomplete) oval.

Curtiss, I.: (*c.* 1820)
Provenance not determined.
Marks recorded include I·CURTISS or I·CURTIS in oblong panel; heraldic eagle (rather crude).

Cutler, David: (1703–1772) Boston, Mass.
Mark ascribed: UTLER (incomplete).

Danforth, Edward: (*fl. c.* 1788) Middletown, Conn. Also (*c.* 1790) Hartford, Conn.
Marks recorded include: lion rampant with EDWARD (above) and DANFORTH (below) in cartouche; lion rampant between initials E D with rim of pellets, in cartouche; E.D in a flattened shield.

Danforth, John: (*fl.* 1773–1793) Norwich, Conn.
Marks recorded include: lion rampant

between columns with JOHN (above) and DANFORTH (below) surmounted by NORWICH with effect of a cartouche; lion rampant between initials J.D in round punch; initials JD in an oblong punch.

Danforth, Joseph: (*fl.* 1782–1788) Middletown, Conn.
Marks recorded include: lion rampant between columns with JOSEPH (above) in curved label and DANFORTH (below) in oblong label, all forming cartouche; initials I·D in oblong punch, or JD in flattened shield punch.

Danforth, Joseph Jr: (*fl. c.* 1807–*c.* 1812) Richmond, Va.
Marks recorded include: American eagle with JD and stars forming circle round it; eagle with JD at feet and stars scattered around its head associated with RICHMOND over WARRANTED in shaped rectangle.

Danforth, Josiah: (*fl. c.* 1825–1837) Middletown, Conn.
Marks recorded include: American eagle with DANFORTH and MIDD.CI around in round panel with serrated edge; J. DANFORTH in oblong panel.

Danforth, Samuel: (*fl.* 1793–1803) Norwich, Conn.
Mark recorded: SAMl DANFORTH in oblong panel; mark ascribed includes the eagle (apparently) with NORWICH in curved panel, presumably as cartouche.

Danforth, Samuel: (*fl.* 1795–1816) Hartford, Conn.
Marks recorded include: American eagle with stars and SAMUEL (above) and DANFORTH (below) curving as cartouche; American eagle perched on SD and ringed with 19 stars, in oval; American eagle between initials S D in upright oval with plain or serrated edge; S.D in small oval punch.

Danforth, Thomas: (*fl.* 1727–1733) Taunton, Mass. Also (1733–1773) Norwich, Conn.
No marks recorded yet.

Danforth, Thomas II: (*fl.* 1755–1782) Middletown, Conn.
Marks recorded include: lion rampant between columns with THOMAS in

curved label attached over, supported on DANFORTH in oblong label forming a cartouche; lion rampant between initials T D in curved cartouche with beaded rim; initials T·D in flattened shield.

Danforth, Thomas III: (*fl.* 1777–*c.* 1808) Rocky Hill, Conn. Also (1807–1813) at Philadelphia, Pa.
Marks recorded include: American eagle with T D above or below, in oval punch; initials T.D in oblong punch, or in upright oblong with canted corners; T. DANFORTH over PHILADA in shaped rectangle.

Danforth, Thomas IV: (1792–1836) Philadelphia, Pa.
No marks recorded as yet.

Danforth, William: (*fl.* 1792–1820) Middletown, Conn.
Mark recorded: American eagle with stars with WILLIAM (above) and DANFORTH (below) in shaped panel.

Day, Benjamin: (1706–1757) Newport, R.I.
Mark recorded: initials BD in flattened octagonal punch.

Derby, Thomas S.: (*fl. c.* 1818–1850) Middletown, Conn.
Mark ascribed: bust surrounded with palm leaves (below) and GEN. JACKSON (above) in circular panel.

Derby, Thomas S., Jr: (*fl. c.* 1840–1850) Middletown, Conn.
Mark recorded T. S. DERBY. in oblong panel.

De Riemer, Cornelius B. & Co: (*fl. c.* 1835) Auburn, N.Y.
Mark recorded: C. B. DE RIEMER & C° over AUBURN, all incised.

Dunham, E.: (after 1825)
Provenance not determined.
Mark recorded E. DUNHAM in oblong panel.

Dunham, Rufus: (*fl.* 1837–1861) Westbrooke, Me.
Marks recorded include: R. DUNHAM in oblong panel with serrated edges, or incised.

Dunham, R. & Sons: (*fl.* 1861–1882) Portland, Me.

Mark recorded: coffee pot over PORT-LAND ME with R. DUNHAM & SONS forming semicircle above.

Edgell, Simon: (*fl.* 1713–1742) Philadelphia, Pa.
Marks recorded include: S·EDGELL in oblong panel; SIMON EDGELL making a semicircle to a bird or such device.

Eggleston, Jacob: (*fl.*-1796–1807) Middletown, Conn. Also (1807–1813) at Fayetteville, N. Carolina.
Marks recorded include: American eagle among stars with J.E (above) in oval; American eagle with stars round its head in upright oval over EGGLESTON.

Elsworth, Williams J.: (*fl.* 1767–1798) New York, N.Y.
Marks recorded include: W.E in oblong punch with canted corners; W·E in oblong panel with serrated edges; lamb with pennant with WILLIAM in curved label (above) and ELSWORTH in curved label (below); mark ascribed, WE conjoined, with a pellet above and below, in an oval.

Endicott, Edmund: (*fl.* 1846–1853) New York, N.Y.
Mark recorded: E. ENDICOTT incised.

Endicott & Sumner: (*fl.* 1846–1851) New York, N.Y.
Mark recorded: ENDICOTT over SUMNER in rectangle with serrated edges, with N.Y. in small oblong punch.

Everett, James: (*fl. c.* 1716) Philadelphia, Pa.
Mark recorded: device resembling a crown between initials I E supported by a hand (?) in oval panel.

Fenn, Gaius & Jason: (*fl.* 1831–1843) New York, N.Y.
Mark recorded: FENN * * * NEW * YORK * * * forming circular label.

Flagg & Homan: (*fl.* 1842–1854) Cincinnati, Ohio.
Mark recorded; FLAGG & HOMAN in an oval panel.

Fuller & Smith: (mid 19th century) New London, Conn.
Mark recorded: firm's name forming a semicircle, incised.

Gardner: (mid 19th century)
Provenance not determined.
Mark recorded: first part incomplete, Y & GARDNER in oblong panel.

Gerhardt & Co: (mid 19th century)
Provenance not determined.
Mark recorded: GERHARDT over & CO incised.

Gleason, Roswell: (*fl.* 1822–1871) Dorchester, Mass.
Marks recorded include: eagle over stars with R. GLEASON above, in oval panel; ROSWELL GLEASON incised.

Graves, Henry H.: (mid 19th century) Middletown, Conn.
Mark recorded: H. H. GRAVES in oblong panel.

Graves, Joshua B.: (*fl. c.* 1844) Middletown, Conn.
Mark recorded: J. B. GRAVES in oblong panel with serrated edges.

Green, Samuel: (*fl. c.* 1778–*c.* 1830) Boston, Mass.
Mark recorded: S. G·BOSTON in curved label.

Griswold, Ashbil: (*fl.* 1807–1842) Meriden, Conn.
Marks recorded include: American eagle with stars above (*c.* 14) and GRISWOLD below, in oval; American eagle with GRISWOLD above in circle with serrated edge; American eagle in circle with ASHBIL in curved label attached (above) and GRISWOLD in curved label attached (below); initials A.G in small oblong.

Griswold, Sylvester: (*fl. c.* 1820) Baltimore, Md.
Mark recorded: S. GRISWOLD BALTIMORE forming circle round eagle (?), in circular panel with serrated edge.

Hall & Boardman: (*fl.* 1849–1857) Philadelphia, Pa.
Mark recorded: HALL over BOARDMAN in shield effect, over PHILA in oblong label attached.

Hall & Cotton: (mid 19th century)
Provenance not determined.

Mark recorded HALL & COTTON in oblong label with serrated edges.

Hamlin, Samuel: (*fl. c.* 1771–1801) Providence, R.I.
Marks recorded include: SAMUEL and HAMLIN in attached curved labels; eagle and stars over HAMLIN in rough circular panel; star (?) in cartouche between initials S H; SH in small square punch with canted corners.

Hamlin, Samuel E.: (*fl.* 1801–1856) Providence, R.I.
Marks recorded include: American eagle in cartouche over HAMLIN; eagle with shield (bearing anchor?) with HAMLIN over, in circle with serrated edge; HAMLIN in oblong panel with serrated edges.

Harbeson, Benjamin: (*fl.* early 19th century) Philadelphia, Pa.
Mark recorded: HARBESON PHILA forming circle in circular panel.

Hera, C. & J.: (*fl.* 1800–1812) Philadelphia, Pa.
Mark recorded: C. & I. HERA in curved label with serrated edges attached to PHILADELPHIA in plain curved label, over small escutcheon.

Heyne, Johann C.: (*fl.* 1754–1780) Lancaster, Pa.
Marks recorded include: crown, over I·C·H in oblong; initials I.C.H in shaped oblong panel.

Hinsdale, John & Daniel: (*fl. c.* 1815) Traded at Middletown, Conn. using as mark: J. & D. HINSDALE over eagle, in flattened oval panel.

Holmes, Robert, & Sons: (*fl. c.* 1853) Baltimore, Md.
Mark recorded: HOLMES & SONS over BALTIMORE in rectangle.

Holt, Thomas R.: (*fl.* 1845–1849) Meriden, Conn.
Mark recorded: T. R. HOLT, incised, or in oblong panel.

Homan, Henry: (*fl.* mid 19th century) Cincinnati, Ohio.
Mark recorded: H. HOMAN.

Homan & Co.: (mid 19th century) Cincinnati, Ohio.
Mark recorded: HOMAN & CO over CINCINNATI.

Hopper, Henry: (*fl.* 1842–1847) New York, N.Y.
Mark recorded: H. HOPPER in oblong panel with serrated edges.

Horan, Johann C.: (*fl.* 1754–1785) Philadelphia, Pa.
Mark recorded: ICH in a shield.

Horsford, E. N.: (*fl.* after 1830)
Provenance not determined.
Mark recorded: E. N. HORSFORD'S over PATENT.

Houghton & Wallace: (*fl.* mid 19th century) Philadelphia, Pa.
Mark recorded: HOUGHTON & WALLACE.

Humiston, Willis: (*fl. c.* 1840) Troy, N.Y.
Mark recorded: W. HUMISTON in curved label attached over TROY NY in oblong panel.

Hunt, S.: (*fl.* after 1830)
Provenance not determined.
Mark recorded: S HUNT.

Hyde, Martin: (*fl. c.* 1857) New York, N.Y.
Mark recorded: M. HYDE.

Johnson, Jehiel: (*fl.* 1815–1825) Middletown, Conn. Also (*c.* 1818) at Fayetteville, N. Carolina.
Marks recorded include: American eagle perhaps with stars, and with initials J J in circular panel.

Jones, Edward: (*fl.* 1837–1850) New York, N.Y.
Mark recorded: not fully decipherable, name surrounding a device, as circular panel.

Jones, Gershom: (*fl.* 1774–1809) Providence, R.I.
Marks recorded include: lion rampant between columns, with GERSHOM in curved label attached (above) and JONES in oblong as support (below); American eagle with stars, surrounded by PROVIDENCE BY G JONES in oval upright panel; initials GJ in square or rectangular punch, associated with an anchor in separate punch; shield bearing an anchor, surrounded by letters; mark ascribed (partly indecipherable): rose with MADE BY .... PROVIDENCE ..

Keene, Josiah: (*fl.* 1801–*c.* 1817) Providence, R.I.
Mark recorded: initials I·K in circle surrounded by scalloped border.

Kilbourn, Samuel: (*fl.* 1814–1830) Baltimore, Md.
Mark recorded: eagle with KILBURN (above) and BALTIMORE (below) in circle.

Kimberly, De Witt: (*fl.* 1845–1849) Meriden, Conn.
Mark recorded: D.W.K in oblong label with serrated border.

Kirby, Peter: (*fl. c.* 1736–*c.* 1776) New York, N.Y.
Mark recorded: initials P K with star between, in circular punch with beaded border.

Kirby, William: (*fl. c.* 1760–1794) New York, N.Y.
Marks recorded include: WM:KIRBY in curved label, forming circle with NEW YORK in curved label, surrounding a device (indecipherable); initials W·K in oblong punch, or circular punch with beaded border, also in square punch with canted corners, associated with a number of emblems, joined.

Kirk, Elisha: (*fl.* later 18th century) York, Pa.
Mark recorded: ELISHA KIRK in oblong label over YORKTOWN in similar label.

Knight, W. W. & Co: (*fl. c.* 1840) Philadelphia, Pa.
Traded using mark: W. W. KNIGHT & CO.

Kruiger, Lewis: (*fl.* 1833) Philadelphia, Pa.
Mark recorded: L. KRUIGER PHILAD forming an open oval.

Lafetra, Moses: (*fl.* 1811–1816) New York, N.Y.
Mark recorded: shield device with M·L (remainder indecipherable) surrounding it, in circular panel.

Leddell, Joseph, Sr: (*fl. c.* 1711–1753) New York, N.Y.
Marks ascribed to him: similar to those used by Joseph Leddell, Jr.

Leddell, Joseph, Jr: (*fl. c.* 1740–1754) New York, N.Y.
Marks recorded include: I·LEDDELL in curved label; initials IL in circular punch.

Lee, Richard: worked variously, as follows: (1788–1790) Grafton, N. H.; (1791–1793) at Ashfield, Mass.; (1794–1802) at Lanesborough, Mass.; (1802–1825) at Springfield, Va.
Marks recorded include: R:LEE in stepped oblong label; RICHARD·LEE in oblong panel with serrated edges; initials R·L in oval with serrated edges.

Lee, Richard, Jr: (*fl. c.* 1795–*c.* 1815) Springfield, Va.
Marks recorded include: fleur-de-lys between initials R L; RICHARD·LEE in oblong label with serrated edges.

Leonard, Reed & Barton: (*fl.* 1835–1840) Taunton, Mass.
Mark recorded: LEONARD REED & BARTON.

Lewis, Isaac C.: (*fl.* 1834–1852) Meriden, Conn.
Mark recorded: I. C. LEWIS.

Lewis, I. C. & Co: (*fl.* 1839–1852) Meriden, Conn.
Mark recorded: ICL & CO.

Lewis & Cowles: (*fl.* 1834–1836) East Meriden, Conn.
Mark recorded: MERIDEN surrounded by LEWIS & COWLES forming open diamond.

Lightner, George: (*fl. c.* 1806–1815) Baltimore, Md.
Marks recorded include: American eagle surrounded by G. LIGHTNER BALTIMORE in large oval with serrated edge; American eagle with stars in large oval with G. LIGHTNER in curved label attached (above) and BALTIMORE in curved label attached (below).

Locke, J. D.: (*fl.* 1835–*c.* 1860) New York, N.Y.
Mark recorded: J. D. LOCKE over NEW YORK all in rectangle, with serrated edges.

Love, I.: (*fl.* after 1840) Baltimore, Md.
Mark recorded: I·LOVE incised.

Lowe, I.: (*fl.* after 1800)
Provenance not determined.
Mark recorded: I·LOWE in curved label.

Lyman, William W.: (*fl.* 1844–1852) Meriden, Conn.
Mark recorded: LYMAN in oblong label.

Manning, E. B.: (*fl. c.* 1850–*c.* 1865) Middletown, Conn.
Mark recorded: E. B. MANNING forming a crescent over PATENT all incised.

Manning, Bowman & Co: (*fl. c.* 1866) Middletown, Conn.
Mark recorded: MANNING BOWMAN & CO.

Marston: (*fl.* after 1830) Baltimore, Md.
Mark recorded: MARSTON over BALTIMORE in shaped rectangle.

McEuen, Malcolm & Duncan: (*fl.* 1793–1798) New York, N.Y.
Mark ascribed: American eagle with stars in broad upright oval, surrounded by band of lettering N. YORK (inscription incomplete).

McQuilkin, William: (*fl.* 1845–1853) Philadelphia, Pa.
Mark recorded: Wᴹ MᶜQUILKIN in oblong label.

Melville, David: (*fl.* 1755–1793) Newport, R.I.
Marks recorded include: DM or D:M in small rectangle; anchor between the initials D M; an anchor on a shield, with stars above and NEWPORT; shield with (incomplete) ADE IN NEW and BY D: MEL over.

Melville, S. & T.: (*fl. c.* 1793–1800) Newport, R.I.
Marks recorded include: anchor on a shield, with stars and curved label S & T·MEL (incomplete) over; S & over T in small rectangle with serrated edges and M in square also serrated.

Melville, Thomas, Jr: (*fl.* 1796–1824) Newport, R.I.
Marks recorded include: initials T and M in small separate rectangles; shield with stars over and NEWPORT.

Meriden Britannia Co: (*fl.* from 1852) Meriden, Conn.
Mark recorded:
MERIDEN
BRITANNIA
CO

Morey & Ober: (*fl.* 1852–1855) Boston, Mass.
Mark recorded: American eagle over MOREY & OBER and BOSTON in curved labels forming an oval.

Morey & Smith: (*fl.* 1857–1885) Boston, Mass.
Mark recorded: American eagle over MOREY & SMITH in curved label over WARRANTED BOSTON in shaped rectangle attached, all with serrated edges.

Munson, John: (*fl.* 1846–1852) Yalesville, Conn.
Mark recorded: J. MUNSON in oblong with serrated edges.

Neal, I.: (*fl. c.* 1842)
Provenance not determined.
Mark recorded: in a circle the words I. NEAL'S PATENT and date MAY 4th 1842.

Nott, William: (*fl.* 1813–1817) Middletown. Also (1817–1825) at Fayetteville, N. Carolina.
Mark recorded: American eagle ringed with stars, over W NOTT, in large oval panel.

Olcott, J. W.: (*fl. c.* 1800) Baltimore, Md.
Mark recorded: American eagle with OLCOTT over, and BALTIMORE under, in circular panel.

Ostrander, Charles: (*fl.* 1848–1854) New York, N.Y.
Mark recorded: OSTRANDER incised.

Ostrander & Norris: (*fl.* 1848–1850) New York, N.Y.
Mark recorded: OSTRANDER in curved label over & NORRIS in curved label, together forming oval.

Palethorp, John H.: (*fl.* 1820–1845) Philadelphia, Pa.

Marks recorded include: J. H. PALE-THORP in oblong, over PHILAD^ in oblong; PALETHORP'S over PHILAD^ in shaped oblong with serrated edges; PALETHORP'S in oblong panel with serrated edges.

Palethorp, Robert, Jr: (*fl.* 1817–1822) Philadelphia, Pa.
Marks recorded include: American eagle in flattened horizontal oval, surrounded by R. PALETHORP PHILA (incomplete); R. PALETHORP J^R over PHILAD^ in shaped rectangle.

Palethorp, R. & J. H.: (*fl.* 1820–1826) Philadelphia, Pa.
Mark ascribed: eagle in oval (incomplete).

Palethorp & Connell: (*fl.* 1839–1841) Philadelphia, Pa.
Mark recorded: PALETHORP over & CONNELL over PHILAD^ each in separate oblong panel.

Parker, Charles, & Co: (*fl.* mid 19th century) Meriden, Conn.
Mark recorded: C. PARKER & CO in oblong panel

Parker, J. G.: (*fl. c.* 1840) Rochester, N.Y.
Mark recorded: N.Y. in small rectangle with J. G. PARKER in curved label over and ROCHESTER in curved label under, together forming oval.

Parkin, W.: (*fl.* after 1830) Provenance not determined.
Mark recorded: W. PARKIN incised.

Parmenter, W. H.: (*fl.* after 1840) Provenance not determined.
Mark recorded: the words GEO. CARR'S PATENT MADE by W. H. PARMENTER arranged in a circular panel.

Pierce, Samuel: (*fl. c.* 1792–*c.* 1831) Greenfield, Mass.
Marks recorded include: eagle with SAMUEL over and PIERCE below, in shaped panel; initials S.P. over cross, in circle.

Plumly & Bidgood: (*fl. c.* 1825) Philadelphia, Pa.
Mark recorded: PLUMLY & BIDGOOD in rectangle.

Porter, Allen: (*fl.* 1830–1840) Westbrook, Me.
Mark recorded: A. PORTER in oblong with serrated edges.

Porter, Freeman: (*fl.* 1835–*c.* 1860) Westbrook, Me.
Mark recorded: F. PORTER WESTBROOK in circular panel.

Porter, James: (*fl. c.* 1795–*c.* 1803) Baltimore, Md.
Mark recorded: American eagle, with JAMES above and PORTER below, in rectangle shaped like cartouche.

Potter, W.: (*fl. c.* 1835) Provenance not determined.
Mark recorded: W. POTTER in oblong.

Putnam, James H.: (*fl.* 1830–1855) Malden, Mass.
Mark recorded: PUTNAM in oblong with serrated edges.

Reed & Barton: (*fl.* from 1840 onwards) Taunton, Mass.
Mark recorded: REED & BARTON.

Reich, John P.: (*fl. c.* 1820–1830) Salem, N. Carolina.
Mark recorded: P. REICH SALEM. N.C. forming circle in circular panel.

Renton & Co: (*fl.* after 1830) New York, N.Y.
Mark recorded: RENTON & CO over NEW YORK.

Richardson, B. & Son: (*fl. c.* 1839) Philadelphia, Pa.
Mark recorded: B. RICHARDSON & SON over PHILADELPHIA.

Richardson, George: (*fl. c.* 1818–1845) Boston, Mass. Also at Cranston, R.I.
Marks recorded include: G. RICHARDSON in oblong alone, or with BOSTON under; G. LENNORE C° in curved label with serrated edges and CRANSTON. R.I. in curved label with serrated edges, both forming an oval about an eagle in a small circle.

Rogers, Smith & Co: (*fl. c.* 1850) Hartford, Conn.
Mark recorded: ROGERS, SMITH & CO·HARTFORD, CT. inside round circle with beaded edge.

Rust, Samuel: (*fl.* 1837–1845) New York, N.Y.
Mark recorded: S. RUSTS PATENT over NEW YORK.

Sage, Timothy: (*fl. c.* 1848) St Louis, Mo.
Mark recorded: T. SAGE in oblong, over ST. LOUIS, MO.

Sage & Beebe: (*fl.* after 1840)
Provenance not determined.
Mark recorded: SAGE & BEEBE.

Savage & Graham: (*fl. c.* 1837) Middletown, Conn.
Mark recorded: MIDD.CT. surrounded by SAVAGE (above) GRAHAM (below) forming circle.

Savage, William H.: (*fl.* 1837–1840) Middletown, Conn.
Mark recorded: SAVAGE MIDD.CT. form oval.

Sellew & Co: (*fl.* 1830–*c.* 1860) Cincinnati, Ohio.
Marks recorded include: eagle surrounded by SELLEW & CO CINCINNATI in oval panel; SELLEW & CO over CINCINNATI.

"Semper Eadem": (*c.* 1760–*c.* 1780) Boston, Mass.
Mark recorded: crowned rose between columns, with SEMPER above and EADEM under, forming a sort of cartouche.

Sheldon & Feltman: (*fl.* 1847–1848) Albany, N.Y.
Marks recorded include: SHELDON & FELTMAN ALBANY arranged in three lines; the same arranged to form a triangle.

Shoff, I.: (*fl. c.* 1785) provenance thought to be Pennsylvania.
Mark recorded: I·SHOFF in oblong.

Sickel & Shaw: (*fl.* mid 19th century) Philadelphia, Pa.
Mark recorded: PHILADᴬ with SICKEL & SHAW arranged above in curve.

Simpkins, Thomas: (1702–1756) Boston, Mass.
Mark recorded: four-petalled flower, crowned, in oval, with name (incomplete) ·SIMPKINS· surrounding it, in a broad oval panel.

Simpson, Samuel: (*fl.* 1837–1852) Yalesville, Conn. Also at New York, N.Y.
Mark recorded: S. SIMPSON in oblong.

Simpson & Benham: (*fl.* 1845–1847) New York, N.Y.
Mark recorded: SIMPSON & BENHAM in three lines.

Skinner, John: (*fl. c.* 1760–1790) Boston, Mass.
Marks recorded include: lion rampant between columns with (?) JOHN above (indecipherable) over SKINNER at foot; I:SKINNER over BOSTON in double label; initials IS in a shield.

Smith, Eben: (*fl.* 1841–1856) Beverly, Mass.
Mark recorded: E. SMITH in oblong.

Smith & Co: (*fl.* 1853–1856) Albany, N.Y.
Mark recorded: SMITH & CO in curved label.

Smith & Feltman: (*fl. c.* 1849–1852) Albany, N.Y.
Mark recorded: SMITH & FELTMAN ALBANY arranged in two lines.

Smith & Morey: (*fl. c.* 1841) Boston, Mass.
Mark recorded: SMITH & MOREY in oblong label.

Southmayd, Ebenezer: (*fl.* 1802–*c.* 1830) Castleton, Vt.
Marks recorded include: sailing ship (incomplete) over name THMAYD (incomplete); sailing ship over initials E·S·

Stafford, Spencer: (*fl.* 1794–1827) Albany, N.Y.
Marks recorded include: S. STAFFORD in oblong label over ALBANY; crowned rose in rectangle.

Stafford, S. & Co: (*fl.* 1817–1824) Albany, N.Y.
Mark recorded: emblem surrounded by S. STAFFORD & CO ALBANY.

Stalkamp, J. H. & Co: (*fl.* mid 19th century) Cincinnati, Ohio.

Mark recorded: J. H. STALKAMP & CO in curved label, over CINCIN-NATI in smaller curved label.

Standish, Alexander: (*fl.* after 1835) Provenance not determined.
Mark recorded: ALEX^R STANDISH.

Starr, William H.: (*fl.* 1843–1846) New York, N.Y.
Mark recorded: W. H. STARR in curved label with serrated edges, over N.Y. in rough oval label with serrated edges.

Stedman, S.: (*fl.* after 1800) provenance not determined.
Mark recorded: S. STEDMAN.

Taunton Britannia Mfg Co: (*fl.* 1830–1835) Taunton, Mass.
Marks recorded include: T. B. M. CO.; TAUNTON BRIT^A over MANF^G CO.

Tomlinson: (*fl. c.* 1843)
Provenance not determined.
Mark recorded: TOMLINSON'S PA-TENT, 1843 in three lines.

Trask, Israel: (*fl. c.* 1825–*c.* 1856) Beverly, Mass.
Mark recorded: I·TRASK in oblong label with canted corners.

Trask, Oliver: (*fl. c.* 1825–*c.* 1839) Beverly, Mass.
Mark recorded: O·TRASK in oblong label with serrated edges.

Treadway, Amos: (*fl. c.* 1785) Middletown, Conn.
Mark recorded: emblem resembling coffeepot on stand, between columns, with AMOS in curved label attached (above) and TREADWAY similarly below; a mark resembling a fleur-de-lys with DDELTOWN in curved label above (incomplete) is ascribed to him.

Vose & Co: (*fl.* after *c.* 1840) Albany, N.Y.
Mark recorded: VOSE & CO over ALBANY.

Wallace, R. & Co: (from 1855) Wallingford, Conn.
Mark recorded: R. WALLACE & CO. in oblong label.

Ward, H. B. & Co: (*fl. c.* 1849) Wallingford, Conn.
Mark recorded: H. B. WARD in plain oblong label.

Warren: (*fl.* after 1830)
Provenance not determined.
Mark recorded: WARREN'S HARD METAL in two lines.

Wayne, C. P. & Son: (*fl. c.* 1835) Philadelphia, Pa.
Mark recorded: C. P. WAYNE & SON in plain oblong label over PHILAD^A in oblong label.

Weekes, James: (*fl.* from *c.* 1820) New York, N.Y. Also at Poughkeepsie, N.Y. (from *c.* 1835)
Marks recorded include: J. WEEKES N Y in oblong label: J. WEEKES alone, or over BROOKLYN.

Weekes, J. & Co: (*fl.* 1833–1835) Poughkeepsie, N.Y.
Mark recorded: WEEKES & CO (incomplete) in oblong label with serrated edges.

Whitcomb, A. G.: (after 1820) Boston, Mass.
Mark recorded: A. G. WHITCOMB. BOSTON arranged around inside edge of circular panel.

Whitehouse, E.: (after 1800)
Provenance not determined.
Marks recorded include: WHITE-HOUSE in oblong label with serrated edges; WHITEHOUSE over WARRANTED.

Whitfield, G. & J.: (*fl.* 1836–1865) New York, N.Y.
Mark recorded: G. &. J. WHITFIELD.

Whitlock, John H.: (*fl.* 1836–1844) Troy, N.Y.
Marks recorded include: crouching animal in lobed panel with WHITLOCK over TROY N Y together in oblong label; WHITLOCK over TROY N.Y. in oblong label with shaped ends.

Whitmore, Jacob: (*fl. c.* 1758–*c.* 1790) Middletown, Conn.
Marks recorded include: crowned rose encircled by JACOB over and WHITMORE below, in separate curved labels; double (quasi-Tudor) rose in circular panel with beaded edge.

Wildes, Thomas: (*fl.* 1833–1840) New York, N.Y.
Marks recorded include: T. WILDES in plain oblong label, or in curved label with serrated edges.

Will, George: (*fl.* 1798–1807) Philadelphia, Pa.
Mark recorded: GW in cursive capitals in oval surrounded by LONG LIVE THE PRESIDENT in circular panel.

Will, Henry: (*fl.* 1761–1775; 1783–*c.*1793) New York, N.Y. Also at Albany, N.Y. (*fl.* 1775–1783).
Marks recorded include: HENRY. WILL over line of pellets over NEW YORK all in rectangular panel; shield between columns with HENRY WILL in curved label (over) attached and NEW YORK in oblong panel (below) attached; crowned rose in cartouche formed of HENRY WILL curved over with NEW YORK curved below; HENRY WILL in slightly-curved label close over NEW YORK similar; crowned rose in rectangle. Other marks ascribed to him are incomplete; sometimes found associated with very small rectangle containing a lion rampant.

Will, John: (*fl. c.* 1752–*c.* 1763) New York, N.Y.
Marks recorded include: initials I. W in circle with serrated edges; I W with a pellet above and below in circle with serrated edges; sailing ship between columns (upper part incomplete) with NEW YORK in oblong attached below; lion rampant in curved cartouche.

Will, William: (*fl. c.* 1770; d. 1798) Philadelphia, Pa.
Marks recorded include: W·W with fleur-de-lys over, in shaped oval; Wᴹ WILL over PHILADELPHIA in two linked curved labels; Wᴹ WILL in oblong label with serrated edges; W. WILL over PHILA· over DELPHIA with small emblem (? a castle) over in shaped rectangle with beaded edges; Wᴹ WILL/PHILADEL/PHIA in three attached labels slightly curved with rounded edges, forming one panel; some incomplete marks also ascribed show an animal or bird in an oval, perhaps surrounded by PHILA WILLI.

Williams, Lorenzo L.: (*fl.* 1835–1842) Philadelphia, Pa.

Mark recorded: L. L. WILLIAMS over PHILADᴬ

Williams, Otis: (*fl. c.* 1826–1830) Buffalo, N.Y.
Mark recorded: eagle surrounded by O. WILLIAMS BUFFALO in upright oval with beaded edge.

Williams & Simpson: (*fl.* 1837) Yalesville, Conn.
Mark recorded: W & S in oblong label.

Woodbury, J. B.: (*fl.* 1835) Philadelphia, Pa.
Marks recorded include: American eagle surrounded by stars (above) and J. B. WOODBURY (below) in circular panel; American eagle surrounded by J. B. WOODBURY (above) and sprinkle of stars (below); J. B. WOODBURY over PHILADᴬ each in oblong label with serrated edges; J. B. WOODBURY in plain oblong label.

Woodbury & Colton: (*fl. c.* 1835) Philadelphia, Pa.
Mark recorded: WOODBURY & COLTON in plain oblong label.

Woodman, Cook & Co: (*fl.* after 1830) Portland, Me.
Mark recorded: WOODMAN, COOK & CO.

Yale, Charles: (*fl. c.* 1818–1835) Wallingford, Conn.
Mark recorded: CHARLES YALE & CO in curved label over WALLINGFORD in curved label, together forming oval shape; the word BRITANNIA may be found associated in plain oblong label.

Yale, Hiram: (*fl.* 1822–1831) Wallingford, Conn.
Mark recorded: bird's head (? eagle) encircled by H. YALE (above) and WALLINGFORD (below) in near-circular panel.

Yale, Hiram, & Co: (*fl.* 1824–1835) Yalesville, Conn.
Mark recorded: H·YALE and WALLINGFORD curved to form horizontal oval about & CO.

Yale, W. & S.: (*fl. c.* 1810–1820) Meriden, Conn.

Mark recorded: (very indistinct) eagle over W & S in upright broad oval panel.

Yale & Curtis: (*fl.* 1858–1867) New York, N.Y.
Mark recorded: YALE & CURTIS N. Y. in pierced semicircular panel.

Young, Peter: (*fl. c.* 1775) New York, N.Y. Also at Albany, N.Y. (*c.* 1785–*c.* 1800) Marks recorded include: initials PY in rectangle with serrated edges; PY in circle with serrated edges; P.Y in oval with serrated edges; crowned rose in rectangle with P and Y in bottom corners; American eagle in curved cartouche with PETER (above), lower part indistinct; PY in small plain rectangle associated with other small punches, e.g. rampant lion.

AMERICAN BICENTENNIAL MARK

In connection with the American Revolution Bicentennial celebrations, this symbol designed by the firm of Chermayeff and Geismar, Inc. has official approbation for use under licence, in various fields. Commemorative and educational-type products may be marked; these include items made of silver or pewter.

The American Revolution Bicentennial symbol is derived from the stars, stripes and colours of the United States flag. The symbol takes the form of an American 5-pointed star in white, surrounded by continuous red, white, and blue stripes, which form a second star. This double star is symbolic of the two centuries that have passed since the American Revolution.

Furniture and Tapestry

English Furniture Marks

Furniture in general, and English furniture in particular, rarely bears a mark or other form of identification of its maker. No powerful trade guild existed, as in France, so no regulations regarding marking were imposed. Marks on English furniture do, however, occur in various forms, and a representative selection is given below. (A comprehensive listing of most known makers is given in the works listed in the bibliography.)

Initials made with a branding iron or punch are sometimes found on joined chairs and stools, on caned walnut chairs of the late Stuart period and on provincial furniture of the Georgian period. They usually appear on an inconspicuous area of the chair and are almost always the initials of journeymen (whose names are unlikely ever to be known) rather than those of the master. They should not of course be confused with the initials of the original owner, prominently and often ornately carved on the backs of joined chairs, and on oak chests, cupboards and similar pieces.

Labels and trade cards, by which makers can be positively identified, originated in the late 17th century and were used throughout the 18th and early 19th centuries, by a few London and provincial furniture-makers. These labels (small, usually circular or rectangular pieces of paper inscribed with the maker's name and address) or larger trade cards (handbills giving the maker's name and address, listing his specialities and often decoratively engraved) are occasionally found pasted to the inside of drawers or the backs or undersides of furniture. In the late 18th and early 19th centuries, brass plaques fulfilled a similar function, especially on patent furniture.

The practice of punching furniture with a name stamp was adopted by, among others, Gillows of Lancaster at the end of the 18th century and, by the 19th century, became relatively common. Many Windsor chairs were marked along the seat edge by this method. Applying a maker's name by means of a stencil was a largely Victorian practice.

Signatures made with a pen or brush, or incised and black-waxed, are the rarest of all marks on English furniture. A signature in pencil on the frame of Victorian upholstered furniture is likely to be that of the craftsman who re-upholstered it.

Discovering a maker's stamp or label on a piece of furniture always adds enormously to its interest and value; the fraudulent addition of such stamps or labels is therefore not unknown.

Makers' labels and trade cards: a selective list

Made by John Belchier *at the Sun in St Paul's Church Yard.*
Small circular trade label found on bureau cabinet, *c.* 1730.

G. Coxed *and* T. Woster. *At the White Swan in St Paul's Churchyard, London; Makes and sells Cabinets, Book-cases, Chests of Drawers, Scrutores and Looking-glasses of all sorts at reasonable rates.*
Trade card of London makers, active 1716–36.

Butler. *13 & 14 Catherine Street. 8 Doors from the Strand. Upholsterer, Cabinet Maker and Chair Manufacturer. Bed Furniture & Mattresses calculated for the East and West Indies. Ship cabbins furnished. Articles particularly adapted and for Travelling and Exportation.*
Trade card of London maker, active 1787–1814.

Giles Grendey, *St John's Square, Clerkenwell, London, Makes and Sells all sorts of Cabinet Goods, Chairs, Tables, Glasses & C.*
Trade card found on japanned chair. Maker active.

George Simson, *Upholder, Cabinet Maker and Undertaker. N. 19 South Side of St Paul's Churchyard, London.*
Trade card found on late 18th-century side table.

Henry Kettle, *successor to Mr Philip Bell CABINET MAKER, Upholder and undertaker at No. 23 St Paul's Churchyard, London.*
Trade card found on late 18th-century mahogany side table.

R. Snowdon, *Cabinet Maker & Appraiser, Northallerton. Every Article of Furniture made after the newest Fashion and in the neatest manner.*
Trade label found on davenport, c. 1821.

From FREEMAN MANUFAC-TURY, ST. ANDREWS, NOR-WICH
Stencil found on mahogany cupboard, c. 1840.

GILLOWS LANCASTER
Stamp punched on drawer of dressing table, c. 1811.

G & R GILLOW & Co
Merchants
& cabinetmakers

Incised mark of John Gumley (*fl. c.* 1694-early 18th century). 'John Gumley, 1703' is also recorded.

GUMLEY

Incised mark of James Moore (1670–1726), found on certain gilt gesso pieces of his making.

MOORE

French Furniture Marks

In 1741 it was laid down by the trade guild concerned (known after 1743 as the "Corporation des Menuisiers-Ebénistes") that every master of the craft (maître) should have an iron to stamp his name (more rarely his initials) on each piece of furniture made by him for sale, and also on pieces made by others when repaired by him. This mark was normally put in some inconspicuous place. A committee examined all work done, or in course of being done, and if it reached the required high standard it was stamped accordingly. Privileged craftsmen working for the French Crown were exempt from Guild regulations, and their work therefore was often unstamped. Other craftsmen exempt from Guild regulations were those living in certain anciently privileged quarters of Paris, including a number of foreign craftsmen. After the trade guilds had been dissolved, during the 19th century makers ceased to stamp their furniture; after the Exhibition at Paris in 1882 interest in the old practice revived, with consequent forgery of "signatures" among dealers trading in furniture.

Numbers found on 18th-century pieces may refer to entries in Crown inventories.

Mark used by the Guild

A Selective List of Makers
of Furniture, Clocks, and Bronzes d'Ameublement
with marks

A.V.
Letters recorded (incised) on the bottom tray of a work-table, period Louis XVI; probably for Adam Weisweiler (q.v.)

Baumhauer, Joseph: (d. 1772)
Cabinet-maker, born in Germany, but working in Paris; soon after 1767 he was awarded the rank of "ébéniste privilégé du Roi".
Stamp recorded:

JOSEPH
Between fleurs-de-lis

Beneman, Jean Guillaume: (fl. 1784–1804)
Cabinet-maker of German birth, who came to Paris, working as an artisan libre; maître-ébéniste in 1785; worked for the Crown; under the Directoire, and during the Consulate.

G · BENEMAN

Berthoud, Ferdinand: (1727–1807)
Parisian clock- and watch-maker; born in Switzerland; moved to Paris c. 1746; elected F.R.S. London.
Stamp recorded:

FERDINAND
BERTHOUD
Inscribed on dial

Boulard, Jean Baptiste: (c. 1729–1789)
French cabinet-maker working at Paris; maître-menuisier 1754; working for Crown from 1777; business carried on by widow, and son Michel Jacques, who received commissions from Napoleon.
Stamp recorded:

J. B. BOULARD
In two varying sizes

Bourbon, Michel: fl. mid 18th century)
Frenchman recorded making sundials at Paris 1753; possibly also made barometers.
Inscription recorded:

BOURBON A PARIS
On dial of cartel barometer

B.V.R.B.
Found on veneered and marquetry furniture, mostly in the rococo style. Thought to be the initials of the Van Risen Burghs, a Dutch family working in Paris in the late 17th to early 18th century. Bernard Van Risen Burgh I (d.1738) became maître by 1730; Bernard II became maître c. 1765 and died c. 1765; Bernard III (d. 1800).

Caffiéri, Jacques: (1678–1755)
French fondeur-ciseleur of Italian descent, working in Paris; did much work for the Crown, in the rococo style.
Stamps recorded:

CAFFIERI

A. PARIS

CAFFIERI A. PARIS

CAFFIERI A. PARIS

FAIt PAR CAFFIERI

Caffiéri, Philippe: (1714–1774)
French fondeur-ciseleur, son of Jacques Caffiéri; working in Paris.
Signed his works:

P. CAFFIERI

Carlin, Martin: (d. 1785)
French cabinet-maker working in Paris; maître-ébéniste 1766; worked for Queen Marie Antoinette.
Stamp recorded:

M▸CARLIN

Coteau, Joseph: (1740–1801)
French peintre-émailleur; noted maker of
clock dials, second half of 18th century.
Usually signed:

> COTEAU

In the enamel, lower
part of dial
Inscriptions recorded include:

> Coteau 1771   10 OCT
> Coteau, Thil 1763 ft

Not to be confused with the miniature
painter, Jean Coteau (*fl. c.* 1739–1812).

Cramer, Mathieu Guillaume
Cabinet-maker of German birth working
in Paris in Louis XVI style. Stamp:

> M. G. CRAMER

Cressent, Charles: (1685–1768)
French cabinet-maker; worked for Philippe, Duc d'Orléans, Regent of France; an
ébéniste who also modelled, cast and
gilded the mounts for his own furniture,
thus infringing guild regulations. Earlier
and best work never stamped.
Stamp recorded:

> C. CRESSENT
> (of doubtful authenticity)

Cronier, Jean Baptiste: (*fl.* 1781–1793)
French clock-maker; became maître-
horloger in 1781.
Inscription recorded:

> Cronier
> A PARIS
> (on dial)

Cronier fils: (*fl.* early 19th century)
French clock-makers, the firm incorporated during the First Empire; still working
1825.

Crowned C
Found stamped on French bronze work;
said to be a hall-mark used on French
bronzes during the period from 5th March
1745 to 4th February 1749; taxes were
levied on works made of the various mate-
rials, which were stamped to suit, e.g. C for
cuivre.

Crowned CT
Found on French furniture in use at the
Château de Trianon.
Mark recorded:

Painted: *c.* 1783

Crowned EU
Found on French furniture in use at the
Château d'Eu.
Mark recorded:

Crowned F
Found on French furniture in use at the
Château de Fontainbleau.
Marks recorded:

Stencilled: on parchment
label, 1780s

F

Stamped: on bronzes
d'ameublement, 1780s

Crowned SC
Found on French furniture in use at the
Château de Saint-Cloud.
Mark recorded:

Stencilled: 1780s

Crowned TH
Found on French furniture in use at the Palais des Tuileries.
Mark recorded:

TH

Stamped: on bronzes d'ameublement, Louis XVI period

Cuvellier, E. J.: (*fl.* 19th century)
French cabinet-maker, whose stamp has been recorded:
E. J. CUVELLIER
Stamped

Daillé, Charles: (*fl. c.* 1722–1760)
Maître-horloger at Paris.
Stamps recorded include:
Daillé AParis

(the AP conjoined)
and
Daillé
horloger de Madame la dauphine

Inscribed on dial, or
engraved on backplate

David
see Roentgen, David

Delorme, Adrien: (*fl.* later 18th century)
Member of family of cabinet-makers working in Paris. Maître-ébéniste in 1748.
Stamp:

DELORME

Delorme, François: (1691–1768)
Member of family of cabinet-makers working in Paris. Stamp:
F.D.

Delorme, Jean Louis Faizelot: (*fl. c.* 1763–1780)
Member of family of cabinet-makers working at Paris: maître-ébéniste 1763.
Stamp recorded:

J ⋆ L ⋆ F ⋆ DELORME

Delunésy, Nicolas Pierre: (fl. second half 18th century)
Maître-horloger (1764) at Paris.
Inscription recorded:
Delunésy AParis

Dimier: (? *fl.* 19th century)
Stamp recorded:

DIMIER

This mark, if found on 18th-century pieces, is probably that of a later craftsman doing a repair.

DR
See Roentgen, David

Dubois, Germain: (*fl. c.* 1757–1789)
French clockmaker at Paris. Maître-horloger 1757.
Inscription recorded:
Gm. Dubois
A PARIS
NB. Many clockmakers of the name Dubois (18th century) are recorded at work, not only in France, but also in Belgium, England and Switzerland.

E.H.B.
Stamp occasionally found on French 18th-century furniture; possibly denoted an owner. Since this stamp has been recorded on a piece belonging to Eugénie Hortense Buonaparte, the initials might stand for her name.

EHB

Erstet, Jean Ulric: (*fl.* 1740–*c.* 1760)
French cabinet-maker, who also sold furniture, in Paris; maîte-ébéniste in 1740.
Stamp recorded:

J·U·ERSTET

Fiéffé, Jean Jacques, père: (*fl.* mid-18th century)
French clockmaker working in Paris.
Mark recorded which may be his:
FIÉFFÉ
DE L'OBSERVATOIRE

Fleur-de-lis mark
Found on bronzes d'ameublement; probably indicates Paris origin.

F.M
Stamp recorded; significance not yet determined; not the mark of a known ébéniste; might be mark of a repairer or of an owner.

Fortier, Alexandre: (*fl. c.* 1725–1760)
Inventor of a certain type of clock movement; known to have collaborated in making the astronomical type of clock. Inscriptions recorded include:
Inventé par A. Fortier
Alexandre fortier jnvenit Stollewerck fecit A paris

Foulet or **Foullet, Antoine:** (d. 1775)
French cabinet-maker in Paris; maître-ébéniste in 1749.
Marks recorded include:

ANT
FOVLLET

Foullet, Pierre Antoine: (*fl.* 1765–*c.* 1780)
French cabinet-maker at Paris; maître-ébéniste in 1765.
Stamp recorded:

foulet

P A FOULLET

(sometimes seen accompanied by a fleur-de-lis)

Furet, André, l'aîné: (*fl. c.* 1690–1740)
French clockmaker; maître-horloger 1691.
Inscription recorded:
FURET L'AINÉ
A PARIS
Inscribed on dial
NB. Other clockmakers of the name of Furet are known to have been working in Paris during the 18th century.

Garnier, Pierre: (*fl. c.* 1720–1800)
French cabinet-maker at Paris; maître-ébéniste in 1742.
Stamp recorded:

P·GARNIER

Gaudreau, Antoine Robert: (*c.* 1680–1751)
French cabinet-maker to Louis XV from 1726; died before regulations enforced.
No marks.

Gaudron, Pierre: (*fl. c.* 1690–1730 or later)
Maker of clocks and watches in Paris.
Inscription recorded:
Gaudron AParis
(the AP conjoined)

Gouchon: (? *fl.* later 18th century)
No record of this clockmaker, but some inscriptions include:
GOUCHON
A PARIS
Painted
Gouchon à Paris
Inscribed

Gourdin, Michel: (*fl.* mid 18th century)
French cabinet-maker at Paris; maître-ébéniste in 1752; worked for the French crown in the 1770s.
Stamp used:

M◆GOURDIN

Gouthière, Pierre: (1732–*c.* 1813)
French bronze worker; maître-doreur in 1758; celebrated ciseleur; worked for the Court (*c.* 1769–1777); known work very rare indeed, and seldom signed.
One example recorded has the words:
PAR GOUTHIERE CIZELEUR ET DOREUR A PARIS, with the address QUAY PELLETIER A LA BOUCLE D'OR 1771.

Guiot: (18th century)
Surname (no Christian names known) of a number of French clock-makers working in Paris.
Inscription recorded:
Guiot AParis
(the AP conjoined)

Hervé, Jean Baptiste: (*c.* 1700–1780)
French clockmaker; maître-horloger in 1726; some clockcases by Charles Cressent were furnished with movements by Hervé.
Inscription recorded:
HERVE
A PARIS

Jacob frères: (*fl.* 1796–1803)
Sons of Georges Jacob, French cabinet-makers at Paris; succeeded by Jacob-Desmalter.
Stamp used:
JACOB FRÈRES RUE MESLEE

Jacob, Georges: (1739–1814)
French cabinet-maker working in Paris; maître in 1765.
Stamp used:

G ◆ I A C O B

with fleur-de-lis (earlier work) between initial and surname, which later became a lozenge.
From 1803 George Jacob collaborated with his surviving and younger son François-Honoré.
See Jacob-Desmalter et Cie

Jacob, Henri: (*fl.* second half 18th century)
French cabinet-maker at Paris; maître-ébéniste in 1779.
Stamp used:
H. JACOB

Jacob-Desmalter et Cie: (*fl. c.* 1803–1813)
French cabinet-makers in Paris; firm consisting of George Jacob (1739–1814) and his son François-Honoré (1770–1841).
Stamp used:
JACOB D. R. MESLEE

NB. Georges Jacob had a house in the Rue Meslée from c. 1789.

Jaquet-Droz, Pierre: (1721–1790)
Swiss clockmaker working at Basle, Neuchâtel, Geneva, and Madrid.
Inscription recorded:
P. Jaquet Droz à La Chaud de Fonds

Jeanselme
Important family of cabinet-makers, active 1824–1930.
Worked for Louis-Philippe and Napoleon III. Marks:

Jeanselme Frères	1824–40
Jeanselme	1840–53
Jeanselme Père et Fils	1853–61
Jeanselme Fils	1858–63
Jeanselme Fils & Godin & Cie	1863–71
Ch. Jeanselme et Cie	1883–1930

Jolly family: (17th and 18th centuries)
Clockmakers working in France, and in England; a number were members of the London Clockmakers' Company.
Inscription recorded:
Jolly AParis
Engraved; the AP conjoined

Joseph
Stamp used by
Baumhauer, Joseph (q.v.)

♥JOSEPH♥

Joubert, Gilles: (1689–1775) also known as Joubert l'aîné.
French cabinet-maker working in Paris; ébéniste du Roi (1763–1774).
Rarely stamped his furniture.
Stamp: 'Joubert' between fleur-de-lis.

Lacroix, or **Vandercruse, Roger**: (*fl.* second half 18th century)
French cabinet-maker of Flemish descent, maître-ébéniste in 1755.
Stamps used included:
R. LACROIX

The initials R V L C with a lozenge between each.

Le Gaigneur, Louis Constantin: (*fl. c.* 1815)
Frenchman owning the Buhl Manufactory, 19 Queen Street, Edgware Road, London.
Inscriptions recorded include:
Le Gaigneur
Louis Le Gaigneur fecit

Lelarge, Jean Baptiste: (1743–1802)
French furniture maker at Paris; maître-menuisier 1775; used the same stamp as his father.
Stamp recorded:

I⋆B⋆LELARGE

Leleu, Jean François: (1729–1807)
French cabinet-maker working in Paris; maître-ébéniste in 1764; in 1780 in partnership with his son-in law Charles Antoine Stadler (*fl.* 1776–1811).
Stamps used included:

J·F·LELEU

and initials J. F. L.

Le Noir: (18th century)
Surname of several French clockmakers,
also of some London clockmakers.
One inscription recorded:
Jean le Noir

Lepaute, Jean André: (1709–c. 1787)
French clockmaker in Paris, one of a family
of clockmakers.
Inscriptions recorded:
Lepaute Hgr DU ROY
Lepaute
DE BELLE FONTAINE
A PARIS

Le Roy, Julien: (1686–1759)
French clockmaker in Paris; maître-
horloger in 1713.
Inscription recorded:
JULIEN
LE ROY
Inscribed on dial

Levasseur, Etienne: (1721–1798)
French cabinet-maker working in Paris;
maître-ébéniste in 1767.
Stamp used:

E·LEVASSEUR

Lieutaud, Balthazar: (d. 1780)
French cabinet-maker working in Paris;
maître-ébéniste in 1749; noted for his fine
clockcases.
Stamp used:

B·LIEUTAUD

Linke, François: (1855–1946)
German cabinet-maker working in Paris.
Specialised in copies of 18th-century furni-
ture. Signed his work 'Linke'.

MA crowned
Monogram for Marie Antoinette, seen
with GARDE MEUBLE DE LA
REINE making a circle around it.

Marchand, Nicolas Jean: (fl. first half 18th
century)

French cabinet-maker in Paris; maître-
ébéniste c. 1735; ceased work c. 1757.
Stamp used:

MARCHAND

Martinière, Antoine Nicolas: (1706–1784)
French enameller working in Paris.
Mark recorded: surname Martinière some-
times accompanied by his address (Rue des
Cinq Diamants) and a date.

*Martiniere Emailleur
et pensionaire du Roi rue
des 5 diamant a paris*

Martinot family: (fl. early 18th century)
French clockmakers in Paris; three were
clockmakers to Louis XIV: Balthazar (fl. c.
1679–1708); Jean Henri (fl. c. 1679–1708);
Jérome (fl. 1695–1732).
Surname Martinot is recorded.

Mellier & Co: (fl. c. 1866–1930s)
London makers of reproduction French
18th-century furniture.
Stamp recorded:

C·MELLIER & C⁰

C. MELLIER & C⁰
CABINET MAKERS
LONDON W

DOM – F*

Michault, J. L.: (fl. late 18th century)
French cabinet-maker at Paris.
Stamp recorded:
MICHAULT

Moinet, Louis: (1758–1853)
French author of a treatise on clock-
making.
Mark recorded:
L. MOINET
A PARIS
May indicate a repair by him,
if found on earlier piece

Molitor, Bernard: (*fl. c.* 1773–1833)
German cabinet-maker working in Paris
from *c.* 1773; maître-ébéniste in 1787.
Stamp used:

B. MOLITOR

Montigny, Philippe Claude: (1734–1800)
French cabinet-maker at Paris; maître-
ébéniste in 1766; specialist in making furniture in the Boulle style; also a repairer of
earlier pieces.
Stamp used:

MONTIGNY

Mynuël: (*fl.* first half 18th century)
Clockmaker, whose name has been found
inscribed:

MYNUEL
Painted on the dial

Oeben, Jean François: (1721–1763)
German cabinet-maker, first recorded
working at Paris 1749; made ébéniste du
Roi in 1754.
Stamp used (in later years):
J. F. OEBEN
Pieces made between 1763 and 1767
stamped with his name; these were probably made in his workshop by Riesener
under Veuve Oeben, before their mar-
riage.

Petit, Nicolas: (1732–1791)
French cabinet-maker working at Paris;
maître-ébéniste in 1761.
Stamp used:

N·PETIT

Piret: (Louis XIV period)
Surname found on bronzes d'ameuble-
ment of the period.
Stamped:

PIRET

Richard, Claude and **Etienne:** (*fl.* second
half 18th century)
French makers (father and son) of springs
at Paris; surname found on clock springs.
Example:

Richard
May be found with a date

Riesener, Jean-Henri: (1734–1806)
German-born cabinet-maker working at
Paris from post 1754; maître-ébéniste in
1768; ébéniste ordinaire du Roi in 1774.
Stamp used:

J·H·RIESENER

Robin, Robert: (1742–1799)
French clockmaker at Paris; horloger to
Louis XV and to Marie Antoinette; clock-
maker to the Republic in 1795.
Inscription recorded:
Robin

Roentgen, David: (1743–1807)
German-born cabinet-maker later established at Paris (after 1779 onward); maître-
ébéniste in 1780.
Stamp used:
DAVID
More frequently he preferred to include his
initials in the marquetry decoration of his
pieces.

R·V·L·C
Initials with lozenge between.
Stamp used by Roger Vandercruse, also
known as Lacroix (q.v.)

R·V·L·C

Schuman, André: (*fl.* 1771–1787)
German-born cabinet-maker working at
Paris; maître-ébéniste in 1771.
Stamp used:

A·SCHUMAN

Stollewerck, Michel: (*fl. c.* 1746–1775)
Made the movements for clocks and also
for musical boxes; maître-horloger in 1746.
Marks recorded include:
Stollewerck fecit A paris
Stollewerck AParis
The AP conjoined

Thuret, Jacques: (*fl.* 1694–1712)
French clockmaker, appointed to the King
(Louis XIV) and to the Observatoire.
Mark recorded:
THURET A PARIS

TW
Found on some bronzes d'ameublement
(18th century); thought to be the mark of
some repairer (not identified).

Vandercruse, Roger: (*fl.* second half 18th
century)
See Lacroix, Roger

Vigier, François: (*fl.* 1744–post 1769) French clockmaker at Paris; maître-horloger 1744.
Mark ascribed to him:
VIGER
A PARIS
Inscribed on dial
Viger AParis
Engraved on back-plate

Vitel: (*fl.* mid 19th century) Dealer trading in Paris; surname may be found ,stamped on 18th-century pieces, perhaps repaired by him:

VITEL·

Weisweiler, Adam: (*fl.* 1778–1810) German-born cabinet-maker later working at Paris; maître-ébéniste in 1778.
Stamp used:

A·WEISWEILER

Zweiner, Joseph-Emmanuel: (1849–) German cabinet-maker working in Paris. Specialised in copies of 18th-century furniture. Example of mark:
Zweiner
Paris
followed by year of manufacture.

Tapestry Marks

In 1528 a regulation was made whereby all Brussels tapestry weavers and dealers in tapestries were required to mark the tapestries. All tapestry weavers in the Low Countries were thereupon required by Charles V to do likewise. Flemish or French weavers emigrating to other countries (e.g. England) naturally continued to follow the same practice. The mark or signature was woven into the selvedge. This unfortunately was often cut away at a later date, so many are now missing.

Representative List of Marks

Antwerp, Flanders
Town mark: two hands on a shield.

Assche, Henri Van: (*fl.* mid-17th century) at Brussels.
Signed his tapestries:

Also: HENDRICK VAN ASSCHE

185

Baumgarten, William: (established 1893) at Williamsbridge, New York City, N.Y. Tapestries marked:

Benne, Jacques: (*fl.* mid-16th century) at Oudenarde, Flanders. Signed his tapestries:

Biest, Hans Van der: (*fl.* early 17th century) Went from Enghien to Munich (1604–1615). Marks used included:

Bradshaw: (*fl.* 1760s) Signature recorded on tapestry made at the Soho factory, London:

BRADSHAW

Brussels, Flanders
Town mark: a red shield, of varying forms, between the initials B B, also of varying styles:

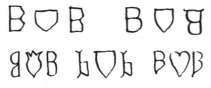

Cammen, Henri Van der: (date not known) at Enghien, Flanders. Marked his tapestries:

Cammen, Jean, or **Jehan, Van der**: (*fl.* later 16th century) at Enghien, Flanders. Signed his tapestries:

Cammen, Philippe Van der: (recorded 1576) at Antwerp, Flanders. Signed his tapestries:

Comans, Alexandre de: (*fl. c.* 1634–1650) Chief tapestry weaver in works at Paris of De Comans & De la Planche. Signed his tapestries:

Comans, Charles de: (d. 1634) Succeeded Marc de Comans at Paris. Signed his tapestries:

Comans, Hippolyté de: (*fl.* later 17th century) at Paris. Signed his tapestries:

Cozette, Pierre François: (*fl.* 18th century) For *c.* 60 years on staff of the Manufacture Royale des Gobelins at Paris; from 1742 director of the high-warp department; his reproducions of paintings, on tapestry, very fashionable *c.* 1781. Signed:

Cozette pixit

Crane, Sir Francis: (d. 1637) at Mortlake factory, Surrey, England. Signed his tapestries:

Crupenn, Remi: (recorded *c.* 1544) at Oudenarde, Flanders. Signed his tapestries:

Delft, Holland
Town mark: a shield between the initials H D:

Demay, Stephen: (*fl.* early 18th century) English tapestry weaver, established *c.* 1700.
Mark recorded:
S. D. M.

Dervael, Jean: (recorded *c.* 1544) at Oudenarde, Flanders.
Signed his tapestries:

Drouais, François Hubert: (1727–1775) French portrait painter; name found woven into examples of Gobelins tapestry woven after his paintings:
Drouais pixit

Enghien, Low Countries
Town mark: a shield, gyronny.

Florence, Italy
Town mark: fleur-de-lis associated with the initials of the weaver.

Fulham, London, England
Tapestry works founded by Peter Parisot (*fl.* first half 18th century).
Marks not recorded.

Geubels, François: (*fl. c.* 1541–1571) at Brussels.
Signed his tapestries:

Gobelins, Paris, France
Tapestry weaving established here in 1667.
Earlier mark:

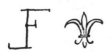

Modern mark:

Hatton Garden, London, England
Tapestry made here for some years from 1679, employing some weavers from Mortlake, Surrey.
Mark a variant of the Mortlake shield:

Also recorded: HATTON GARDEN.

Hecke or **Hecque, Leo(n) Van den**: (recorded 1576) at Antwerp, Flanders.
Probably at Brussels.
Marked his tapestries:

Hove, Nicholas Van: (recorded 1576) at Brussels.
Marked his tapestries:

Hyckes or **Hickes, Richard**: (*fl.* later 16th century)
English weaver working in Warwickshire.
Signature recorded:
Ric = Hykes

Karcher, Jehan (?): (*fl.* 16th century)
Flemish weaver working at Ferrara, Italy.
Signed his tapestries:

Karcher, Nicholas: (recorded mid 16th century)
Flemish weaver said to have worked at Florence, Italy.
Marked his tapestries:

Lambeth, London, England
Workshop set up here (*c.* 1670) by William Benood.
Recorded on a tapestry before 1675:
MADE AT LAMBETH

Maecht, Felipe: (*fl.* later 16th century) perhaps working in Spain, and of Flemish or Dutch extraction.
Signature ascribed to him:

Maecht, Philip de: (recorded 1620s)
Master weaver of Dutch or Flemish origin working at Mortlake, Surrey. Thought to have worked previously with de Comans at Paris.
Signed his tapestries:

Maelsaeck, François Van: (d. 1638) at Brussels.
Marked his tapestries:

Morris, I.: (*fl.* early 18th century)
English tapestry weaver.
Mark recorded (*c.* 1723)
I. MORRIS

Mortlake, Surrey, England
Tapestry weaving established here in 1619, flourishing until *c.* 1703.
Mark: a white shield, of various forms, with the red cross of St George:

Neilson, Jacques: (*fl.* 1749–1788)
Artist of Scottish origin, in charge at the Gobelins tapestry works, Paris.
Signature found:
J. NEILSON

Orley, Michael Van: (*fl.* mid-16th century) probably at Oudenarde, Flanders.
Mark ascribed:

Oudenarde, Flanders
Town mark:

Pannemaker, Wilhelm de: (*fl.* mid-16th century) at Brussels.
Marks used include:

Paris, France
Mark used: a fleur-de-lis and the letter P, accompanied by the initials of the master weaver.

Poyntz, Francis: (d. 1685)
English weaver, connected with Mortlake or Hatton Garden.
Marks included:
FRANCUS POYNTZ
also F P with a shield; or with
HATTON GARDEN.

Raes, Jean: (*fl.* early 18th century) at Brussels.
Marked his tapestries:

Reymbouts, Martin: (recorded 1611–1615) at Brussels.
Marked his tapestries:

Royal Manufactory, Madrid, Spain
Mark recorded:

Santa Barbara factory, Madrid Spain
Tapestry factory founded here in 1720 by
Philip V; closed 1808, reopened 1815.
Mark: a weaver's shuttle.

Saunders, Paul: (*fl.* second half 18th century) at Soho, London, England.
Signature recorded (*c.* 1761):
    P. SAUNDERS LONDINI

Schrijner, Peter: (*fl.* later 17th century)
possibly at Mortlake, Surrey.
Monogram ascribed (on Mortlake piece):

NB. This mark might alternatively be that
of the weaver Paul Steen.

Segers, Jan: (*fl.* later 17th century) at
Brussels and at Paris.
Marked his tapestries:

Segers, Wilhelm: (recorded 1688) at Brussels.
Marked his tapestries:

Soho, London, England
Tapestry woven here mid-18th century.
No special mark recorded.

Spierincx, Armand: (recorded 1555) at
Delft, Holland.
Marked his tapestries:

Spierincx, François: (recorded 1576 and
1607) at Delft, Holland.
Marked his tapestries:

Tayer, Hans: (*fl.* mid 17th century)
Master weaver at Paris before 1662. Some-
times called Jean Taye.
Marked his tapestries:

Thomson, W. G.: (*fl.* early 20th century) at
Edinburgh, Scotland.
Mark recorded:

Tournai, Flanders
Town mark: a castle:

Vanderbank, John: (*fl.* later 17th century)
at Hatton Garden, London.
Recorded between 1689 and *c.* 1727.
Marks included: initials J.V.D.B.; name
having various spelling.

Vos, Jos de: (recorded 1705) at Brussels.
Mark recorded: I. D. VOS.

Vos, Judocus: (*fl.* early 18th century) at
Brussels.
Signature recorded:
    JUDOCUS DE VOS

Wezeler, Georges: (recorded 1534) at
Brussels.
Goldsmith of Antwerp and noted mer-
chant.
Mark:

Ceramics

European Marks

Aalmis, Jan: (1714–post 1788)
Ceramic painter, Rotterdam

Abaquesne, Masseot: (d. *c.* 1560)
Faience potter, Rouen (*fl. c.* 1530–60)

found on drugpots

Absolon, William: (1751–1815)
Pottery decorator, and china and glass dealer at Yarmouth (*fl.* from *c.* 1790)
Mark, painted in red, occurs on wares bought from Turner, Wedgwood, Shorthose, and Leeds (impressed with their marks):

Other marks:

Painted

Abtsbessingem, Thuringia, Germany
Faience pottery from mid-18th century.
Mark, a fork plus painter's initials:

Adams, Benjamin: (1787–1828)
Greengates, Tunstall, Staffordshire.
Managed family business from 1805; sold out to Meir of Tunstall in 1820. Works bought back by Adams family in *c.* 1858.
B. ADAMS
Impressed

Adams, J., and Co.: (*fl* later 19th century)
Styled J. Adams & Co. until 1873, then known as Adams & Bromley.
Marks, impressed, include:
ADAMS & BROMLEY
J. ADAMS & Co.

Adams, John: (1882–1953)
Pottery manufacturer and designer; joint founder (1921) and managing director (1921–49) of Carter, Stabler and Adams, Poole Pottery, Dorset.

Personal mark

Adams, William: (1746–1805)
Owner of Staffordshire potworks.
ADAMS & Co.
Impressed: on cream-coloured earthenware
1770–1800
ADAMS & Co.
Impressed: on solid jasper
1780–90
ADAMS
Impressed: on stoneware, transfer-printed earthenware, jasper
1787–1805
W. ADAMS & Co.
Impressed: on jasper

Adams, William: (1772–1829)
Potter at Burslem (until 1804), then at Cliff
Bank, Stoke, in partnership with his sons
from 1819; works continued as part of the
Wedgwood group.

ADAMS

ADAMS ADAMS

Impressed: 1804–64
(except on blue transfer-printed ware)

1804–40   *c.* 1879–
On blue transfer-printed earthenware.
Variations occur

W. ADAMS & SONS
STOKE . UPON . TRENT

Printed: 1819–64
on bone china, ironstone china,
enamelled earthenware

W A . & S.

1819–64; on various wares

Sample post-1891 marks

Adams, William: (1798–1865)
Owned the Greenfield pottery, Stafford-
shire, from 1834.
ADAMS
Impressed

Ahrenfeldt, Charles & Son: (fl. 1886–1910)
Factory at Limoges and at Altrohlau. Also
an importer with office in New York.

At Limoges

Importer's marks

Aire, Pas-de-Calais, France
Faience made here *c.* 1730 to 1790.
Reputed marks:

Albissola, northern Italy
Maiolica centre during the 17th and 18th
centuries. See also SAVONA.

Alcock & Co., Samuel: (*fl* 1828–59)
The Hill Pottery, Burslem, Staffordshire.
Marks found both impressed and printed:
ALCOCK & CO.
HILL POTTERY   S.A. & Co.
   BURSLEM

Sam/Alcock & Co.

Alcora, Valencia, Spain
Faience made *c.* 1726–*c.* 1780; cream-coloured earthenware from *c.* 1780; hard-paste porcelain from *c.* 1774.
Marks: letter A incised, in colours or in gold, used from 1784.

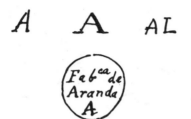

Transfer-printed in red
Early 19th century

Altenburg, Thuringia, Germany
Earthenware, late 18th to early 19th century.

Impressed

Altrohlau, Bohemia, Czechoslovakia
Cream-coloured earthenware and porcelain made by Benedict Hasslacher from 1813 to 1823; taken over by August Nowotny in 1823; closed 1884.

Altwasser, Silesia, Germany
Hard-paste porcelain from 1845 by Tielsch & Co.

Amberg, Bavaria, Germany
Faience made from 1759 (by Simon Hetzendörfer); cream-coloured earthenware and hard-paste porcelain made from 1790. The factory continued until 1910.

Amstel, near Amsterdam, Holland
Hard-paste porcelain from 1784 to 1820.

In blue
See also OUDE LOOSDRECHT and WEESP

Andreoli, Giorgio: (*c.* 1465/70–*c.* 1553)
Maiolica painter, working at Gubbio; especially noted for lustre. Called Maestro Giorgio. Marks occur on pieces dated from 1518 onward:

Principal mark

194

The mark of Maestro Giorgio has been forged.

Over-neat and careful in rendering: Mark on 19th-century reproduction

Angarono, near Bassano, Italy
Cream-coloured earthenware figure groups, late 18th century.

Angarono 1779

Angoulême, Charente, France
Faience, 1748–late 19th century

ANGOULEME

Annecy, Haute-Savoie, France
White earthenware, 1800–08, marked:

ANNECY

Ansbach, Bavaria, Germany
Hard-paste porcelain, 1858–62; moved to Castle of Bruckberg, 1762–1806; sold 1806; continued to 1860.

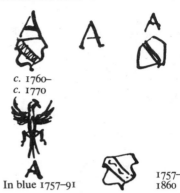

c. 1760–
c. 1770

In blue 1757–91   1757–1860

Various artists' marks appear.

Antonibon, Giambattista:
Made earthenware at Le Nove, Italy, from 1728 to 1741, when his son Pasquale took over from him. His monogram occurs on porcelain made *c.* 1762, perhaps in his honour:

Appel, Johannes Den:
Owner of Delft factory, De Vergulde Boot, from 1759; registered his mark in 1764 as:

IDA

Aprey, Haute Marne, France
Faience factory *c.* 1740 to *c.* 1860.

APREY

Artists here included Jacques Jarry, responsible for a certain type of bird painting; mark:

Apt, Vaucluse, France
Earthenware made here from 1728. Factory founded by César Moulin, and eventually in the hands of the widow Claire Arnoux (end of the 18th century).

Impressed

Mark of Claire Arnoux, being the initials VVA for veuve Arnoux.

Arbois, Jura, France
Faience made here from c. 1745 to c. 1800.

Arkhangelskoie, near Moscow, Russia
Site of porcelain factory, privately owned by Prince Nicholas Yussopoff, from 1814 to 1831.

Arnhem, Holland
Tin-glazed earthenware made here during third quarter of 18th century.

Arras, Pas-de-Calais, France
Soft-paste porcelain made here c. 1770–86.

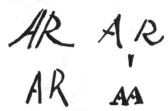

In blue, crimson or purple

Arzberg, Bavaria, Germany
Carl Schumann made hard-paste porcelain here from 1880.

Aschach, northern Bavaria, Germany
William Sattler made general pottery here, 1829–60.

W. S. & S.
Impressed

Ashby Potters' Guild, 1909–22
Manufacturers of earthenwares, including art pottery, at Woodville, near Burton-on-Trent, Derbyshire.

Ashtead Potters Ltd, Ashtead, Surrey
Manufacturers of earthenware 1926–36.

Ashworth, Geo. L., & Bros Ltd
Trading at Hanley from 1862; sold out 1883 to J. H. Goddard, whose descendants continue to present day, using designs of C.J. Mason. Firm retitled Mason's Ironstone China Ltd in 1968.

ASHWORTHS
REAL
IRONSTONE
CHINA

1862 onwards
Transfer-printed and impressed. Variations occur. "England" added after 1891.

1862 onwards
Transfer-printed and impressed.
Variations occur.

Astbury, Richard Meir: (1765–1834)
Potter and merchant; worked the Foley Pottery, Lane Delph, Staffordshire, from 1780 until 1797.
R.M.A. or ASTBURY

Augsburg, Swabia, Germany
Important centre for decoration of Meissen porcelain by outside decorators (Hausmaler) from *c.* 1725. Hausmaler included Johann Auffenwerth (d. 1728) who produced a small quantity; much attributed to him more likely came from the workshop of Bartolomäus (*c.* 1730–35).

Ault, William (*fl.* 1887–1923)
Made art pottery at Swadlincote, near Burton-on-Trent, Staffordshire, some (1891–96) from designs by Christopher Dresser. Ault & Tunnicliffe Ltd 1923–37; Ault Potteries Ltd 1937 to present.

1887–1923

Aultcliff
MADE IN
ENGLAND

1923–37

Chr Dresser

1891–96

Auxerre, Yonne, France
Faience factory established here by Claude Boutet in 1785.

BOUTET   *Fayence d'Auxerre*

Aveiro, Portugal
Faience made here from *c.* 1780, found marked F.A. (Fabrica Aveiro).

F.Aº   F.AVEIRO

Avisseau, Jean Charles: (1796–1861)
Made pottery in style of Palissy and Henri Deux wares at Tours. Signed in monogram, rarely in full.

Aynsley, Henry & Co.: (1873–)
Made various earthenwares in Longton, Staffordshire. "Ltd" appears in marks from 1932.

Aynsley, John and Sons: (1780–1809)
Made cream-coloured earthenware and porcelain at Longton, Staffordshire. Some black transfer-printed wares signed:

Aynsley, Lane End

J. Aynsley, Lane End

Aynsley, John and Sons: (1864)
Made bone china at Longton, Staffordshire.

From 1891

Baddeley, John: (d. 1772)
Made salt-glazed stoneware and cream-coloured earthenware at Shelton, Staffordshire; his family continued the business until c. 1802.

Incised inscription (not mark)

Baden-Baden, Germany
Zacharias Pfalzer directed a porcelain factory here, 1770–78. Earthenware was made by François Antoine Anstett from 1793.

Pfalzer

Anstett

| In blue on porcelain | In colour on faience | On earthenware |

Baguley, Isaac: (fl. 1842–55)
Painter at Derby; bought part of Rockingham works on its closure in 1842 to decorate china, buying wares from Minton; Brown, Westhead, Moore & Co., and others.
Mark:
"Baguley Rockingham Works" with or without the griffin crest.

Bailey & Batkin: (c. 1815–29)
Made lustred pottery at Lane End, Staffordshire.
Mark recorded:
Bailey & Batkin,
SOLE PATENTEES

Baker, Bevans & Irwin: (c. 1813–38)
Firm working at Swansea, Wales; closed 1838/39.
Marks:
The words BAKER, BEVANS & IRWIN with SWANSEA forming a circle round the Prince of Wales's feathers (impressed); the initials:
BB & I or BB & Co
Transfer-printed

Balaam, W.: (c. 1870–81)
Slipware potter at Ipswich.
Mark recorded:
W. Balaam, Rope Lane Pottery,
IPSWICH

Ball, Isaac: (fl. late 17th to early 18th century)
Potter at Burslem, Staffordshire.
Mark possibly his:
Initials I.B. on early Staffordshire posset pots, dated 1696–1700.

Baranovka, Volhynia, Poland
Porcelain factory founded here by the two Mezer brothers in 1801, continued until 1917 or later.

Barangwka

In black, brown or other colour

Barker family: (fl. mid-18th/end 19th century) Staffordshire
Various members potted at different works, e.g. at Fenton, Lane End, Lane Delph, etc. Barker Bros recorded in 1876.

198

LONGTON

1912–30

Barker, Sutton & Till: (*fl.* 1833–*c.* 1850)
Potters at Burslem, Staffordshire, making
earthenware, lustre ware, and figures. By
1850 Thomas Till sole owner, later taking
sons into partnership.
Marks:
"B.S. & T. Burslem" and TILL impressed

Barron, Paul: (1917–1983) Studio potter.

Bassano, Venice, Italy
Maiolica made here from the 16th to the
mid-18th century.

See also TERCHI

Bates, Elliot & Co.
Bates, Walker & Co.: (*fl.* 19th century)
Potworks at Dalehall, Longport, Staffordshire, passed through various ownerships,
from Joseph Stubbs (d. 1836) to Bates,
Walker & Company (1875–78)
Marks:
BATES WALKER & CO. impressed
or B.W. & CO.

Bayeux, Calvados, France
Factory established here in 1810, making
hard-paste porcelain; in 1849 owned by
F. Gosse.

1851–78

Bayreuth, Bavaria, Germany
Faience factory founded *c.* 1713 by Johann
Georg Knöller (d. 1744).
Mark, in blue, B.K. for Bayreuth-Knöller.
Initials used during succeeding ownerships:

B.F.S. (Bayreuth-Fränkel-Schreck,
1744–47)
B.P.F. (Bayreuth-Pfeiffer-Fränkel,
1747–60)
B.P. (Bayreuth-Pfeiffer, 1760–67)

WEZEL occurs impressed after 1788,
when cream-coloured English-type earthenware was exclusively made. These marks
often found with initials of painters and
decorators:

RIP	**Johann Kaspar Ripp** 1714
C	**Johann Clarner** 1731–48
G.A.H.	**G. A. Hagen** 1733–48
In full	**Johann Christoph Jucht** 1736–63
W.H.P.	**Wolfgang Heinrich Parsch** 1729–38
POPP	**Johann Albrecht Popp** 1745–47
O.S.	**Johann Martin Anton Oswald** 1764
J.M.H.	**Johann Markus Hagen** (1737–1803) 1760–1803
In full	**Johann Henrich Steinbach** (d. 1761) 1760–61

Porcelain made at times during the 18th
century. J. C. Schmidt founded a factory in
the early 19th century, for making hardpaste porcelain, stoneware, and creamcoloured earthenware; some products
were impressed with the "counterfeit mark
of Wedgwood."
See under METSCH, Johann Friedrich

Bell, J. & M. P. & Co. (Ltd).
Founded Glasgow pottery in 1842; china
and earthenware made from 1842; firm
closed down 1928.

Standard mark to present day

Bellevue, Meurthe-et-Moselle, France
Faience made here from 1758; factory in
control of Charles Bayard and François
Boyer in 1771. Bayard and his son started a
separate factory a few years later at Toul,
nearby. English-type earthenware made in
the 19th century.

Belle Vue Pottery, Hull
Established 1802; acquired 1825 by William Bell, making cream-coloured and
transfer-printed wares; factory closed
1840.
Marks recorded:

Transfer-printed

Printed or impressed

Belleek, Fermanagh, Ireland
Factory established here in 1863, making
china, parian, ironstone, and painted,
printed, and gilded earthenware, and a
curious lustred porcelain, which is still
made today.
Marks include

BELLEEK
Co. FERMANAGH and
FERMANAGH
POTTERY
Crowned harp rarely used 1863–80.

Transfer-printed

Berlin, Prussia, Germany
Faience made here from late 17th to 18th
century by various firms. Hard-paste
porcelain made by various manufacturers,
including Wilhelm Kaspar Wegely (1752–

Standard mark 1862–90

77) and Johann Ernst Gotzkowsky (1761–63), whose factory was acquired by Frederick the Great in 1763. It was renamed Königliche Porzelann Manufaktur and continues to the present day. From 1835, hard-paste porcelain was also made by A. Schumann at Moabit, near Berlin.

1835–

Berlin, Gotzkowsky's Factory and the Royal Factory

Porcelain made from 1761 onward. The letter G, in underglaze blue, was used in Gotzkowsky's time; from 1763 the sceptre mark was generally used.

K.P.M. with an orb, in blue or red
or with a sceptre impressed
(1830s)
KPM accompanied by Prussian Eagle
(late 1840s)

c. 1763–1800

1832–

1837–

Berlin, Wegeley's Porcelain Factory
Hard-paste porcelain made 1752–57.

In blue, or impressed, sometimes with numerals arranged one above the other in two or three tiers. These perhaps indicated mould numbers.

Bevington, John:
Made decorated porcelain at Hanley, 1872–92.

Blue-painted

Billington, Dora May: (d. 1968)
English studio potter; also decorated industrial pottery made by Meakins, c. 1912–60.

Incised
(variations occur)

Bing & Grondahl:
Established at Copenhagen, Denmark, by Harold Bing in 1853, making porcelain, stoneware, and earthenware.

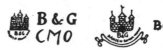

Bingham, Edward:
Made pseudo-Tudor and 17th-century pottery at Castle Hedingham, Essex, c. 1864–1901.

Birch, Edmund John: (*fl. c.* 1796–1814)
Staffordshire pottery firm of Birch &
Whitehead recorded 1796; in 1802 under
Birch only; made black basaltes and jasper
wares in Wedgwood style, marked:
E. I. B., BIRCH or "Birch"·(impressed)

Birks, Alboin: (1861–1941)
Artist in pâte-sur-pâte; worked for Mintons Ltd (1876–1937).

Bishop & Stonier (*fl.* 1891–1939)
Manufacturers of china and earthenwares
at Hanley, Staffordshire.
Marks: initials "B & S", printed or impressed, often with name of pattern, 1891–
1919.

"Bisto."

"Bisto."

BISHOP
MADE IN
ENGLAND

With or without "Bisto" below, 1891–1936
Printed or impressed, 1936–39

Blashfield, John Marriott: (*fl. c.* 1840–75)
Produced architectural terracotta and
statuary, at Stamford, Lincolnshire, from
1858; Stamford Terra Cotta Co. formed
1874; closed 1875. Firm made busts,
statues, and animals (1862 International
Exhibition).
Marks:
J. M. BLASHFIELD (impressed)
BLASHFIELD, STAMFORD

Boch frères, of Keramis, Le Louvière,
Hainault, Belgium
Earthenware factory established 1841; tiles
made at branch factory opened at
Mauberge in France, in 1861.

Bodenbach, Bohemia, Czechoslovakia
Terracotta and imitation Wedgwood made
here 1829–1855 by Schiller & Gerbing.

S & G

Impressed

F. Gerbing   W. Schiller & Sons

WEDGWOOD

Impressed

Bodley & Son: (*fl.* 19th century)
Potters at Burslem, Staffordshire; Edwin
J. D. Bodley sole owner in 1875, continuing until 1890s; made parian, china,
and earthenware.

Boisette, near Melun, Seine-et-Marne, France
Faience factory established *c.* 1732, also made porcelain from 1777 until *c.* 1792.

In blue or black. The form of the B is variable

Bologna, Italy
Lead-glazed earthenware made from the 15th to the 18th centuries. Some 17th-century marks:

Maiolica made by Aldovrandi's factory from 1794, and cream-coloured earthenware, with mark CARLO ALDOVRANDI impressed. Imitation Italian Renaissance maiolica made from 1849 by Angelo Minghetti & Son:

Bonn, Rhineland, Germany
General pottery factory founded by Franz Mehlem in 1755. Continues to present day. Mark "Franz Ant. Mehlem Bonn A/Rhein" in circle around FAM monogram, or

Boote, T. & R.: (*fl.* 1842–94)
Founded by Thomas Latham Boote and Richard Boote; made parian statuary and vases at Burslem, Staffordshire.

T. & R.B.

Booths Ltd (*fl.* 1891–1948)
Manufacturers of earthenware at Tunstall, Staffordshire.
Marks: "Booths Royal Semi-Porcelain Staffordshire England" in lozenge below crown, 1891–1906; "Booths Silicon China" with crown, 1906–; "BBB England" below crown, 1930–48.

Bordeaux, Gironde, France
Faience made from *c.* 1711 onward, at several factories.

David Johnston
1834–45

Impressed
J. Vieillard
1845 onward

Hard-paste porcelain made from 1781 to 1787 by Pierre Verneuilh and his nephew Jean.

In gold or underglaze blue
Verneuilh and nephew

Stencilled
Alluard & Vanier making porcelain, from 1787 to 1790

LR.

Lahens & Rateau, from 1828

Bornholm Island, Denmark
A German, Johann Spietz, founded an earthenware factory here in 1792, which continued until 1858.

Spietz

Impressed

Bott & Co.: (*fl.* early 19th century)
Made earthenware busts and figures; also
silver lustre wares and blue-printed earthenware.

Bott & Co

Impressed

Boullemier, Antonin: (1840–1900)
Painted figure subjects on porcelain; work-
ed at Sèvres until 1870, when he worked at
Mintons, England.

a Boullemier

Boumeester, Cornelis: (*c.* 1650–1733)
Painter of Dutch tin-enamelled pottery:

C:BM

C:BOVMEESTER

Found in blue

Bourg-la-Reine, France
Faience and porcelain made here from
1774 to 1806 by Jullien and Jacques.

BR B.R.

Incised

Bourne, Charles: (*c.* 1807–30)
Made porcelain at Foley, Fenton, Staffordshire.

$$\frac{CB}{N^o 1} \qquad \frac{CB}{N^o 3}$$

Bourne & Son: (*fl.* 1809 to present day)
Stoneware manufacturers, first at Belper
(1812) and Denby, Derbyshire; from 1834
at Denby only.

Bovey, Tracey, Devonshire
Several potworks here in 18th century;
Bovey Tracey Pottery Company formed in
1841 to make Staffordshire-type earthenware, continuing until 1956.

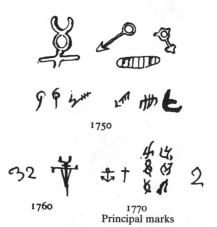

Bow, London
Porcelain made here from *c.* 1750 until
1776.
Numerous factory and workmen's or repairers' marks recorded; most generally
recognised Bow marks (*c.* 1760–76) are an
anchor and dagger in red or under-glaze
blue. Mock Chinese characters also
appear. Most Bow porcelain is unmarked.

1750

1760

1770
Principal marks

Brain, E. and Company: (*c.* 1903–63)
Founded by Edward Brain at Foley, Longton, Staffordshire, to make china.

204

ENGLISH BONE CHINA
PAINTED BY HAND.

Mark introduced in 1936

ESTABLISHED

FOLEY CHINA.

FOLEY ART CHINA
PEACOCK
POTTERY
ENGLAND Rᵈ

Early printed mark
c. 1903+

Printed mark
c. 1905

Brameld, William: (d. 1813)
Took over Rockingham factory in 1806; succeeded after his death by his three sons; porcelain made from 1826 to 1842.

Painted in red
c. 1826–30;
in puce 1830–

Impressed

Brannam, C. H. (Ltd): (1881–)
Took control of Litchdown Pottery, Barnstaple, Devon, in 1881, continuing to present day. Manufactured earthenware, including Barum Ware.
Marks: a wide variety incorporating "C. H. Brannam", "Barum Ware". "Ltd" added from 1914.

Breeze, John & Son
Made earthenware and porcelain at Tunstall, 1805–12

Mark may be that of various potters of this name.

Bretby Art Pottery, near Burton-on-Trent, Derbyshire.
Established by Henry Tooth at Woodville in 1883.

Mark to present time

Brianchon, Jules Joseph Henri:
Took out an English patent in 1857 for an improved method of colouring porcelain, etc.: a mother-of-pearl lustre sheen, popular in later 19th century, and characteristic of Irish Belleek porcelain. Brianchon partner in Gillet & Brianchon, Paris:

G.B
BREVETE
PARIS

Briddon, Samuel & Henry (*fl.* mid-19th century)
Manufacturers of Stonewares at Brampton, Derbyshire.
Mark: "S. & H. BRIDDON", *c.* 1848–*c.* 1860.

Bridgwood, Sampson:
Firm recorded in 1805, making earthenware; later made bone china, now making earthenware again, at Longton.
S. BRIDGWOOD & SON (impressed)

Impressed: 1860
(on fine white earthenware)

Impressed: 1870+

Bristol,
Soft-paste porcelain made here from *c.* 1749 until 1752, when the factory amalgamated with Worcester.
Hard-paste porcelain made here from 1770 until 1781.
Marks in underglaze blue and blue enamel.

205

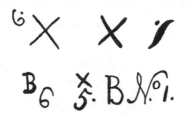

Copies of Meissen marks.

Brownfield, William: (d. 1873)
Made earthenware at Cobridge, Staffordshire, from 1850; took son William Etches into partnership 1871, when bone china was also made; factory closed in 1900.

or: BROWNFIELD & SON
COBRIDGE STAFFS

upon a scroll enclosing two globes

Brown-Westhead, Moore & Co., (1862–1904)
Manufacturers of Earthenware and porcelain at Hanley, Staffordshire.
Marks: initials "B.W.M." or "B.W.M. & Co." printed or impressed in various designs, with "Cauldon" or "Cauldon Ware".

Brunswick, Germany
Faience made from 1707; various factories:

Von Hantelmann
1711–49

Reichard & Behling
1749–56

Rudolf Anton Chely
1745–57

Buen Retiro, Madrid, Spain
Porcelain made here from 1759 to 1808, after transference of Royal factory from Capodimonte, Naples.
Mark of Bourbon fleur-de-lys used from 1760 to 1804, in various forms:

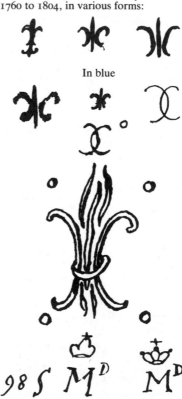

In blue

In red   1804–8   In red

In colour   In red   Impressed

Arists working here whose marks are recorded include:
Salvatore Noferi, sculptor (1759–85), transferred from Capodimonte:

Caetano Fumo, modeller:

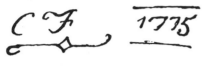

Incised

Bullers Ltd:
At Milton, Staffordshire, made image toys, decorative pottery, etc. from 1937 until 1955.

Incised

Artists:
Anne Potts, figure maker

Agnete Hoy Bohrer, modeller and decorator

Incised   Painted

James Rushton, decorator

Burmantofts pottery, Leeds
Established 1858 making fire-clay wares; art pottery made 1882–1904; later reverted to terra-cotta faience.

BURMANTOFTS
FAÏENCE
(Impressed)

or: B F in monogram

Caduceus mark
Mark found on some Meissen porcelain, from c. 1723. Thought to represent, not the caduceus of classical Rome, but perhaps the tail of the so-called Chinese kite mark, also found on Meissen ware. It has been suggested that it was considered more acceptable to Levantine merchants dealing in Meissen porcelain than the crossed-swords mark, which perhaps resembled too nearly the Christian symbol.

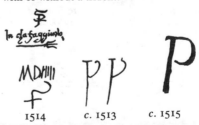

Caen, Calvados, France
Hard-paste porcelain made here, c. 1793–1806, at factory of d'Aigmont-Desmares and Ducheval.

caen
CAEN
Stencilled in red

Cafaggiolo, near Florence, Italy
Maiolica made here during the 16th century.
Marks recognised include: the inscription "in Chafagguolo"; a monogram of the letters S F or S P crossed with a paraph, with or without a trident.

1514   c. 1513   c. 1515

c. 1510   c. 1515

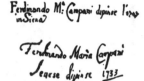

c. 1540 c. 1545–50 Alessandro Fattorini
c. 1545–50

(A cock is also the mark of the Arnhem factory in Holland.)

Campani, Ferdinando Maria: (1702–71)
Maiolica painter working in the istoriato style of Urbino, known to have worked at Siena. A dish in the Victoria and Albert Museum is signed: Ferdinando Ma: Campani dipinse l'1747 in Siena:

Campolide
Marks found on 19th-century traditional pottery, made at Lisbon:

Painted in blue   Painted in blue

Cantagalli, Ulysse: (d. 1901)
Proprietor of maiolica factory founded in Florence in 1878, making reproductions of early Urbino, Faenza, Deruta and della Robbia wares etc.

Capodimonte, Italy
Soft-paste porcelain factory opened 1743, transferred to Buen Retiro, Madrid, late 1750s.

Impressed

On tablewares
(very variable, often smeared)

In gold

Cardew, Michael: (1901–83)
Studio potter, making slipware at his Winchcombe Pottery, Gloucestershire, 1926–39; made stoneware at Wenford Bridge, Cornwall, 1939–42, then left for the Gold Coast.

Carey, Thomas: (d. c. 1847)
Made earthenware and china at Lane End, Staffordshire; firm listed as Carey and Son in 1818, later as Thomas and John Carey (dissolved 1842)

Incised on lustre wares produced by Carter before 1921; also Carter & Co.

Impressed 1921–24. After 1924, with word "Ltd" added

Impressed after 1921; also in black underglaze

From 1950–51 black underglaze Later variations

POOLE
ENGLAND

Impressed after 1921

Carlton Ware Ltd: (1958–)
Manufacturers of earthenware at Stoke, Staffordshire (owned by Wiltshaw & Robinson, 1890–1957)

c. 1894–

1958–

"Carlton Ware Handpainted Made in England Trade Mark", handpainted, c. 1925–

Carouge, near Geneva, Switzerland
Cream-coloured earthenware made from 1812, notably by Baylon & Co.

Impressed

Carter, Stabler & Adams: (1921–63)
Making tablewares and "fancies" at Poole, Dorset. Firm retitled Poole Pottery Ltd in 1963.

Casa Pirota mark
Conventional representation of a fire wheel or fire bomb (pyrrhus rota, used as a canting device) as a pottery mark by the leading maiolica workshop at Faenza, the Casa Pirota, worked by the Pirotti family:

16th century
See also FAENZA

Cassel, Hesse-Nassau, Germany
Hard-paste porcelain made here from 1766 until 1788.

Both in underglaze blue
(The Frankenthal lion has a single tail)

Casteldurante, Urbino, Italy
Made Renaissance maiolica (from *c.*
1508). The factory continued into the 18th
century.

A nearly similar inscription
includes the date 1525

Castelli, Abruzzi, Italy
Maiolica made from 16th to 18th centuries.
From end of 17th century dominated by the
Grue and Gentili families.

Caughley, Shropshire, England
Porcelain made here from 1775 by Thomas
Turner; John Rose of Coalport took over
the factory 1799; it closed down in 1814.
Most notable marks, letters S or C in blue,
or word "Salopian" in upper or lower case
letters, impressed.

C   S   S×   SALOPIAN

In blue   Impressed

Chamberlain's Worcester: (*c.* 1786–1852)
Founded by Robert Chamberlain at
Worcester, making porcelain from 1792;
amalgamated with the main Worcester
factory in 1840; trading as Kerr and Binns
in 1852; became the Worcester Royal
Porcelain Co. in 1862.
Various marks used:

c. 1786–1810

c. 1786–1810

Chamberlains
Worcester
403

Chamberlain's
Regent China
Worcester
&155
New Bond Street,
London
Printed in red
c. 1811–20

H Chamberlain
& Sons
Worcester

c. 1811–27

CHAMBERLAIN'S   Chamberlains
Both
c. 1847–50

Chantilly, Oise, France
Soft-paste porcelain made from *c.* 1725
until 1800.
Mark, a hunting horn (much imitated).

In red   In red   In blue

In red   In red   In red

In underglaze   In underglaze   In
blue   blue   red

Chantilly

In blue: with the
hunting horn: rare

In blue

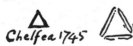

In blue

Early marks usually carefully drawn in red
without accompanying sign or initials; later
marks in blue more carelessly drawn,
smudgy in appearance, and frequently with
workman's initials, painted, or incised in
the paste. Word "Chantilly" with hunting
horn in blue is late 18th-century. The
hunting horn in gold occurs only on early
"red-dragon" ware.

Chaplet, Ernest: (1835–1909)
French artist-potter.

Chelsea, London, England
Factory established here *c.* 1745, making
porcelain, until 1784; under different man-
agements, eventually bought by William
Duesbury and John Heath of Derby. The
products of the years 1770 to 1784 known
as Chelsea-Derby. Closed down 1784.
Four clearly defined periods of Chelsea
manufacture recognised: Triangle 1745–
49; Raised Anchor 1750–53; Red Anchor
1753–58; Gold Anchor 1758–70.

Incised

Incised
1745–49

In applied
relief
1750–53

In under-
glaze blue
1749

Various red painted anchors, *c.* 1753–58

Various gilt anchors, *c.* 1758–70. These
marks are widely faked.

Chetham family: (*fl.* end 18th century to
1875)
Made earthenware, pearlware, etc., at
Longton, Staffordshire, from *c.* 1796; factory eventually controlled by H. Aynsley
and Company in 1875.

CHETHAM

Chetwynd, David: (*fl.* 1851–76)
Pottery modeller, 1851–65, at Hanley and
Burslem, Staffordshire; partner with
Cockson at Cobridge, 1866–76.
Mark, the Royal Arms and the name:

IMPERIAL IRONSTONE CHINA,
COCKSON & CHETWYND.

Child, Smith: (1730–1813)
Established a factory at Tunstall, Staffordshire, in 1763, making transfer-printed and
other decorated wares, working until 1790.
Mark:

CHILD
Impressed 1780–90

Made earthenware with J. H. Clive, 1806
to 1813, as Child & Clive.
Mark also occurs:

CLIVE
Impressed 1802–11

"Chinese" marks
Marks imitating Chinese characters appear
fairly frequently on porcelain made at
Bow, Worcester, and Caughley, or by
Spode and Mason in north Staffordshire,
18th and early 19th centuries. Also common on 18th-century English redware.

"Chinese" marks on European porcelain
Examples:

Vienna   Meissen

Choisy-le-Roy, Seine, France
Paillard & Hautin (1824–36) and Hautin & Boulanger (1836–) made porcelain and white earthenware here.

HB & Cⁱᵉ
CHOISY
LE ROI

On hard-paste porcelain

Cleffius, Lambertus:
Proprietor of De Metale Pot, Delft, 1660–91.

Clementson, Joseph: (1794–1871)
Started in partnership with Jonah Read (Read & Clementson) making earthenware at the Phoenix Works, Shelton, Staffordshire, 1832–39; bought the Bell Works in 1856.

Clerici, Felice:
Maiolica worker at Milan, 1745–80. Probably related to the Clérissys of St Jean du Désert and Moustiers.

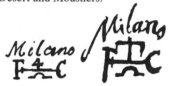

Clérissy, Pierre: (1651–1728)
Founded the Moustiers faience industry in 1679.

See also MOUSTEIRS.

Clermont-Ferrand, Puy-de-Dôme, France
Faience made here at two periods: (1) from c. 1730 to 1743; (2) from 1774 to c. 1784.

Clews (Clewes), Ralph and James: (*fl.* 1815 to 1835)
Made blue-printed earthenware at Cobridge, Staffordshire, mainly for the American market; also made ironstone china.

Transfer-printed

Impressed

Clignancourt, Paris
Hard-paste porcelain made here during the later 18th century. Mark of a windmill:

In blue

In gold   1771–75

M, for   Stencilled in red
Monsieur   initials L S X, for
                        Louis-Stanislas-
                        Xavier, 1775–93

The factory was under the protection of Louis-Stanislas-Xavier, Comte de Provence, also known as "Monsieur", being then
the King's brother.

Stencilled in red
1775–93

Clowes, William: (d. *c.* 1815/16)
Made earthenware and black basaltes at Longport, Burslem, Staffordshire, from *c.* 1783; firm styled Henshall, Williamson & Clowes in 1796; and Henshall & Williamson in 1805.
Mark recorded:

Impressed

Coalport or Coalbrookdale, Shropshire
Factory established here *c.* 1796 by John Rose, making porcelain, continued by his descendants until 1862. In 1880 owned by a member of the Bruff family; in 1924 sold to Cauldon Potteries Ltd, moving to Staffordshire in 1926, where Messrs Coalport continue today as part of the Wedgwood group.

1820

c. 1810–25
Painted in blue

c. 1830–50   1820–

JOHN ROSE & Cᵒ
COALBROOKDALE
SHROPSHIRE

c. 1830–50

c. 1851–61   *c.* 1861–75

copy of Chelsea mark *c.* 1845–55

Coffee, William: (*fl.* 1794)
Modeller, employed at Derby porcelain factory 1794–95; later made terracotta. Reputed mark on terracotta, *c.* 1805–16.

W. COFFEE DERBY
Incised in script

Conta & Boehme, Pössneck, Germany. (1790–)
Manufacturers of hard-paste porcelain

Coombes, or Combes: (*fl. c.* 1780–1805)
Repairer of china, who re-marked and
re-fired pieces, at an address in Queen
Street, Bristol.

Rare, printed
c. 1847–51

Standard printed
c. 1851–85

Standard printed marks on earthenwares

Cooper, Susie OBE (b. 1902)
Decorated wares for A. E. Gray & Co.
1925–30. Designed pottery for various
firms 1930–. Founded Susie Cooper China
Ltd *c.* 1950, renamed Susie Cooper Ltd
c. 1961. Incorporated into Wedgwood
Group
1966.
Marks: "Susie Cooper" printed, in script.

c. 1867–90

c. 1875–90

c. 1894–1910

c. 1891 to
20th century

Copenhagen, Denmark
Soft-paste porcelain made here, *c.* 1760
until 1765

Usual marks for Frederick V, 1760–65

Copeland & Garrett:
Made earthenware, parian, porcelain etc
at Stoke, 1833–47. See also SPODE.

Copenhagen, Denmark
Royal Copenhagen Porcelain Manufactory, making hard-paste from 1775.
Mark, three wavy lines in blue, emblems of
the three principal Danish waterways into
the Baltic, adopted in 1775.

Painted in blue 1775 onwards

Incised

Copeland, W. T. & Sons:
Followed Copeland & Garrett, 1847–1970.

214

1889   1894

1925   modern

Philip Schou (1838–1922) director in 1884; connected with faience factory "Aluminia" which worked with the porcelain factory from 1885.

1903   19th century impressed   1929

Copenhagen, Store Kongensgade Factory
Faience made here during the 18th century.

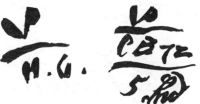

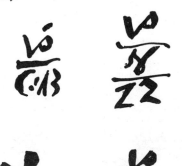

Cork & Edge:
Earthenware, Burslem, *c.* 1846–60.

CORK & EDGE

C & E

Printed

Corn, William and Edward: (*c.* 1864–1904) Began to make earthenware at Burslem, Staffordshire, in 1837; in the 1890s firm gave up making tablewares, and became the Henry Richard Tile Co.

W & EC

Crane, Walter, R. W. S.: (1846–1915) English general designer, also of pottery and tiles (Wedgwood, 1867–77, Mintons and Pilkingtons); helped to found the Arts and Crafts Society in 1888.
Personal mark:

Creil, Oise, France
English-style earthenware made here from *c.* 1794 to 1895.

'CREIL' CREIL.

Impressed

The transfer-printed mark, in black, of Stone, Coquerel and Legros d'Anisy, as a monogram, occurs on white ware printed by these Paris agents, 1807–49:

Creussen, Bavaria
Stoneware made here during the 16th and 17th centuries, the chief potters being the Vest family, who flourished from 1512 onward.

Lorenze Speckner 1618

Limbach, crossed L's with the star similar to Meissen mark of Marcolini period

Volkstedt, rather like 2-pronged forks

House marks of the Vest family

La Courtille, Paris, in underglaze blue; crossed flambeaux freely drawn

Worcester

Crossed arrows mark
See LA COURTILLE

Crossed L's mark
See SÈVRES.

Crossed swords mark
Taken from the Electoral arms of Saxony, and adopted as the Meissen porcelain factory mark c. 1724. On early Meissen the mark is more carefully drawn, with the swords at a wide angle to each other. In the later 18th century, the mark was drawn more freely. For variations see under MEISSEN.

Weesp, Holland, crossed swords with 3 dots placed near the blades

In the 19th century, apart from deliberate forgeries, some firms adopted misleadingly similar signs, e.g. Samson & Co, Paris:

Some other 18th-century factories were using this mark, often a close imitation, e.g. at Limbach and Volkstedt in Germany, Weesp in Holland, La Courtille, Paris, in France, and Worcester in England; also much copied by various 19th-century firms.

Crossed torches mark
Used by the hard-paste factory of La Courtille, Paris. May be mistaken for a carelessly drawn Meissen mark. The factory was established in 1773, apparently intending to produce imitations of German porcelain.

Crown Staffordshire Porcelain Co. Ltd:
Made porcelain at Fenton from c. 1889 to present day.

Printed marks, *c.* 1889+

Cutts, James: (*fl.* 1834–70)
Of Shelton, Staffordshire; designer and engraver of printed earthenware and china, working for Wedgwood, Pinxton and Davenport.

In gold

Cyfflé, Paul Louis: (1724–1806)
Sculptor, working at Lunéville from time to time. Marks on his figures:

All impressed

Cyples family: (*fl. c.* 1784–1840)
Manufacturers of earthenware at Lane End, Staffordshire. Joseph Cyples active *c.* 1784–95; Mary, *c.* 1795–1812; Jesse, *c.* 1805–11; Lydia *c.* 1812–34; Richard and

William *c.* 1834–40. Absence of initials in name-marks makes dating difficult. Examples:

I. CYPLES OR CYPLES

J CYPLES

Dale, John: (*fl.* early 19th century)
Engraver and pottery figure maker, at Burslem, Staffordshire.
Mark recorded:

J . DALE
BURSLEM

Impressed

Dallwitz, Bohemia, Czechoslovakia
Factory founded here 1804 to make earthenware; in 1830 permission was obtained to make porcelain. Various owners included W. W. Lorenz (*c.* 1832), F. Fischer (1850–55), and Franz Urfus (1855–*c.* 1875).

D DALWITZ

W.W.L.
DALWITZ

FF FFD F&U
D   U
DALWITZ

Dalou, Jules: (1838–1912)
French sculptor, who made terracotta figures (various sizes), and also did some work for the Sèvres porcelain factory, between 1879 and 1887.

DALOU

Damm, Aschaffenburg, Germany
Earthenware factory founded here in 1827; became known for reproductions of 18th-century porcelain figures made at Höchst.

The letter D with the old wheel sign of Höchst was used on these.

Dammouse, Pierre-Adolphe: (b. 1817) Modeller and designer of figures and ornament at the Sèvres factory from 1852 until 1878, and for Pouyat of Limoges.

Daniel, Henry and Richard (*fl.* 1822–46) Manufacturers of pottery and porcelain at Stoke-on-Trent and Shelton, Staffordshire. After death of Henry Daniel in 1841, Stoke factory continued by Richard. Marks: "H. & R. Daniel" in script, 1820–41; "H. Daniel & Sons", in script, 1829–41.

Daniell, A. B. & R. P.: (*c.* 1825–1917) Dealer whose mark is found on Coalport and other fine porcelains.

Dannhöfer, Johann Phillipp: (1712–90) Decorator of pottery and porcelain at the Vienna factory and elsewhere, e.g. Höchst, Fulda, and Ludwigsburg.

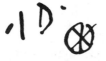

On Höchst faience

Darte frères: (*fl.* from 1795) French manufacturers of hard-paste porcelain, in rue de Charonne, Paris.

Stencilled in red

Davenport family: (*fl.* 1793–1887) Manufacturers at Longport, Staffordshire; made blue-printed earthenware, creamware, porcelain, and ironstone china.

DAVENPORT
LONGPORT

DAVENPORT
LONGPORT
STAFFORDSHIRE

Impressed. "Longport" may occur in place of "Davenport". Numerals each side of anchor referring to last two digits of year, *c.* 1795–*c.* 1860.

Impressed, *c.* 1805–20.

Printed on porcelain *c.* 1870–86.

Painted in blue on porcelain, *c.* 1850–70. In black or other colour pre-1830.

See also CUTTS, JAMES

Davis, Harry: (1910–86) Studio potter.

Dawson, John & Co: (*fl.* 1800–64)
Manufacturer of pottery at Sunderland, Co. Durham.

DAWSON
Impressed

Deck, Théodore: (1823–91)
Generally regarded as the first of the studio potters. Worked in Paris; was appointed Director at Sèvres in 1887.

Impressed	Impressed, incised, or transfer-printed

H DECK

Impressed

Delaherche, Auguste: (1857–1940)
Made stoneware near Beauvais and worked in Paris; in 1904 began to make his own shapes at La Chapelle-aux-Pots near Beauvais.

Incised or impressed

Delft: De Drie Klokken (The Three Bells)
Factory working from 1671 to 1840. During the 18th century, mark of the three bells, rather crudely drawn, was used. About the same time Van der Goes also registered the mark WD conjoined. Van Putten & Company worked the factory from 1830 to 1840.

Delft: De Drie Porseleyne Flessies (The Three Porcelain Bottles)
In various ownership from 1679 to after 1764. Hugo Brouwer, coming into possession in 1762, registered his mark in 1764:

HB

Delft: De Drie Vergulde Astonnen (The Three Golden Ashbarrels)
Factory founded in 1655, working under various owners, viz. the Kam family (1674–1720); Zacharias Dextra (1712–59); Hendrick van Hoorn (1759–1803). Continued for a short time by Hoorn's daughter.

G. P. Kam
(also at de Paauw)

Z.DEX   Z:DEX

Zacharias Dextra

astonne

Mark registered in 1764

H ✓ H

H. van Hoorn

Delft: De Dubbele Schenkkan (The Double Jug)
Factory apparently founded in 1648, continuing until second half of the 18th century. Most important potter was Louwys Fictoor; his mark was almost identical with that of Lambertus van Eenhoorn.

Louwys Fictoor
here 1689–1714
(or Lambertus van Eenhoorn)

Mark registered in 1764

Delft: De Gekroonde Theepot (The Crowned Teapot)
Managed or owned from 1671 until 1708 by Ary Jansz de Milde, followed by his son-in-law and widow.

Delft: De Grieksche A (The Greek A)
Pottery started 1658; Adriaenus Kocks owned it 1687–1701; Jan Theunis Dextra held it 1759–65; Jacobus Halder (or Jacobus Halder Adriaensz) from 1765. The factory closed down in 1820.

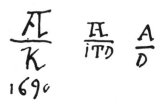

Adriaenus Kocks   Jan Theunis Dextra

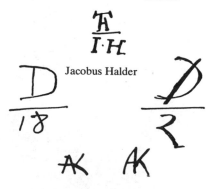

Jacobus Halder

Delft: De Lampetkan (The Ewer)
Factory working from 1609 or 1637 until

1811. For most of the period, the mark was a variant of the initials L.P.K.

Delft: De Metale Pot (The Metal Pot)
Established 1638, worked under various owners until 1764.

Ɛ

Lambertus Cleffius
(owner, 1660–91)

Lambertus van Eenhoorn
(owner, 1691–1721)

Eenhoorn's mark cannot be distinguished from that of Louwys Fictoor

M̃

Mark registered by Pieter Paree
(owner, 1759–64)

Delft: De Paauw (The Peacock)
Founded 1651, closed down c. 1779. Various owners:

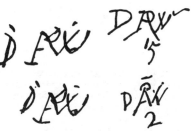

Gerrit Pietersz Kam (c. 1700) signed:

220

Delft: De Porseleyne Bijl (The Porcelain Hatchet)
Factory working from mid-17th century until 1802 or 1807.

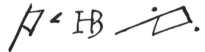

Hugo Brouwer, owner (1716–1807).

Delft: De Porseleyne Fles (The Porcelain Bottle)
Factory working from 1655 until after 1876. Owners included Dirck Harlees (1795–1800) and H. A. Piccardt in 1800.

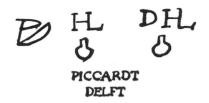

PICCARDT
DELFT

Impressed

Delft: De Porseleyne Klaeuw (The Porcelain Claw)
Factory working from 1662 until 1850. Claw mark used, freely rendered in many variations:

In conjunction with numerals and initials of owners.

Delft: De Porseleyne Schotel (The Porcelain Dish)
Factory flourishing from 1612 until late 18th century. Among important owners were Johannes Pennis (1702–88) from 1725 to 1764, and Johannes van Duyn from 1764 to 1777.

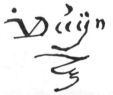

Delft: De Romein (The Rummer)
Factory under various owners from c. 1613 until 1769. Among recorded signatures:

Petrus van Marum (1756–64)

Johannes van der Kloot (1764–69)

Delft: De Roos (The Rose)
Factory working from c. 1666/7 until after 1848.

Dirk van der Does (proprieter, 1760)

18th-century marks

Delft: De Twee Scheepjes (The Two Little Ships)

Factory working from mid-17th century until end of 18th century. Adriaen Pynacker here registered his mark as the monogram AP.

Delft: De Twee Wildemannen (The Two Wildmen)

Factory dates given variously as 1661–1780, 1704–78, and 1756–94.
Willem van Beek was connected with it from 1760 to after 1778.

$$W : V : B$$

Delft: De Vergulde Blompot (The Golden Flowerpot)

Factory working from 1654. Initials B P are main mark.

Delft: De Vergulde Boot (The Golden Boot)

Factory recorded working from 1613 until after 1764.

A. Reygens or Reygensberg
(owner 1663–66)

G. L. Kryck,
who took over in 1666; mark
similar to that of G. P. Kam

Dirck van der Kest
(manager 1698–1707)

Johannes den Appel
(working 1759)

Delft: De Witte Starre (The White Star)

Faience factory established 1663, working until its closure in the early 19th century. In succession from 1720 came: Cornelis de Berg, Justus de Berg, Albertus Kiell (1763–72) and Johannes de Bergh.

Cornelis de Berg   Justus de Berg   Albertus Kiell

Johannes de Bergh   The White Star

Delft: 'T Fortuyn (The Fortune)

Factory working from c. 1661 until after 1770.

$$P \; \varphi \; B$$

P. van den Briel
(took over 1747)

$$WVD\,B$$
$$W\,\varphi B$$

Widow van den Briel
(registered mark in 1764)

't *Frerkingh*

JhF

J. H. Frerkingh
(here in 1769)

LVD LV♦

Marks sometimes wrongly attributed to this
factory

Delft: 'T Hart (The Hart)
Founded 1661, working through the 18th
century.

t'hart

T HART HVMD

**Delft: 'T Oude Moriaenshooft (The Old
Moor's Head)**
Factory working from mid-17th century to
around end of 18th century.

R·

Rochus Hoppestein (d. 1692)
proprietor

Delft: See also: APPEL, DEXTRA,
EENHORN, HOORN, HOPPE-
STEIN, KOCKS, PENNIS,
PIJNACKER, REYGENS,
VIZEER.

Del Vecchio, Cherinto:
Made cream-coloured earthenware at
Naples, late 18th century:

F D V
N

Standing for Fabbrica del Vecchio Napoli

del Vecchio
N

Della Robbia Co. Ltd: (1893–1900)
Manufacturers of earthenware, tiles and
plaques at Birkenhead, Cheshire.
Marks: "Della Robbia", incised or impressed. Incised initials are those of decorator.

De Morgan, William Frend: (1839–1917)
English potter noted for making reproductions of 16th- and 17th-century Syrian
wares; rediscovered the process of reduced
lustre decoration. Worked first in London,
then at Merton Abbey, Surrey (1882–88); in
partnership with Halsey Ricardo at Fulham
(1888/9 and again 1898/1907).

W. De Morgan & Cº
London 1891

Painted

Painted

Impressed

Impressed

Initials of certain painters are sometimes encorporated, e.g.:
J.J. for **Joe Juster**
C.P. for **Charles Passenger**
F.P. for **Fred Passenger**

Denuelle, Domeniquei:
Hard-paste porcelain manufacturer at Paris and Saint-Yrieix.

Derby
Soft-paste porcelain made by Andrew Planché and John Heath c. 1750–56. Derby Porcelain Works (1756–1848), under various owners.

1756–97 Duesbury period.
Establishment of Derby Porcelain Works, under control of William Duesbury I. On his death in 1786, factory passed to William Duesbury II, who from 1795 worked in partnership with Michael Kean. William Duesbury II died in 1797 and factory passed to Michael Kean.

1770–84 Chelsea Derby period.
Purchase of Chelsea factory by William Duesbury I in 1770 and manufacture of Chelsea-style porcelain at Derby.

1814–48
Factory under control of Robert Bloor. From c. 1828, small factory maintained successively by Locker & Co., Stevenson & Hancock, Sampson & Hancock and others.

Derby Crown Porcelain Ltd founded 1878. Renamed Royal Crown Derby Porcelain Co. Ltd in 1889. Continues today.

Most Derby porcelain up to 1780 is unmarked.

Incised
1750

Painted
1780

1784

Chelsea Derby
1770–82

c. 1784–1840

Imitation
Meissen

Imitation
Sèvres
c. 1825–48

Printed
c. 1820–40

Without wording
c. 1878–90
With wording c. 1891 onwards
plus "England".
or (in 20th century)
"Made in England"
With year cyphers from 1882

Deruta, Umbria, Italy
Decorative maiolica made here from before
1500, and continued through the 17th
century.

*IN DERVTA
EL FRATE PENSE*

*1 5 3 7
fran^{co} Vrbini*

Dextra, Zacharias:
Manager from 1712 at De Drie Vergulde
Astonnen.

Z. DEX   Z: DEX
                3
            astonne

Dicker Pottery, Lower Dicker, Sussex
(1843–1959)
Maker of earthenwares.

'DICKER WARE'

20th-century mark

Dillwyn & Co: (*fl.* early 19th century)
English potters at Swansea (q.v.) trading
1810 to 1817 (previously as Haynes,
Dillwyn & Co, 1802–10); owners again from
1831 to c. 1850.

DILLWYN &Co

Dimmock & Co., Shelton and Hanley,
Staffordshire (c. 1828–59 and 1862–1904)
Maker of earthenware.

1828–59

1828–59   1862–1904

Dirmstein, near Worms, Germany
Faience and cream-coloured earthenware
made here 1778–88; factory founded by the
Bishop of Worms.

Taken from the arms of the episcopal see of
Worms; very uncommon.

Dixon & Co: (*fl* 19th century)
English firm working the North Hylton
Pottery at Sunderland, Co. Durham
(founded 1762 by C. Thompson and J.
Maling); later trading as Dixon, Austin &
Co; and Dixon, Phillips & Co.
DIXON & CO.
DIXON, AUSTIN & CO.
SUNDERLAND
Impressed

Doat, Taxile-Maximilien: (b. 1851)
English sculptor at Sèvres from 1879 to 1905
or later; worked in porcelain and stoneware. Mark the monogram TD:

Doccia, near Florence, Italy
Porcelain made here from 1735 onward, at
first under the Ginori family; from latter
part of 19th century working as Richard-
Ginori.

Blue, red,   18th century Incised   In red
or gold

Incised

On imitation Capodimonte

1873–1903   1847–73

N
1850–1903

GI

GIN

19th century

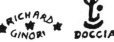

1874–88   1884–91   1883–1900

Late 19th century

Dolphin mark
(For Dauphin) found stencilled in red on
hard-paste porcelain made at Lille from
1784 until 1790 by Leperre-Durot, under
the protection of the Dauphin.

Donaldson, John: (1737–1801)
Scotsman, enameller and miniaturist, who
came to London (*c.* 1760); became a no-
table outside porcelain decorator, e.g. for
Chelsea and Worcester.
Monogram mark recorded:

Donath: (*fl.* later 19th century)
Dresden decorator of porcelain from 1872.

226

Don Pottery, Swinton, Yorkshire
Earthenware of various types and stone-wares made from *c.* 1790 until 1893; factory trading as Greens, Clark & Co (1807); as John William Green & Co (1822); remaining with the Greens until taken over by Samuel Barker in late 1830s.

Painted   Impressed

Transfer-printed *c.* 1800–34

Dorotheenthal, near Arnstadt, Thuringia, Germany
Faience made here from 1716 until the beginning of the 19th century. A number of painters are recorded:

R.L.   Johann Michel Rasslender 1725–40
MF   Johann Martin Frantz   1717–29
MB   Johann Martin Meiselbach 1733–58

The monogram AB stands for Augusten-burg, which was the seat of the Dowager Elizabeth Albertine of Schwarzburg-Sondershausen, sometime patron of the factory.

Douai, Nord, France
Two factories here made English-type earthenware: (1) Leigh's, 1781–1831; and (2) under Dammann 1799–1804, followed by an Englishman, Halfort, 1804–07. Marks: Douai, Leigh & Cie, Martin Dammann, Halfort.

Douai   Douai

Doulton: (*fl. c.* 1815–)
John Doulton (1793–1837) became partner in Doulton & Watts (1815) at Lambeth, London, making salt-glazed stoneware; firm traded as Doulton & Co. from 1854, continuing to present day at Burslem, Staffordshire. Decorative stoneware made at Lambeth from 1870 onward, and at Burslem, also, from 1877. Bone china made from 1884.

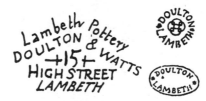

Before 1836   *c.* 1869+

Artists' (Lambeth) marks recorded include:

 Barlow, Arthur Bolton: 1871–78 various forms of decoration

Barlow, Florence: *c.* 1873–1909 animal decorations

Barlow, Hannah Bolton: *c* 1872–1906 incised animal decoration

Broad, John: 1873–*d.* 1919 figure modeller

Butler, Frank A.: *c.* 1873–1911

Davis, Louisa: *c.* 1873–90

Edwards, Louisa E.: *c.* 1873–90

Huggins, Vera: 1932–50

Lee, Francis E.: *c.* 1875–90

Marshall, Mark Villars: 1876–1912, figure modeller and decorator

Mitchell, Mary: *c.* 1874–87

Pope, Frank G.: 1880–1923 modeller

Roberts, Florence C.: *c.* 1879–1930

Rowe, William: *c.* 1883–1939

Simeon, Henry: 1894–1936

Simmance, Eliza: *c.* 1873–1928

Tabor, George Hugo: *c.* 1878–90

Thompson, Margaret E.: 1900

Tinworth, George: 1867–1913, modeller

Dresden, Saxony, Germany
Faience made from 1708 to 1784.

Initials D.H. for "Dresden: Hörisch" used from 1768 until 1784, when Sophie von Hörisch was proprietor, her son being director during 1784.
Number of 19th-century manufacturers working here in Meissen style, some using marks closely imitating original Meissen:
DONATH
HAMANN
HIRSCH
KLEMM
LAMM
MEYERS & SON
   HELENA WOLFSOHN
Madame Wolfsohn used the Augustus Rex monogram of the Meissen factory.
Other Dresden marks included:

Dudson Bros: (from mid-19th century) James Dudson made earthenware at Hanley, Staffordshire, from 1835; firm became Dudson Bros in 1898 and so continues.

Printed 1935–45

Dunn, Constance: (dates unknown)
Studio potter.

Dux, Bohemia, Czechoslovakia
Duxer Porzellan-Manufaktur founded by
E. Eichler in 1860. Continues to present
day.

C.N.

Eastwood, Hanley, Staffordshire, England
(*fl.* 18th and 19th centuries)
Cane and brown wares made here by
William Baddeley from *c.* 1750; son
continued, adding cream ware and black
basaltes; many imitations of Wedgwood
made, late 18th and early 19th centuries.
EASTWOOD
Impressed
c. 1802–22

Eckernförde, Schleswig, Germany
Faience made here 1764 to 1785.

Edge, Joseph: (1805–93)
Partnered Benjamin Cork (1847) at
Burslem, Staffordshire, making Egyptian
black, lustred wares, and stonewares; in
1864 firm became Cork, Edge & Malkin; in
1875 Edge, Malkin & Co; pottery was then
abandoned for tile-making.

Edge & Grocott: (*c.* 1830)
Manufacturers of earthenware figures in
Tunstall, Staffordshire.
Mark: "Edge & Grocott".

Eenhoorn family: *c.* 1658–85.
Samuel van Eenhoorn worked at De
Grieksche A potworks Delft (*q.v.*),
1674–85. His mark is frequent:

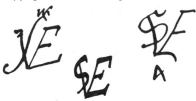

Eenhoorn, Lambertus van: d. 1721
Bought De Metale Pot, Delft (*q.v.*), 1691.
His widow continued until 1724.

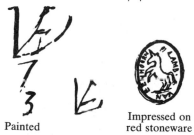

Painted   Impressed on
red stoneware

Eichwald, Bohemia
Hard-paste porcelain made here from 1870.

E

Eichwald

Elbogen
Porcelain manufacture established in 1815
by Rudolf Haidinger. Owned by Springer
and Company from *c.* 1900.

Ellis, James: (*fl.* early 18th century)
Modeller (1818), and earthenware toy manufacturer (1830), at Shelton, Staffordshire.

J. ELLIS & Co

Impressed

Elton, Sir Edmund (*fl.* 1879–1920)
Manufacturer of earthenwares at Clevedon, Somerset, and founder of Sunflower Pottery (1879–1930).
Marks: "Elton" in script, painted or incised. Painted, with cross, 1920–30 (after Elton's death in 1920).

Emens, Jan: (*fl.* 1568–94)
German stoneware potter. Used his initials IE, IEM, or full name YAN EMENS.

Emery, James: (*fl.* 1837–61)
Made earthenware at Mexborough, Yorkshire, England.

J Emery
Mexbro

Incised   1838

English redware
Made in Staffordshire *c.* 1750–70s. Bears imitation Chinese marks not attributable to any individual maker. David and John Philip, Dutch brothers making red earthenwares in Fulham and Vauxhall, London, *c.* 1690–1700, have been incorrectly associated with these makers.

Este, northern Italy
Cream-coloured earthenware made here from 1785 by Gerolamo Franchini.

ESTE
G   GF

Impressed

Étiolles, Seine-et-Oise, France
Hard-paste porcelain made here from 1768 to *c.* 1780, by Dominique Pellevé and Jean-Baptiste Monier, with the mark:

MP

Other marks are recorded:

E Pellevé 1770

Incised

Etiolles
x bre 1770
Pellevé

Incised

Faber, Johann Ludwig: (*fl.* 1678–93)
Nuremberg hausmaler painting on glass and faience in schwarzlot, signing with monogram or initials, J.L.F.

Fabriano, Urbino, Italy
Manufacture of maiolica *c.* 1527 inferred from an inscribed plate:

fabriano
1527

Faenza, Emilia, Italy
Influential centre of maiolica production from mid-16th century onward.

1510–15

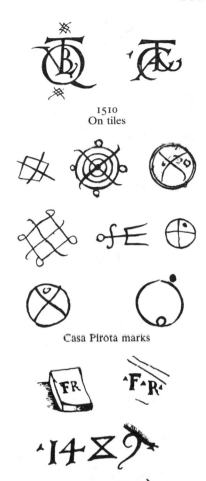

1510
On tiles

Casa Pirota marks

See also FARINI, FERNIANI, CASA PIROTA.

Farini, A.:
Potter at Faenza, from 1850.

Faubourg Saint-Denis, Paris
(or Faubourg Saint-Lazare)
Hard-paste porcelain made here from 1771
to 1810.

In blue	Stencilled in red	In colour
1771–76	1779–93	1800–10

FLEURY

early 19th century

Fell, Thomas, & Co.: (*fl.* 1817–90)
Manufacturers of earthenware and cream-
ware at Newcastle-on-Tyne.
"F", "Fell & Co", "F & Co" or "T.F. &
Co.", sometimes with anchor and cable, or
arms of Newcastle, in blue.

FELL

Impressed 1817–30.

Féraud, Jean Gaspard:
Founded faience business in Moustiers in
1779; continued to 1874, worked by his
descendants.

Ferniani, Count Annibale:
Made maiolica at Faenza from 1693; factory
continued by descendants to present day.

231

18th-century marks

Ferrybridge, near Pontefract, Yorkshire, (1792–)
Earthenware made here first by Edwin Tomlinson & Co. Firm traded later as Wigglesworth & Ingham, then as Reed, Taylor & Company until 1851. Other firms followed.

FERRYBRIDGE
(impressed)
TOMLINSON & CO.
(impressed)

F.F., F.F.F., and F.F.O. marks
Attributed to Flaminio Fontana:

See FONTANA FAMILY

Finch, **Raymond:** (*b.* 1914)
Studio potter.

Fishley family: (*fl.* from end 18th century through 19th century)
Made pottery at Fremington, Devon. Five generations included: George Fishley (until 1839); Edmund Fishley (d. 1861); Edwin Beer Fishley (1832–1912).
Mark of latter recorded:
E. B. FISHLEY
FREMINGTON

Fletcher, Thomas: (*fl. c.* 1786–*c.* 1810)
Black-printer, in partnership with Sampson Bagnall the younger (1786–96), making earthenware at Shelton, Stoke-on-Trent, Staffordshire; on his own account at

Shelton from 1796 to *c.* 1810. His prints signed.
T. Fletcher Shelton
or
T. FLETCHER, SHELTON

Fleur-de-lis mark
At Capodimonte, Naples, painted in blue; also in gold, and impressed, 1743–59. At Buen Retiro, Madrid, 1760–1808, the same; incised fleur-de-lis rare.
At Marseilles faience factory of Honoré Savy, *c.* 1777 onward.
At Sèvres, the fleur-de-lis above the word "Sèvres" and the figures "30", transfer-printed in blue, August-December 1830 only. The Sèvres painter, Taillandier, also used the fleur-de-lis.

Florence, Tuscany, Italy
Centre of great ceramic activity during the Renaissance. Some unidentified marks:

On early 15th-century jar made at or near Florence

Near the base of a Florentine albarello *c.* 1450–70

See also MEDICI and CANTAGALLI

Folch, Stephen: (*fl.* 1820–30)
Made earthenware and ironstone china at Stoke-on-Trent, Staffordshire.
FOLCH'S GENUINE
STONE CHINA

Fontainebleau, Seine-et-Marne, France
Hard-paste porcelain factory set up here in 1795. Works bought by Jacob and Mardochée Petit in 1830.

Jacob Petit   Godebaki & Co
1875

Fontana family:
Celebrated family of maiolica potters and artists, working in Italy. Originally named Pellipario, of Castel Durante, and mentioned from *c.* 1515 to 1605.
Nicola Pellipario: worked at Castel Durante, *c.* 1515–27; signature found on various pieces, some dated 1521, 1528.

1521

1528

Orazio Fontana: grandson of Nicola, working from before 1565, died in 1571.

On dish dated 1541

Other marks on face of dish,
possibly painter's signatures

Ford, Charles (*fl.* 1874–1904)
Manufacturer of porcelain at Hanley, Staffordshire.
Marks: "CF" impressed or printed monogram 1874–1904; in swan mark *c.* 1901–4.

Forli, Italy
Maiolica made here, 16th century or earlier.

FATA
IN
FORLI   ·FATA·IN·
FORLI·

Forsyth, Gordon Mitchell: (1879–1952)
Pottery craftsman, designer, and teacher. Connected with various firms, notably Pilkingtons, Manchester, England (1906–19); produced finely painted lustre pottery; designed pottery shapes and decoration for Brains of Longton, Pountney of Bristol, etc. (period 1920–44); and finely gilded and lustred pieces (from 1944) for Grimwades. Mark: four interlacing scythes, or initials G.M.F. incised.

Incised

Fouque family: (*fl.* 1750 onward)
Made faience at Moustiers q.v., *c.* 1750–1852.

Fowke, Sir Frederick, Bart: (*fl.* early 19th century)
Established a terracotta works at Lowesby, Leicestershire, in 1835, which existed for a few years only.

233

Foy, Peggie:
Studio potter

Frankenthal, Palatinate, Germany
Porcelain made here from *c.* 1755 to *c.* 1800.

| In blue 1771 | In blue *c.* 1756 | In blue 1756–59 (The Cassel lion has a double tail) |

In blue
1762–93

In blue
1771

From 1770 to 1788 the last two figures of the year were added.

Frankfurt-an-der-Oder, Brandenburg, Germany
Faience and earthenware made here from 1763 by Karl Heinrich, who signed HF or FH, placed one above the other, and separated by a stroke.

Frankfurt-am-Main, Germany
Faience made here from 1666 to 1772.
Mark: letter F with initials of painters; dated examples are known.

F.R. or F.L.R. painter: (*fl. c.* 1522)
Initials identified as those of a notable Faenza figure painter.

Frijtom, Frederick van: (*fl. c.* 1658–)
Delft painter.

Fulda, Hesse, Germany
Faience made here from 1741.

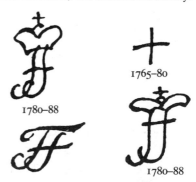

Porcelain made here from 1765 to 1790. Marks: the letters FF for "Fürstlich-Fuldaisch", forming the letter H for Heinrich von Bibra, who founded the factory.

1765–80

1780–88

1780–88

Between 1788 and 1803, FF was arranged to form a letter A, for Adalbert von Harstall; this is rare.

Fulham, London
John Dwight of Fulham took out a patent in 1671 to make "transparent earthenware" and stoneware: followed by Margaret Dwight and others of the family; no certain marks known. In 1862 factory owned by MacIntosh & Clements; in 1864 by a Mr Bailey; trading today as the Fulham Pottery and Cheavin Filter Co.
Mark:

FULHAM POTTERY
LONDON
See also: DE MORGAN

Fürstenberg, Brunswick, Germany
Porcelain made here 1747–1859, and onward.

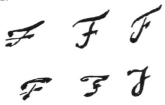

Impressed
on biscuit reliefs

In blue on
19th-century
reproductions
from old moulds

Modern mark

All in blue

Galle, Emile: (1846–1904)
Artist at Nancy; did experimental work in
the ceramic field.

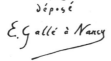

**GALLE
NANCY**

E. G allé à Nancy

E F G.
déposé

Garrison Pottery, Sunderland, Co.
Durham.
Various earthenwares made here from the
early 19th century; factory first owned by
Phillips & Co.
> PHILLIPS & CO.
> Sunderland (date)
> PHILLIPS & CO.
> Sunderland Pottery

Later the firm was Dixon, Austin Phillips
& Co.
> DIXON, AUSTIN & CO.
> Sunderland Pottery
> DIXON & CO.
> Sunderland Pottery

Gély, J.: (fl. 1851–88)
Decorative artist at Sèvres, working in the
pâte-sur-pâte technique.

I.G.

Gera, Thuringia, Germany
Faience made here 1752–c. 1780.

Gien
Factory here made imitations of 16th-
century Italian maiolica.

Giovine, Raffaele: (fl. 1826–60)
His workshop decorated imported French
porcelain.

Giovine in Napoli

In red

Giustiniani family: (fl. c. 1760 onward)
Made porcelain and earthenware at
Naples.

Giustiniani   GIUSTINIANI

Impressed

G   Giustiniani
I ⚱ N

Other marks:
BG or BG over an N, for Biagio
Giustiniani
F.M.G.N.   for Fabbrica Michele Giusti-
niani Napoli
F.G.N.   for Fratelli Giustiniani
Napoli

Glass, John: (fl. c. 1784–1838)
Made earthenware and black basaltes etc
at Hanley, Staffordshire.
> GLASS
> HANLEY
> Impressed

Glienitz, Silesia, Germany
Faience factory established here in 1753; in 19th century turned to cream-coloured earthenware and white-glazed earthenware.
18th-century mark: letter G or GG painted, the latter standing for Gaschin-Glienitz (Countess Anna), 1767–80.
Mark from 1830: place-name GLINITZ over letter M (for Mittelstadt), or letter G impressed.

Goincourt, Oise, France
Faience factory called "L'Italienne" started here in 1793.

Impressed

Goebel, William (1879–)
Manufacturer of hard-paste porcelain at Oeslau, Bavaria, Germany.

Goode, Thomas & Co. (Ltd)
London retailer whose marks occur on many pieces from the 1860s onwards.
Marks including "Ltd" date from 1918 onwards.

Gordon, William: (*fl.* 1939–56)
Sculptor and studio potter; experimented at Chesterfield, Derbyshire, England, in 1939, making salt-glazed stoneware at the Walton Pottery Co., 1946–56.

Goss, William Henry, F. G. S.: (1833–1906)
Manufacturer of earthenware, parian and porcelain at Stoke-on-Trent, Staffordshire (1858–1944). Noted for Goss's Armorial China; made decorative objects in third quarter of 19th century. Renamed "Goss China Co. Ltd" *c.* 1934 when acquired by Cauldon Potteries Ltd.

W H GOSS COPYRIGHT

Impressed or printed, *c.* 1862–

Printed crest mark *c.* 1862; with "England" below, 1891–.

Gotha, Thuringia, Germany
Hard-paste porcelain factory established here in 1757; continues.

1757–83   1783–1805

1805–   1802–*c.* 1830

Gouda, Holland
Tin-enamelled earthenware made here from 1621 (originator Willem Jansz). Three modern factories exist here.

236

Goult, near Apt, France
Faience made here from 1740 to *c.* 1805.

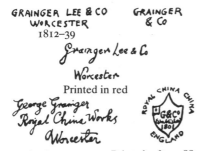

Grainger, Thomas: (d. 1839)
Founded porcelain factory at Worcester, in 1801; later made porcelain with mark of Grainger Lee & Co., finally absorbed by Royal Worcester firm, 1889.

GRAINGER LEE & CO
WORCESTER
1812–39

GRAINGER
& Co

Grainger Lee & Co

Worcester

Printed in red

George Grainger
Royal China Works
Worcester

In red: 1839+

Printed: after 1889

Gray, A. E. & Co,: (1912–61)
Pottery-decorating business at Hanley, Staffordshire, moving to Stoke in 1934. Used "white" wares from Johnson Bros and others. Renamed "Portmeirion Pottery" in 1961.
Many marks incorporating a ship.

Transfer-printed in colours 1834–61.

Green, Stephen: (*fl. c.* 1820–58)
Made salt-glazed stoneware at Lambeth, London; factory bought by John Cliff in 1858; closed down in 1869.

Or: "Stephen Green, Imperial Potteries, Lambeth" (impressed).

Green, T.A. & S.:
Porcelain at Minerva Works, Fenton, *c.* 1876–89. Became Crown Staffordshire Porcelain Co (*q.v.*) from 1889.

Printed mark, *c.* 1876–89

Green, T. G. & Co: (*fl. c.* 1864–)
Made earthenware at Church Gresley, Derbyshire, from 1864, succeeding previous firms.
Numerous marks used, with name of firm, type of ware, or pattern, and often incorporating a church.

1930s

Greenock, Renfrewshire, Scotland
White and cream-coloured earthenware made here from 1810s, at several factories, including the Clyde Pottery (1816–1903), and Greenock Pottery (1820–60).

237

Grenzhausen, Rhineland, Germany
Hard stoneware made in the Westerwald district here, from 15th century onward, and again in the 19th century.

Mark of Merkelbach & Wick (from 1873)

Groszbreitenbach, Thuringia, Germany
Hard-paste porcelain made here during later 18th century. From 1869 the firm was Bühl & Söhne.

c. 1778–   1869–

Grünstadt, Rhineland, Germany
Factory run by Bordello family; flourished from 1812 to late 19th century.

Gubbio, Urbino, Italy
Maiolica and lustred wares made here during the 16th century. Famous lustre painter Giorgio Andreoli, or Maestro Giorgio, worked here (c. 1518 onward), likewise his son Vincenzo.

Note also the 19th-century firm of Carocci, Fabbri & Company.

Gudumland, Denmark
Cream-coloured earthenware and faience made here from 1804 until 1820.

In brown   Impressed

Gustafsberg, Sweden
Pottery made from 1786 and during the 19th century, up to the 1860s. Modern revival from c. 1900.

Gutenbrunn
Porcelain made here 1769–75.
Mark of initials PZ found, standing for Pfalz-Zweibrücken, where the Gutenbrunn factory had originated in 1767.

Haarlem, Holland
Maiolica made here from c. 1572.

238

Probably Cornelis
Lubbertsz

Probably Hans Barnaert
Vierleger

Hackl, Joseph: (*fl. c.* 1749–68)
German factory owner and modeller of
faience, perhaps also an outside decorator.

Mark attributed to him

Hackwood, William (d. 1849) **& Son**:
(*fl.* 1818–53)
Made earthenware at Shelton, Staffordshire, under various partnerships.

Transfer-printed *c.* 1846–49

Hadley, James & Sons (Ltd):
Earthenware and porcelain, Worcester,
c. 1896–1905.

1896–97

Printed: 1902–05   Printed: 1900–02

Hague, The, Holland
Hard-paste porcelain made here *c.* 1776–
94; also decorating of Meissen and
Ansbach hard-paste porcelain and of Tournay soft-paste porcelain.

In blue
overglaze or underglaze

Haile, Sam: (d. 1948)
English potter and teacher.

c. 1936–48

Halfort: (*fl.* 1804–07)
English potter at earthenware factory at
Douai.

HALFORT

Halfort & Cⁱᵉ

Hall, John and Ralph: (1802–22)
Staffordshire potters working together at
Tunstall and Burslem; then separately:
Ralph at Tunstall, as Hall & Co, or Hall &
Holland (*c.* 1846–49); John, with sons, at
Burslem (bankrupt 1832).
Blue-printed earthenware for the Amer-
ican market made by both firms.
Mark recorded on enamelled figures:

Impressed

239

Hamann: (working *c.* 1866)
Dresden porcelain decorator.

Hammond, Henry: (1914–89)
Studio potter.

Hanau, Hesse Germany,
Fayence made here 1661–1806.
Marks: incised crescent with letter, e.g. y,
h, f, k; Hanau.

Hancock, Robert: (1729/30–1817)
Engraver working at Worcester (partner
1772–74); joined Turner at Caughley 1775.

R. Hancock fecit

RH. Worcester

RH Worcester

R. H. f.

Harding, W. & J.: (*fl.* 1862–72)
Made cream-coloured and transfer-printed
ware, etc., at the New Hall factory, Shelton, Staffordshire (recorded 1864–69).
Mark: W. & J. H.

Harley, Thomas: (1778–1832)
Worked as enameller, black printer, and
earthenware manufacturer (from 1801); in
1818 the firm styled Harley and Seckerson;
at Lane End, Staffordshire.
T. Harley Lane End
HARLEY
Impressed

Harmer, Jonathan: (*fl.* 1800–1820)
English potter making terracotta insets for
gravestones and tombs, working at Heathfield in Sussex.
Some found signed:

HARMER FECIT

Harvey, Charles & Son: (*fl.* first half 19th
century)
Made china, earthenwares, gold lustre,
etc. at Longton, Staffordshire, from 1799
for some years; and again 1835–53.

Transferprinted

Hauer, Bonaventura Gottlieb: (1710–82)
Painter at Meissen.
Work signed with initials B G H or, rarely,
in full.

Haviland & Co:
Founded 1892 to make Limoges porcelain
mainly for the American market.

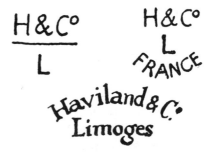

Haviland, David: (*fl.* 1842–)
American who became a naturalised
Frenchman, and founded a pottery works
at Limoges (*q.v.*).

Haviland
France

Haviland, Theodore (d. 1919)
Founder of hard-paste porcelain factory at Limoges in 1893.

Théodore Haviland Limoges FRANCE

Hawley, Thomas: (*fl.* early 19th century)
Identity doubtful. Potters of this surname working in both Yorkshire and Staffordshire in the 19th century.
Mark recorded on a bust of John Wesley:

THO HAWLEY

Impressed

Heathcote, C. & Co.: (*c.* 1818–24)
Made decorated earthenware at Longton, Staffordshire.
Mark recorded:
C. HEATHCOTE & CO. often with pattern name and Prince of Wales feathers in arc above.

Heel, Johann: (1637–1709)
Nuremberg decorator of faience.

I·H

Heinrich & Co: (founded 1904)
Made hard-paste porcelain at Selb in Bavaria.

Helchis, Jacobus: (*fl. c.* 1738–*c.* 1748)
Porcelain decorator, believed to have worked some time at Vienna. Covered cup (British Museum, London) signed "Jakob Helchis fecit".

Herculaneum Pottery, Liverpool: (*c.* 1793–1841)
Factory founded 1793; passing through various ownerships; made earthenware, stoneware, and, from 1801, porcelain of the Staffordshire type.

HERCULANEUM

Impressed
c. 1796–1833

(so-called
liver bird)

Both *c.* 1833–36

Variants recorded:
Crown enclosed by a garter inscribed HERCULANEUM;
HERCULANEUM POTTERY impressed;
liver bird surrounded by a floral wreath, with the word HERCULANEUM in an arc above, and a scroll inscribed LIVERPOOL beneath (printed in red).

Herend, Hungary
Porcelain factory founded 1839, directed by Moritz Fischer; specialised in copies of European and Oriental porcelain, especially Sèvres, Capodimonte, etc.

HEREND

HEREND

MF

Herold, Christian Friedrich: (1700–79)
Decorator at Meissen from 1726, best known for chinoiserie harbour scenes, etc. Cup and saucer, with gold relief applied to the porcelain (British Museum, London) is signed:
C. F. HEROLD INVT. ET FECIT A MEISSE 1750.d.12 Sept.

Herold, or Höroldt, Johann Gregor: (1696–1776)
Director at Meissen, 1731–56, and again 1763–65. Chemist responsible for many fine colours. Signed pieces noted: on a vase with yellow ground "Johann Gregorius Höroldt inv Meissen den 22 Jann Anno 1727"; on another vase "J. G. Höroldt fec. Meissen 17 Augusti 1726".

Heron, Robert & Son: (*c.* 1850–1929)
Manufacturers of earthenware, including Wemyss Ware, at Sinclairtown, Kirkaldy, Scotland. Initials "R H & S" incorporated into various printed marks.

Printed, 1920–9.

Herrebóe, near Friedrichshald, Norway
Factory founded here by Peter Hofnagel (1721–81), making the first Norwegian faience in 1759; factory making domestic ware until *c.* 1778.
Marks, 2-tiered arrangement of initials, HB for Herrebóe over those of the decorator.
Artists:
Johann Georg Kreipe, foreman or manager, 1760–64.
Joseph Large (1742–93), painter
Gunder Large (1744–1818), modeller
H.F.L. Hosenfelder (1722–1805) working 1762–72

Heubach, Gebr.: (1820–)
Manufacturers of hard-paste porcelain at Lichte, Thuringia, Germany.
Marks: "DEP" in triangle; HC monogram and "Schutz-Marke" in circle under setting sun; "HEUBACH".

Hicks & Meigh: (*fl.* 1806–22)
Hicks, Meigh & Johnson: (*fl.* 1822–35)
Manufactured decorated earthenware and ironstone china at Shelton, Staffordshire.

Printed

High Halden, Kent
Country pottery existed here in the 18th century, using slip decoration and inlaid technique.
Mark recorded:
HALDEN POTTERY
On a 19th-century moneybox, with inlaid name, J. G. DUDEN

Hilditch: (various 19th-century firms)
English potters at Lane End and Lane Delph, Staffordshire:
Hilditch & Co. (*c.* 1805–13)
Hilditch & Martin (1818)
Hilditch & Son (1820s)
Hilditch & Hopwood (1830–67)

Hirsch, Franziska:
Decorator of porcelain at Dresden, 20th century.

242

Hispano-Moresque pottery
No potters' marks can be identified with certainty.

Höchst, near Mayence, Germany
Porcelain made here from 1750 to 1798.

Wheel mark in red or other coloured enamel, c. 1750–62; wheel mark in blue 1762–96; crowned wheel mark c. 1765–74; impressed wheel mark, of six spokes, c. 1760–65.
Faience made here from 1750 to 1758.
Marks used: the four- or six-spoke wheel together with painted initials or signatures. Rare forms include an eight-spoke wheel surmounted by a crown and a circle enclosing a six-point star:

Artists:
Georg Friedrich Hesse 1746–51
Ignatz Hesse 1746–51
Johannes Zeschinger 1748–53
Adam Ludwig 1749–58
Joseph Philipp Dannhöfer 1747–51
Pressel 1748

Holdcroft, Joseph:
Made parian, maiolica, and lustreware at Longton, Staffordshire 1865–1939.

Impressed

Holdsworth, Peter (fl. 1945–)
Founded the Holdsworh Potteries at Ramsbury, near Marlborough, Wiltshire, England, in 1945.

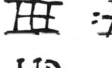

Holitsch, Hungary
Maiolica factory founded here in 1743.
Usual mark the letter H:

In blue, manganese purple, or light green.
Other marks included:
H.F for Holitscher Fabrik
HH for Holitscher Herrschaft
HP for Holicske Panstvi
On cream-coloured earthenware the mark consisted of the word HOLICS, HOLITSCH or HOLITSH, impressed.

Hollins, T. & J.: (fl. c. 1795–1820)
Potters making stonewares in the Wedgwood style at Hanley, Staffordshire; business founded by the father, Richard Hollins, in 1750.

T. & J. HOLLINS
Impressed

Honiton Pottery, Devon
Established in 1919 by Charles Collard, who sold to Norman Hull in 1947. Honiton Pottery Ltd since 1956.

COLLARD
HONITON
ENGLAND

1918–47

NORMAN HULL
POTTERY

N.T.S. Hull

1947–55

Honoré, François-Maurice:
Founder of hard-paste porcelain factory in Paris in 1785; also associated with Dagoty until the 1820s.

Dagoty
à paris

Hoorn, Hendrik van: (d. 1803)
Recorded as owner of De Drie Vergulde Astonnen factory, Delft (*q.v.*), in 1759.

HVhoorn

Hoppestein, Jacob Wemmersz:
Proprietor of T'Oude Moriaenshooft, Delft (*q.v.*), about 1680.

Hoppestein, Rochus Jacobs: (d. 1692)
At T'Oude Moriaenshooft, Delft (*q.v.*); his widow carried on until 1714.

Hubertusburg, Saxony, Germany
Faience factory established here in 1770, continuing until 1814, when it passed to the Government. Weigel and Messerschmidt manufactured here from 1835 until 1848.

Impressed
K.S.ST.F. stands for Königliche sächsische Steingut-Fabrik.

Hunslet Hall, Leeds, Yorkshire, England
Cream-coloured and blue-printed earthenware made here from *c.* 1792 by Petty and Rainforth.

RAINFORTH & CO.
Impressed: 1790s
Continued until 1880 or later, under various names:
1818, Petty & Co.; 1822, Petty & Hewitt; 1825, Samuel Petty & Son; 1847, John Mills

Hunting horn mark
Adopted by the Chantilly factory in 1725; rendered in many forms.

The mark was imitated on porcelain made at Worcester.

Hutschenreuther, C. M.: (*fl.* 1814 onward)
Founded hard-paste porcelain factory at Hohenberg, Bavaria, which was continued by his widow and descendants. Both useful and luxury porcelain was made from 1860.

244

Hutschenreuther, Lorenz: (*fl. c.* 1856–)
Firm founded at Selb, Bavaria, making hard-paste porcelain.

Ilmenau, Thuringia, Germany
Hard-paste porcelain factory founded here in 1777 by C. Z. Gräbner; bought by Christian Nonne in 1808, who worked it with his son-in-law, named Roesch.

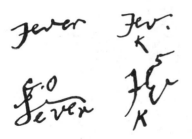

Jever, Oldenburg, Germany
Faience factory working from 1760 to 1776.

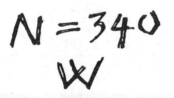

Johanneum mark
Named after the building in Dresden which housed the Royal Saxon collection of porcelain, including Chinese and Japanese export ware. Collection begun by Augustus the Strong, and porcelain identified by inventory marks engraved on the wheel and coloured black:

$$N = 340$$
$$W$$

Johnson Bros: (1883–)
English potters, whose firm was founded in 1883 by four brothers; making earthenwares at Hanley and Tunstall, Staffordshire, continuing today.

Johnson, Reuben and Phoebe: (*fl.* 1818–40)
Reuben Johnson recorded as making lustred china and fancy earthenware at Hanley, Staffordshire, in 1818; factory listed in 1834 under name of his widow, Phoebe Johnson (Phoebe Johnson & Son, 1836).

Jones, A. G. Harley:
Decorative earthenware at "Royal Vienna Art Pottery", Fenton, *c.* 1907–34.

Printed

Jones, George (& Sons Ltd):
Decorative earthenware and maiolica-style pieces, *c.* 1861–1951.

Printed or impressed
c. 1874–1924

Keeling, Anthony: (1783–1815)
Made pottery at Tunstall, Staffordshire, from 1783 to 1810; in 1802 Anthony and Enoch Keeling were working two factories in Burslem, with the mark:

A. & E. KEELING

Keeling, Toft & Co.: (*fl.* 1806–26)
Made black basaltes and other earthenwares; succeeded by Toft & May, working until 1830.

KEELING, TOFT & CO.
Impressed

Kellinghusen, Holstein, Germany
Faience made here from *c.* 1765.

Carsten Behren's factory *c.* 1765 onwards

Joachim Möller, 1785–95

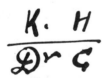

Dr Sebastian Grauer, 1795–1820

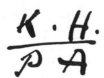

c. 1800

Kelsterbach, Hesse-Darmstadt, Germany
Faience factory founded at Königstadt *c.* 1758; transferred to Kelsterbach in 1761, closing 1835. Cream-coloured earthenware made in the later years.

For Königstadt or
Kelsterbach; early mark

In blue or impressed on
cream-coloured ware
late 18th century

Hard-paste porcelain made here from 1761 to 1768, and again from 1789 to 1802.

In blue:
rare before 1789

In blue:
Lay's period (*c.* 1789)

Kemp, Dorothy: (20th century)
English studio potter and teacher; makes lead-glazed earthenware, slip-decorated pottery, and stoneware.

Kiel: Holstein, Germany
Faience factory established here in 1763, under J. S. F. Tännich, succeeded by J. Buchwald, and closing *c.* 1788.
Marks usually three-tiered, with initial of factory, manager, and artist, and occasionally, last figures of date and other figures.

Kiel/Tännich/Christopherson
Artists
C for Christopherson
K for Kleffel
A.L. for Abraham Leihamer

Kiev, Russia
Cream-coloured earthenware made here
from end of 18th century.

Porcelain made by M. Gulina is marked:

Kilnhurst pottery, Swinton, Yorkshire
Kilnhurst Old Pottery established in 1746
by William Malpas; eventually taken over
by Joseph Twigg & Brothers in 1839;
continued in hands of Twigg family until
1881, using the marks:

TWIGG'S

Impressed

Kishere, Joseph: (*fl.* up to 1843)
Made salt-glazed stoneware at Mortlake,
Surrey, England; pieces found marked:
Kishere Pottery, Mortlake, Surrey.

Klemm, K. R.: (*fl.* from *c.* 1869)
Decorator at Dresden, in style of Meissen
factory.

Klösterle, or Klásteric, Bohemia, Czechoslovakia
Porcelain and earthenware factory established here in 1793, continuing through 19th century.

Kloster-Veilsdorf, Thuringia, Germany
Hard-paste porcelain factory established
here in 1760.

| 1760 onwards | 1765 | 1760 onwards |

| Imitation
Meissen | Also used on
Ilmenau, Grosz-
breitenbach and
Limbach porcelain | Modern
mark |

Kocks, Adriaenus: (*fl.* 1687–1701)
Proprietor of De Grieksche A pottery,
Delft (*q.v.*), from 1687 until his death in
1701.

Korzec, or Kóretzki, Poland
Hard-paste porcelain made here from *c.*
1790 until factory transferred in 1797 to
Gorodnitza, where it closed in 1870. Mark,
an eye drawn in geometric convention:

Kunersberg, near Memmingen, Germany
Faience made here from 1754 to *c.* 1768.

Other marks recorded: the initials KB,
separately, or in monogram.

La Charité-sur-Loire, Nièvre, France
Earthenware factory established here in
1802.

LA-CHARITÉ
Impressed

La Courtille, or Rue Fontaine-au-Roy, or
Basse Courtille, Faubourg du Temple,
Paris
Hard-paste porcelain factory established
here in 1771, closing in 1841.
Mark similar to Rue de la Roquette (Les
Trois Levrettes)

Incised   In blue   In blue

Lake, W. H.: (1872–)
English manufacturer of earthenware and
redware at Truro, Cornwall.

Mark:

LAKE'S
CORNISH
POTTERY
TRURO
Probably 20th-century

Lakin & Poole: (*fl.* 1791–95)
Potters at Burslem, Staffordshire, making
blue-printed earthenware, etc.; trading as
Poole, Lakin, & Shrigley in 1795; soon
after, Lakin withdrew, Poole and Shrigley
becoming bankrupt in 1797.
LAKIN & POOLE
Impressed

Lamm, A.: (*fl.* from 1887)
Dresden porcelain decorator working in
the Meissen style.

Lammans, B., Andenne, Belgium
Made white and cream earthenware from
1794 until 1820.

Impressed   On transfer-printed ware

La Moncloa, or Florida, Madrid
Factory working from 1817 until 1850.

Landais: (*fl.* 19th century)
Copyist of Henri Deux and Palissy wares.

Landore Pottery, Swansea, South Wales
Earthenware factory established in 1848 by

John Forbes Calland; closed down in 1856.
J F CALLAND & CO
LANDORE POTTERY
CALLAND
SWANSEA

Langenthal, Switzerland
Porcelain factory established here in 1906.

La Rochelle, Charente-Inférieure, France
Faience made here in the 18th century, from 1722. Most important factory was that of De Bricqueville, founded in 1743. Marks recorded:

La Tour D'Aigues, Vaucluse, France
Faience factory founded here in 1753, using the mark:

Leach Pottery:
Established by Bernard Leach, at St Ives, Cornwall, in 1921.

 For Leach Pottery impressed: c. 1921 to present day

 For Bernard Leach

 David Leach (son of Bernard Leach)

Leach, Margaret: (*fl.* 1947–56)
Studio potter, making slipware, marked:

Leeds, Yorkshire, England
The Old Pottery: (*c.* 1760–1878)
Established at Hunslet, Leeds (not to be confused with the later factories of Hunslet Hall, and Rothwell, in the same district), *c.* 1760 by the two Green brothers, later trading as Hartley, Greens & Co, and making fine cream-coloured earthenware in quantity (*c.* 1780–1820) with pierced or basket-work; sold in 1825, trading successively as S. Wainwright & Co; the Leeds Pottery Co; and Warburton, Britton & Co.

Impressed

Impressed
Marks also appear on 20th-century wares

Lefebvre, Denis: (*fl.* 1631–49)
Painter working at Nevers.
Mark recorded:

249

Lei, Pietro: (*fl.* 18th century)
Maiolica painter at Sassuolo and Pesaro.
Dated mark recorded:

Leigh, Charles and James:
English potters trading at Douai from 1781; faience factory continued to 1831.

Impressed

Le Montet, Saône et Loire, France
Mark used on white stoneware, of 19th-century date:

Le Nove, Italy
Porcelain made here *c.* 1762 to 1835.
Monogram G B A stands for Giovanni Battista Antonibon, original founder. The usual mark from 1781 was a six-point star, or the word N O V E incised on figures, etc. The letter N incised on later tablewares may stand for Nove or be a workman's mark.

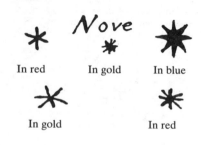

In red   In gold   In blue

In gold   In red

In gold

In colour   In blue

Unexplained marks, possibly of owners:

In gold   In red

Lenzburg, Switzerland
Faience made here from 1763 for a few years by Heinrich Klug. Faience painter Jacob Frey or Hans Jacob Frey had a workshop from 1775 to 1790.
Numerous marks; initials accepted:
      LB for Lenzburg
      HK for Heinrich Klug
      HF for Hans Frey

Leroy, Louis: (d. 1788)
Faience manufacturer at Marseilles from 1750. Signature recorded:
Fabque De Marslle Le Roy

Lessore, Emile: (d. 1876)
Pottery painter: at Sèvres until 1850, then in Paris; in England 1858, a few months at Mintons, then at Wedgwoods at Etruria until 1863; then returned to France.

Lesum, near Bremen, Germany
Faience factory established here in 1755 by Johann Christoph Vielstick (1722–1792/1800). Mark: the letter V or VI over initial of the painter separated by a dash.

Liège, Belgium
Faience made here from 1752 until 1811. The name "Boussemaert" also occurs.

Lille, France
Faience and soft-paste porcelain made here by Jean François Boussemaert and Barthélémy Dorez from 1711 until 1730. Mark ascribed:

Jean-François Boussemaert

Barthélémy Dorez

Hard-paste porcelain made here by Leperre-Durot, from 1784 to 1790; after which it
passed from hand to hand, closing down in 1817.

Stencilled

The dolphin was adopted because the factory was protected by the Dauphin.

Faience made here from 1696 to 1802; a tileworks also flourished from 1740 to 1808.

Used on later
copies

Limbach, Thuringia, Germany
Porcelain factory founded here in 1772 by Gotthelf Greiner, worked after his death (1797) by his sons, trading as Gotthelf Greiner-Sohne.

1772–88   1788

Limoges, Haute-Vienne, France
Faience factory established here, working from 1736 to 1773.
Mark recorded:
The place-name, Limoges, with various dates.
Hard-paste porcelain factory established in 1783 by Massie, Fourniera and Grellet; taken over by the King of France, 1784; Grellet junior was succeeded as manager by Alluaud 1788; firm traded as Alluaud during the first half of the 19th century, becoming Charles Field Haviland in 1886. A large number of factories worked from the 1820s onward, the best known being Haviland & Company, and Charles Field Haviland (1833–96) (*q.v.*).

For the Comte d'Artois
protector of the factory until 1784

Selection from large number of 19th-century marks:

Serpaut

C. Tharaud

Martial Redon
from 1853
(d. 1890)

C F H
G D M
FRANCE

Charles Field
Haviland
in green
1881–91

Porcelaine Mousseline

Theodore Haviland & Company
(Theodore died 1919)

J.P.

J. Pouyat

L. Sazaret
from c. 1850

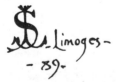

L. Sazaret

In green

Haviland
France
Impressed
Haviland and Co.

Haviland
France

A. Lanternier E. Madesclaire J. Granger
1855   jeune   et cie

Lindemann, George Christoph: (*fl.* 1758–*c.* 1767)
Painter on porcelain, e.g. flowers, landscape and figure subjects, at Nymphenburg (1758–60).
Mark recorded: initials of artist, G.C.L., with date, 1758; another signature (Meissen) dated 1767; also occurs on Tournay pieces.

Linthorpe, Yorkshire
Factory established here in 1879 by John Harrison, making art pottery of extravagant form; closed 1889. Christopher Dresser worked here.

Impressed

Lisieux, France
Faience tiles and pottery made here from mid-17th century.
Mark recorded:

Lissim, Simon: (1900–)
Stage and ceramic designer, working in France, *c.* 1921 to 1940, in U.S.A. from 1940 onward.
Mark: the initials S L in monogram.

Liverpool, Lancashire
Delftware made here (*c.* 1710–*c.* 1780) and porcelain (second half 18th century), but marks are almost unknown; numerals occur on various types of delftware. See also SEACOMBE POTTERY.

Livesley, Powell & Co: (*fl. c.* 1851–66)
China and earthenware made at Hanley, Staffordshire, by William Livesley & Co;

firm traded successively as:
Wm. Livesley & Co.
Livesley, Powell & Co., *c.* 1851–66
Powell & Bishop, *c.* 1866–78
Powell, Bishop & Stonier, *c.* 1878–91
Bishop & Stonier, 1891–1939

Impressed
c. 1851–66

Lloyd, John: (1805–51)
and Lloyd, Rebecca:
Made earthenware and china toys at Hanley, Staffordshire (*c.* 1834 to after 1851).

Impressed

Locke & Co. (Ltd):
Made porcelain at Worcester, *c.* 1895–1904.

Printed: *c.* 1895–1900 Printed: *c.* 1900–04

Lockett firm: (*fl.* from *c.* 1786 onward)
Staffordshire potters trading successfully under the family name with variations; Timothy and John Lockett made earthenware at Burslem, Staffordshire (1786–*c.* 1802); moved to Lane End (1802), then as J. & G. Lockett; later names:
John Lockett & Co (1818–30s)
John Lockett (d. 1835) & Son
John & Thomas Lockett (recorded 1851 and 1875)
John Lockett & Co. (1889 onward)

Mark recorded:

J. LOCKETT
Impressed *c.* 1821–58

Lodi, Lombardy, Italy
Maiolica made here by Simpliciano Ferretti from 1725.
Mark: SF in monogram.
See also ROSSETTI

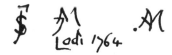

Lodovico, Maestro: (*fl. c.* 1540)
Venetian maiolica painter; inscription recorded:
In Venetia in Cotrada di Sto Polo in botega di Mo Lodouico

Longton Hall Works, Staffordshire: (*c.* 1749–60)
Manufacturers of porcelain. William Littler and Aaron Wedgwood trading as Littler & Co. Most Longton Hall porcelain is unmarked.

In blue
under the glaze

Longwy, Lorraine, France
Faience and earthenware made here during 18th and 19th centuries; factory owned by Huart de Northomb *c.* 1840.

Impressed

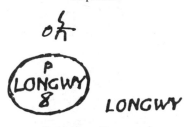

In black and impressed

Lovatt's Potteries, Langley Mill, Nottingham, England, *c.* 1895–
Manufacturers of earthenware.

Another 20th-century mark: words "LANGLEY Pottery" superimposed upon a windmill.

Löwenfinck, Adam Friedrich von: (1714–54)
First a painter of porcelain (Meissen 1727–*c.* 1736), then at Bayreuth and Chantilly; made faience at Fulda (1741–45), where signature recorded: F.v.L. with arms of Fulda. Made faience at Höchst (*c.* 1745–49) and later at other places.

Lowestoft, Suffolk, England
Factory making soft-paste porcelain established here in 1757, lasting until 1799.
No mark consistently used, but numerals up to 28, often in underglaze blue, inside the footring, are found on some pieces. Factory marks of Worcester, Meissen, and other factories sometimes imitated:

Lücke, Johann Christoph Ludwig von: (d. 1780)
Ivory carver known to have been modeller and repairer at Vienna in 1750; signature recorded on Vienna porcelain figures, etc., as "L. v. Lücke."

Ludwigsburg, Württemberg, Germany
Hard-paste porcelain made here from 1758 until 1824. Marks are similar to those of Niderviller.

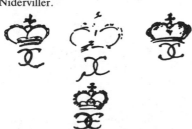

Usually in blue, occasionally in red: 1758–93

Painted in blue: 1758–93

Stags horns, from arms of Württemberg, painted in blue: late 18th or early 19th century

Duke Ludwig
1793–95

King William
1816–24

King Friedrich
1806–16
impressed, or
painted in gold
or red

A number of painters' and repairers' marks are known, including the L of Jean-Jacob Louis (d. 1772).
A painted arrow sometimes occurs on ware produced 1760–70.

Incised
Jean-Jacob Louis,
"chief repairer" 1762–72

The Letters WPM found under various Ludwigsburg marks indicate the modern factory at Schorndorb, and signify Württembergische-Porzellan-Manufaktur.
Faience made at Ludwigsburg from 1756, using mark of Niderviller, namely that of Comte de Custine:

Lunéville, Meurthe-et-Moselle, France
Faience made here during the 18th century
from 1731; successive owners included:
Cambrette, Loyal, Keller & Guerin
(1788), Cufflé, etc.

Lyons, France
Faience made here from *c.* 1520 until
c. 1758. Some pieces have inscriptions in-
clud-
ing name of maker, place-name, and date.
Mark recorded:

Maastricht, Holland
Pottery called "De Sphinx" established
here in 1836, by Petrus Regout (b. 1801).

Machin & Potts: (*c.* 1833–37)
Made drab stonewares with relief decora-
tion and blue-printed earthenware at Burs-
lem, Staffordshire.
Mark on piece in British Museum:
PUBLISHED
AS THE ACT DIRECTS
June 20th, 1834, by
Machin & Potts
Burslem, Staffordshire
(stamped)

MacIntyre, James & Co.:
Earthenware, Burslem, *c.* 1860 to present
day.

Printed
post 1894–1927

Mafra & Son, Caldas da Rainha, Portugal
Firm making earthen ware form 1853.
Made pieces often with Whieldon-type
tortoisehell glazes; work usually marked,
but otherwise might easily pass for authen-
tic Whieldon wares.

Magdeburg, Hanover, Germany
Faience made here from mid-18th century
for about 30 years, under direction of
Johann Philipp Guichard (1726–98). From
1786 Guichard made English-type earthen-
ware, with mark:
M
(GUISCHARD)
Impressed

Makkum, Holland
Faience made here from *c.* 1669 onward.
Modern mark used by Freerk Jans Tiche-
laar:

Maling family: (*fl.* 1762–1815)
North Hylton Pottery, near Sunderland,
Co. Durham, 1762–1815, founded by William Maling and worked by his sons Christopher and John. Ouseburn Pottery, near

Newcastle, 1817–59, established by Robert Maling. A & B Ford Potteries, Newcastle-on-Tyne, *c.* 1859–90, worked by C. T. Maling; 1890–1963 worked by C. T. Maling & Sons. Marks: "MALING" impressed *c.* 1800–90; "C.T.M.", *c.* 1859–90; "CTM" in triangle, "Trade Mark. Established 1762" *c.* 1875– *c.* 1908; "CTM & Sons" below castle.

c. 1908–

c. 1924–

Malkin, Samuel: (1668–1741)
Slipware potter at Burslem, Staffordshire (*fl.* 1710–30); pieces known with dates (1712 and 1726); dishes usually signed on the face S. M.

Malta
Mark recorded on stoneware jars given to Sèvres museum in 1844:

Manara, Baldassare: (*fl. c.* 1530–36) Maiolica painter of Faenza.
Mark, signature in full or initials:

Marans, Charente-Inférieure, France
Faience made here from 1740 to 1745;
factory transferred to La Rochelle in 1756.

Similar cancellations were used at Vienna
and Sèvres:

Vienna   Sèvres

Marieberg, near Stockholm, Sweden
Faience and porcelain factory working
here from 1758 to c. 1788.
Marks on faience:

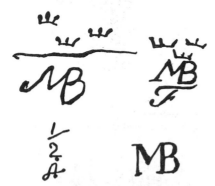

In blue   MB, Marieberg-Berthevin
(Pierre Berthevin, 1766/9)

Marks on porcelain:

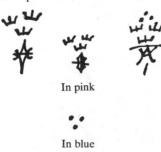

In pink

In blue

Marks, cancellation
Outmoded or defective wares sold "in the
white" to outside decorators (hausmaler)
were marked with a stroke through the
original factory mark, by firms that had
regard for the quality of their wares; practice originated at Meissen, where one
stroke is said to indicate wares sold as
defective to decorators, two or more
strokes to indicate imperfectly decorated
factory products:

Marks, ownership
These include: signs of hospitals or phar-
macies on Italian drugpots; names of
châteaux or palaces on French porcelain
and faience; court inventory marks on
German and Russian porcelain; all generally marks of ownership; not to be taken
for factory marks.
Examples:

Pharmacy mark

Mark of the
Carthusian
order

Pharmacy mark

Mark of owner or
maker: Florentine jar

Mark of Jan Emens and
merchant's mark

Pharmacy sign

257

Pharmacy mark:
Hispano-
Moresque
drugpot

Merchants' mark:
Siegburg stoneware

Nymphenburg
workman's mark

Höchst:
repairer's mark

Π:К.

Russian court
inventory mark:
Meissen porcelain

Made for the
Château d'Anet:
Sceaux

Sèvres: painters' marks

K.H.C.

Königliche Hof-
Conditorei
(Royal Pantry):
Meissen porcelain

Meissen: lustre
mark

 Meissen: lustre
mark

Marktredwitz, Bavaria
Hard-paste porcelain made here by firm of
F. Thomas, from mid-19th century.

On Italian maiolica plate
as part of decoration, and
on the reverse

Marseilles, Bouches-du-Rhône, France
Hard-paste porcelain made here from
c. 1770, by Joseph Robert:

Faience made here from 1677 until about
1827. Important factories included those of
Fauchier, Leroy, Perrin, Savy, Robert,
and Bonnefoy.

Marks, workmen's
These include artists' signatures or initials,
and the initials or signs of gilders, repairers, etc.; they were used to assist factory
organisation, and as a means of checking
faulty workmanship; artists' and gilders'
signs used at Sèvres are well-
authenticated.
Selection of examples:

On Sèvres porcelain

St Jean du Désert factory
(worked by Joseph Clérissy, 1677–85)

Fauchier factory *c.* 1711–95

Factory of Veuve Perrin (*fl.* 1748–93)
These marks are said to be much forged

Honoré Savy *c.* 1770

J. G. Robert *c.* 1750–95

B

Bonnefoy, late 18th century

Martin Bros: (*fl* 1873–1915)
English potters making salt-glazed stone-ware at Southall, Middlesex.

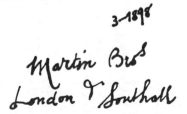

Incised

Mason, Miles: (1752–1822)
English manufacturer, recorded at Liverpool, Lancashire (1796–1800), and at Lane Delph, Staffordshire (1796–1813), with different partners; made bone china, a hard porcelain and earthenware.
Marks:
M. MASON or MILES MASON (impressed); a square seal with MILES above and MASON below.

Pseudo-Chinese seal
Transfer-printed in blue
on bone china

Mason, William: (1785–1855)
Made blue-printed earthenware at Lane Delph, Staffordshire, from 1811 to 1824.
Mark:

W. MASON
In blue: transfer-printed

Mason family: (*fl.* 1795–1854)
Staffordshire potters; Miles Mason (1752–1822), made porcelain at Fenton (from 1800), bone china (1807–13); succeeded by G. M. Mason (withdrew *c.* 1829) and C. J. Mason (bankrupt 1848), making porcelain, bone china, and ironstone china; C. J. Mason started up again at Longton (1851), but closed in 1854.

Transfer-printed

Variations in crown

Transfer-printed

Transfer-printed

Massier, Clément and Jérôme: (*fl.* from 1870s)
Made decorative pottery, with flambé and lustre glazes, at Golfe Juan and Vallauris, France.

Painted   Impressed

Lucien Levy was artist and designer.

Mathews, Heber: (?1905–59)
Studio potter

HM.

Mayence, Germany
Cream-coloured earthenware made here during early 19th century.
Mark: name MAINZ or initials MZ impressed.

Mayer, E. & Son: (*fl. c.* 1805–34)
Made earthenware at Hanley, Staffordshire.
Marks recorded:
E. Mayer
E. Mayer & Son
Impressed

Mayer, Thomas: (1762–1827) and Newbold, Richard: (1758–1836)
Staffordshire manufacturers in partnership (*c.* 1817–33) at Lane End; made porcelain and various earthenwares.

Mayer, T. J. & J.:
Earthenware, parian and porcelain at Dale Hall Pottery, Burslem, *c.* 1843–55.

Printed: 1843–55

Meakin, J. & G.: (*fl.* 1845 onward)
Earthenware factory established 1845 by James Meakin at Lane End, Staffordshire; transferred to Hanley in 1848/50; continues to present day.

20th-century marks

Medici porcelain, Florence, Italy
Soft-paste porcelain made from 1575 until 1587, and again possibly *c.*, 1613.
Marks recorded included the six balls of the Medici arms, and the dome of Florence Cathedral, with or without the letter F.

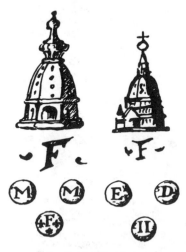

Painted in blue
The initials MMFEDII stand for Franciscus Medicis Magnus Dux Etruriae Secundus.

Meigh family: (*fl.* 1790–1860)
English manufacturers of earthenware at Hanley, Staffordshire; traded as Job Meigh & Son (1812–35); Charles Meigh (1835–49); Charles Meigh, Son & Pankhurst (1850); Charles Meigh & Son (1851–61).

The firm was known as the Old Hall Earthenware Co Ltd, 1862 to 1887, and as Old Hall Porcelain Co Ltd, from 1887 to its closure in 1902.

J.M.S.	MEIGH'S
M. & S.	CHINA
C.M.	C.M.S. & P.

Job Meigh & Son: 1812–34

Charles Meigh: 1835–49

Charles Meigh Son & Pakhurst: 1850

Charles Meigh & Son

Charles Meigh & Son: 1851–61

Meillonas, near Bourg-en-Bresse, Ain, France
Faience made here from 1761 until *c.* 1804.

Meir, John & Son:
Earthenwares at Tunstall, *c.* 1837–97.

Meissen, near Dresden, Saxony, Germany
Red stoneware made here in early 18th century until *c.* 1730, chiefly under J. F. Böttger (*fl.* 1704–19).

Impressed, incised, or moulded

Hard-paste porcelain in production here by 1713, but not systematically marked until 1724.

Pseudo-Chinese mark occurring on blue-and-white porcelain (*c.* 1720–25) and on stoneware:

N 27 is Johanneum Inventory No. 27
So-called Caduceus mark first used *c.* 1723:

First clearly identifiable factory marks were initials, for Königliche Porzellan Manufaktur or Königliche Porzelann Fabrik, sometimes with the crossed swords.

1723–24

The crossed swords mark was introduced *c.* 1724, continuing in use until the 20th century. Various forms:

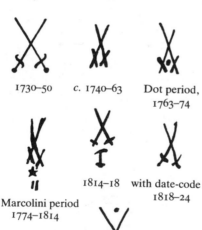

1730–50   *c.* 1740–63   Dot period, 1763–74

Marcolini period 1774–1814

1814–18   with date-code 1818–24

1924–1934

Some variations of the crossed swords mark with unexplained additions:

Incised on biscuit porcelain 1774–19th century

Variant of the gilded mark on the right

14

Mark in blue number in red

Crossed swords in blue. Centre mark in gold and inventory mark incised

Sub-standard ware cancelled thus:

The Augustus Rex cipher was placed in blue on especially fine pieces intended as royal presents, or for the Royal Palace, generally 1725–30; much forged in the 19th century:

Rare mark is the monogram F.A. for Frederick Augustus II of Saxony (1733). Wares for special departments marked:
K.H.C.W. (Königliche   Hof-Conditorei Warschau)
K.H.C.   (Königliche Hof-Conditorei)

K.H.C.W.   K.H.C.

A number of pieces are marked B.P.T. with word "Dresden" and date, 1739. Believed to be Palace marks:

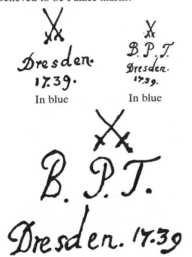

Dresden.   B.P.T.
17.39.   Dresden.
              17.39.

In blue   In blue

B.P.T.

Dresden. 17.39

In blue

Inventory marks were engraved on the wheel and coloured over in black:

Z90   N=494.
 W   W

J. G. Heintze frequently incorporated the factory mark and date in his paintings; artists sometimes signed their work, e.g.

C.F Herold
invt: et.fecit a meissē
1750. ʒ 12 Sept:

Melchior, Johann Peter: (1747–1825)
Modellmeister at Höchst, 1767–79; at Frankenthal, 1779–93; and at Nymphenburg from 1796 until 1822.
Signatures recorded:

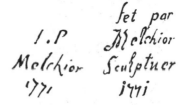

J.P   fet par
Melchior   Melchior
'771   Sculptuer
               1771

Mennecy, Seine-et-Oise, France
Porcelain made here from 1734 to 1748, then at Bourg-la-Reine, 1773 until 1806.

DV   .D.V.

Incised   In blue
        Mennecy

BR
B.R.   N   MŌ

Late 18th century   Initials of
Bourg-la-Reine   Christophe Mŏ
                     from 1767

Mesch, Quirynus: (*fl.* 1702–19)
Delft painter.

MQ
M29

Methven, David (& Sons):
Made decorated earthenwares at Kirkcaldy, Fifeshire, Scotland, first half of 19th century to *c.* 1930.

STONE WARE
D. METHVEN & SONS

Metsch, Johann Friedrich: (*fl.* 1732 to after 1751)
Enameller at Dresden (1731); Hausmaler at Bayreuth (1735–51); later at Fürstenberg.
Signatures recorded:

On Meissen porcelain

F. M.
Bäyreith
1744

On Chinese porcelain

Mexborough Old Pottery, Mexborough, Yorkshire, England
Established in 1800 by Sowter & Bromley; taken over 1804 by Peter Barker, and worked by the Barker family until its closure in 1844; chiefly made printed earthenware.

SOWTER & CO
MEXBRO
Impressed

Meyers & Son: (late 19th century)
Dresden decorators in the Meissen style, using mark closely resembling the crossed swords mark:

Middlesbrough Pottery Co., Middlesbrough, Yorkshire
Factory established 1834; from 1844 to 1852 traded as the Middlesbrough Earthenware Co; from 1852 as Isaac Wilson & Co; closed 1857.
Made painted and printed earthenwares.

Impressed

Midwinter, W. R. (Ltd): (*c.* 1910–)
Manufacturers of earthenware at Burslem, Staffordshire, now part of the Wedgwood Group.
Marks: variations on "W. R. Midwinter Burslem", sometimes with "porcelain" or "semi-porcelain"; beneath crown *c.* 1945–.

Milan, Italy
Maiolica made here in the 18th century.
Mark recorded of potter named Cesare Confaloniere (1775–82), working in the oriental style:

Firm of Julius Richard and Company established in 1833, working until 1873, when linked to Ginori of Doccia.
Mark:

In black

Milland Pottery, Liphook, Hampshire
Earthenware potworks started 1948.
Mark, a windmill between the words:

MILLAND/POTTERY

Minton, Stoke-on-Trent, Staffordshire
Factory founded in 1793, working under various titles until the present day. By 1817, trading as Thomas Minton & Son; Minton & Boyle, 1836–41; Minton & Co., 1841–73; Minton & Hollins, 1845–68; Mintons Ltd from 1883; joined Royal Doulton Group in 1973.

Painted marks
c. 1805–16

1822–36

Transfer-printed, c. 1840s

Printed or
impressed
after 1851

MINTON

Impressed 1861 onward

Transfer-printed
1863–72

Minton & Co: 1841–75

MINTONS   B B New Stone

Impressed   Impressed
20th century

Transfer-printed
Minton & Hollins: 1845–68   Transfer-printed, uranium glaze, 1918

Year marks (impressed). Used in conjunction with main mark. Forms may vary.

1842–50

1851–59

1860–68

1869–77

1878–86

1887–95

1896–1904

1905–13

1914–22

1923–31

1932–40

Signatures recorded:

Birks

Birks, Alboin: (1861–1941) 1874–1937
decorator, pâte-sur-pâte

A Boullemier

Boullemier, Antonin: (1840–1900)
figure painter

A CARRIER

Carrier-Belleuse, Albert: after 1854
sculptor and figure modeller

JEDean

Dean, Edward J.: (1884–1933)
painter of fish and game

L Solon   LEON·Y SOLON

Solon, Leon Victor: (1872–1957) 1909
art director

Solon, Marc Louis: (1835–1912)
1870–1904
decorator, pâte-sur-pâte

Wadsworth, John William: 1935–1955
art director

Wright, Albert:
fish and flower painter
c. 1871 into 20th century

Miragaya, near Oporto, Portugal
Faience factory established here in late
18th century.

Mô, Christophe and Jean: (*fl* from 1767)
Modellers and repairers working at
Mennecy. Jean continued as a repairer at
Bourg-la-Reine.
Marks recorded include: "J Mo" and
"Mo" (incised) also e.g. "BR, Mo" and
DV, Mo".

Monaco
Pottery established here in 1874.

Monterau, Seine-et-Marne, France
English-type pottery made here from 1748;
by Clark, Shaw et Cie from 1775 and
various owners afterwards.
MONTEREAU M^{AU} No 1
Impressed

Moorcroft Ltd, W.: (1913–)
Manufacturers of earthenware, including
art pottery, at Burslem, Staffordshire.
Founded by William Moorcroft. After his
death in 1945, continued by his son Walter.

William Moorcroft, 1913–45 (but also
appears on pieces decorated by Moorcroft
while at James Macintyre & Co.)

Other marks include "Moorcroft Burslem" and initials "W.M." in script for
Walter Moorcroft.

Moore, Bernard: (1853–1935)
English china manufacturer at Stoke-on-
Trent, Staffordshire, from 1905.
Factory marks:

    Painted

    BM

Artists' marks:

    Adams, John: (1882–1953)

Beardmore, Hilda

Billington, Dora May:
(1890–1968)

    Buttle, George A.:
(1870–1925)

Jackson, Gertrude

    Lindop, Hilda

    Ollier, Annie: (1878–1978)

Tomlinson, Reginald R.: (1885–1978)

Wilkes, Edward R.: (1861–1953)

Moore Brothers: (*fl.* 1870–1905)
English china manufacturers at Longton, Staffordshire.

c. 1902–05

Moore & Co: (*fl.* 1803–74)
English potters working the Wear Pottery at Sunderland, Co. Durham, taking it over shortly after it was founded by Brinton & Co in 1803.

MOORE & CO.
SOUTHWICK

MOORE & CO.
Impressed

Morley, Francis (*fl.* 1845–58)
First partner in firm of Ridgway, Morley, Wear and Co; sole proprietor in 1845, trading under his own name, or as Morley & Co (1850–58), or Morley & Ashworth (1858–62); purchased the Mason moulds and engravings.

Printed

Morris, Rowland James: (1847–1909)
English ceramic sculptor; modeller to the trade, e.g. to Bernard Moore at Longton, Staffordshire, and to J. S. Wilson, parian manufacturer at Longton.

Incised

Mortlock John, or Mortlocks Ltd: (*fl.* 1746–c. 1930)
London retailer who bought undecorated porcelain from various manufacturers (e.g. Swansea, Nantgarw, and Coalport), to be painted to his order by Randall, Robins, and other artists. His name is found on various articles, including Rockingham brown-glazed "Cadogan" teapots (made *c.* 1813–26).

Moscow, Russia
Francis Gardner's factory established here, making porcelain from 1758.

Ç

ГАРДНЕРЪ

In blue

Impressed

Transfer-printed

Popov factory established in 1806, closing 1872.

Moseley, John: (*fl. c.* 1802–22)
Perhaps two English potters of this name; Moseley & Dale recorded at Cobridge, Staffordshire (1802–18); a John Moseley recorded as making black basaltes at Burslem (*c.* 1809–22); also a John Moseley recorded as an earthenware manufacturer at Cobridge.

Moulds, marked (Staffordshire)
Examples dated and inscribed recorded:
A.W. Aaron Wood
R.W. with dates, Ralph Wood
J.B. John Baddeley

Moustiers, Basses Alpes, France
Faience made here from 1679 until 19th century. Various names associated with it.

Jean-Gaspard Féraud 1779–1817	Joseph-Gaspard Guichard *c.* 1755

	ferrat moustiers
Jean-François Thion 1758–88	Jean-Baptiste Ferrat 1718–91

Müller, E. & A.: (1890–)
Manufacturers of hard-paste porcelain at Schwarza-Saalbahn, Thuringia, Germany. Marks: "Corona" beneath a star; M in script; S V monogram in shield below crown.

Müller, Paul:
Founded hard-paste porcelain factory at Selb in 1890, using marks:

Münden, Hanover, Germany
Pottery made here from 1737.
Marks, three crescents from the arms of the founder, Carl Friedrich von Hanstein.

Murray, William Staite: (*fl.* 1919–40, d. 1962)
Studio potter, making stonewares; worked in England until 1940, then left for Southern Rhodesia.

Myatt Pottery Co.: (19th century)
Manufacturer of earthenwares at Bilston, Staffordshire.
Mark:

MYATT

N.B. Many potters of this name worked in the Potteries from *c.* 1790 to the 19th century.

Nantgarw, Glamorgan, Wales
Porcelain factory founded here in 1813 by William Billingsley; transferred to Swansea for a short time; Billingsley again at Nantgarw 1816 until 1820.

NANT·GARW
C.W.

Naples, Italy
Maiolica made here from end of 17th century; notably at factory of Biagio Giustiniani (end 18th century).
Marks recorded include:

269

Naples, Italy: Royal Factory
Soft-paste porcelain made here from 1771 to 1807; sold to Jean Poulard Prad et Cie, working at Capodimonte until 1834.

In colour or gold

Impressed   In blue   In red

In blue   In blue   In blue

Neale, James: (1740–1814)
English potter making earthenware at Hanley, Staffordshire (1778); trading as Neale & Wilson after Robert Wilson made a partner in 1786; as Neale & Co when other partners admitted; factory in hands of David Wilson & Sons (1801–17).

NEALE & Co

NEALE & Co

NEALE

Impressed

NEALE & CO

G

NEALE & WILSON

Impressed

Nevers, Nièvre, France
Faience industry founded here after arrival of Augustin Conrade from Albissola (c. 1585). One considerable factory working in 19th century, of H. Signoret and his successor A. Montaignon.
Marks recorded:

New Hall, Shelton, Staffordshire
Factory making hard-paste porcelain, c. 1782–c. 1812; bone china, from c. 1812 until closure in 1835
Marks:
On porcelain, pattern numbers prefaced by N or No in cursive style; on bone china, the words "New Hall" in a circle.

Initials and pattern number painted before 1812; circular mark transfer-printed 1812–35.

Niderviller, Lorraine, France
Faience made here from 1754 onward; porcelain made from 1765 by Beyerlé, followed by Comte de Custine in 1770–71

(*fl.* 1770–93). Factory reopened by Lanfrey (d. 1827), followed by M.L.G. Dryander. Marks are similar to those of Ludwigsburg.

Beyerlé

Beyerlé

In black Custine Custine In black
Custine

Impressed

Impressed
late 18th century

Lanfrey Lanfrey
Early 19th century

Dryander

Noël, Gustave (*fl.* 1755–93)
Painter at Sèvres.
Not to be confused with 19th-century faience painter of same name. Used the mark:

Nuremberg, Bavaria, Germany
Faience made here, 16th century onward.

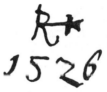

Reinhard Nuremberg

Initials used by hausmaler working at Nuremberg include:

A.H.   Abraham Helmhack (*fl.* 1675–1700)
I.H.   Johann Heel (1637–1709)
I.M.G. Johann Melchior Gebhard
J.L.F. Johann Ludwig Faber (*fl.* 1678–93)
M.S.   M. Schmidt

Nuremberg factory, Mark of under J. von Schwartz:

1880

Nymphenburg, Bavaria, Germany
Hard-paste porcelain made here 1755 to 1862, and onward.
Inventory marks:

Painted in purple

C. H
Zöhrgaden, 1773.

Churfürstliche Hof Zöhrgaden
(Electoral Court storeroom)

271

C.H. Conditoreij

j7.

j > 7j.

Churfürstliche Hof Conditoreij
(Electoral Court Confectionery)

Factory marks:

Impressed   Impressed

1763–77

Modern marks
Modellers' marks include:

F.B

Franz Bustelli
(fl. 1754–63)

J: Peter
Melchior

Johann Peter Melchoir
(fl. 1787–1822)
Painters' marks include:

J.W.
CCL   C Pusſher

Hausmalers' marks include those of
Amberg, J. A. Huber, etc.

.iAH.   Amberg 1774

K·

A:A·

With dates 1765, 1778

Nyon, near Geneva, Switzerland
Hard-paste porcelain factory founded here
in 1781 by Jacques Dortu, director until
1813.

In underglaze blue

Oettingen-Schrattenhofen, Bavaria, Germany
Pottery established at Oettingen about
1735, transferred later to Schrattenhofen.
Later products marked with name "Schrattenhofen" in one or two lines, with the
name of the painter or owner.

Ofen, Hungary
Factory making cream-coloured earthenware established c. 1795 here.
Mark: word OFEN impressed.

Offenbach, near Frankfurt-am-Main, Germany
Faience factory established here in 1739,
still in existence in 1807.

OFF   OFF

Offenbach

Oldfield & Co.: (c. 1838–88)
English manufacturers of stoneware at
Brampton near Chesterfield in Derbyshire.

OLDFIELD & CO MAKERS   **J. OLDFIELD**

Impressed   Impressed

Old Hall Earthenware Co. Ltd:
At Hanley, *c.* 1861 to July 1886; Old Hall Porcelain Works Ltd 1886–1902.

Printed or
moulded
c. 1861–86

Printed
Registered 1885
continued to 1902.
From 1891
"England" added

Olerys, Joseph (d. 1749) working with Laugier, Joseph:
Made faience at Moustiers, France, factory continuing under same name until 1790.

In ochre   In green

O'Neale, Jefferyes Hamet: (1734–1801)
Irish artist and ceramic decorator; worked at Chelsea (soon after 1752), and later as outside decorator for Worcester; his work is found on Worcester and Chelsea porcelain.

Orléans, Loiret, France
Soft-paste porcelain made here from 1753; hard-paste after 1770.

In blue

In red
Benoist le Brun 1806–12

Heraldic label found on Orléans soft-paste porcelain (1753–70).

Faience made here from the 17th century. Marks found on marbled ware made late 18th century:

GRAMMONT

LAINE FABQT

A ORLEANS

ORLEANS

Impressed

Ottweiller, Nassau-Saarbrücken, Germany
Hard-paste porcelain made here from 1763, but earthenware only during the last years (closed down 1797).

In gold, underglaze blue or incised

Oude Loosdrecht, Holland
Hard-paste porcelain factory transferred here from Weesp in 1771, working until 1784, then transferred to Amstel.

M . O . L M : o L M . O . L
✳   In blue   ✳

273

In blue	Incised

Oxshott Pottery, Surrey: (1919–)
Mark: OXSHOTT. Studio potters working individually here:

Denise K. Wren	Rosemary Wren

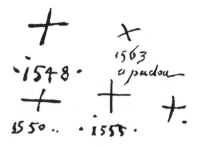

Henry D. Wren (d. 1947)

The marks are scratched into the rough clay, on the base of the pot.

Padua, Italy
Maiolica and lead-glazed earthenware made here from the end of the 15th century until about the end of the 18th century.

Two marks recorded on porcelain, and attributed to Padua are as follows: the date 1627 and initials I.G.P.F.; date 1638 and initials G.G.P.F. The initials P.F. might stand for "Padovano fece"; a cross potent and a hatched imitation Chinese character also appear, e.g.:

Palais Royal, Paris
Important decorating shop run here in early 19th century by Darte frères, using stencilled marks;

DARTE
Pal Royal
Nº 21

DARTE
FRERES
A PARIS

Darte also ran workshops (1790–1840) at rue de Charonne, rue de la Roquette, rue Popincourt, and rue Fonaine-au-Roi.

Palmer, Humphrey: (*fl. c.* 1760–78)
Earthenware manufacturer at Hanley, Staffordshire; rival and imitator of Wedgwood.

PALMER

Palsjö, near Helsingborg, Sweden
Faience factory established here by Michael Anders Cöster in 1765; taken over by Heinrich Wolff in 1770, closing down in 1774.
Mark: letters PF (Palsjö Fabrik) or PFC (Palsjö Fabrik-Cöster) with date and other numerals.

Pardoe, Thomas: (1770–1823)
English porcelain decorator (mostly flowers); worked for Derby, Worcester, and Swansea (*c.* 1785–1809); independent enameller at Bristol (1809–21); at Nantgarw in 1821.
Signatures recorded:

Pardoe, Fecit Bristol.

Pardoe
Cardiff

Painted

Passau, Bavaria, Germany
Hard-paste porcelain made here from 1840
by Dressel, Kister & Co.

Reproductions of Höchst porcelain figures
made here from old moulds, using the
Höchst (*q.v.*) "wheel" mark.

Patanazzi family: (at Urbino)
Had maiolica workshop; signed pieces by
four members of the family are recorded;
Antonio (1580); Alfonso (1606); Francesco (1617); and Vincenzio (1620).

ALF.
P.F.
VRBINI
1606

FATTO·IN VRBINO

ALFONSO PATANAZZI
FECIT
VRBINI 1606
ALF.
P.F.
VRBINI
1606

Pattison, James: (*fl. c.* 1818–30)
English earthenware toy manufacturer at
Lane End, Staffordshire.
Name and date recorded:

Pecs, Fünfkirchen, Hungary
Factory established at Fünfkirchen in 1855
by W. Zsolnay using these marks:

ZSOLNAY
PÉCS

Impressed

In lustre   In blue

Impressed   Impressed

Pellatt & Green: (*fl. c.* 1802–30)
Dealers' name occurring as mark on English porcelain, notably on Swansea.

Pellipario, Nicola (*fl.* 1515–*c.* 1550)
Maiolica painter, working successively at
Castel Durante, doubtfully at Fabriano,
and at Urbino.
See FONTANA FAMILY.

Pennis, Anthony: (*fl.* 1756–70)
Owner of Delft (*q.v.*) factory De Twee
Scheepjes (The Two Little Ships), which
continued under his widow (1770–82), and
then under his son Jan.

Pennis, Johannes: (1702–88)
Proprietor of De Porceleyne Schotel (The
Porcelain Dish) at Delft (1725–64).
Mark attributed to him:

Pesaro, near Urbino, Italy
Maiolica made here during late 15th and
16th centuries; revived in 18th century.

Painted on Pesaro maiolica
16th–18th centuries

Possibly Pesaro Gabice
16th century

Casali and Caligari

Modern mark on imitation Urbino
ware by Magrini & Co.
established in 1870

Petit, Jacob (b. 1796) **and Mardochée**:
Made hard-paste porcelain from 1830 at
Fontainebleau and later at Belleville. This
factory sold out in 1862, and another
opened in Rue Paradis Poissonière. Models, moulds and marks in use until 1886 and
later.

j.P.

Meissen models and marks copied.

Petite Rue St Gilles, Paris
Porcelain factory founded 1783 by F. M.
Honoré, working until *c.* 1822(?).

Picasso, Pablo: (1881–1973)

Pijnacker, Adriaen: (*fl.* 1675–1707)
Worked De Porceleyne Schotel with his
brother-in-law Cornelisz Keyser (d. 1684)
and brother Jacobus Pijnacker; worked De
Twee Scheepjes (1690–94); foreman of De
Wildeman (1696-1707)
Mark ascribed to Cornelisz Keyser and
Adriaen Pijnacker:

Mycock, W. S.

Rodgers, Gwladys

Pilkingtons Tile & Pottery Co.: (1892–
1938) **Pilkingtons Tiles Ltd** (1938–) Clifton
Junction, near Manchester.
Manufacturers of earthenwares, tiles and
art pottery; and 'Royal Lancastrian'
ornamental wares from *c.* 1897.

Impressed
c. 1914–35

Factory mark *c.* 1904–14. Roman numeral
below refers to year.

Artists' marks recorded:

Pillivuyt & Company:
Made porcelain at three factories, at
Foescy, Mehun and Noirlac, established in
1817.

In gold

Barlow, A.

Pinxton, Derbyshire
Porcelain made here *c.* 1796–*c.* 1812. Most
of it is unmarked.

Cundall, Charles E.

Crane, Walter
(1846–1915)

Rarely, name "Pinxton" in script or initial
"P" preceding a pattern number.

Pirkenhammer, Brezova, Bohemia
Factory established 1830 by Friedrich
Höcke; let to Granz & Brotthäuser 1806;
sold to Martin Fischer and Kristof
Reichenbach 1811; traded as Fischer &
Mieg for a time, and as Christian Fischer
1845–53.

Day, Lewis F.

F&R

Impressed

C.F.

F&M

Impressed

Pirotti family: (*fl.* 16th century)
Made maiolica at Faenza, from *c.* 1500. Inscriptions recorded include: FATOIN FAENZA IN CAXA PIROTA; and FATE. IN. FAEnza. IOXEF. In CAsa PIROTE 1525.
Workshop mark: a globe scored across at right angles, with a circle or pellet in one segment sometimes with a flame issuing from it.
See FAENZA.

Plant, Benjamin: (fl. *c.* 1870–*c.* 1820)
Made tablewares and lustred and enamelled figures; his son Thomas Plant (1801–53) also made pottery figures.

B.Plant
Lane End

TP

Painted

Plant, R.H. & S.L. (Ltd):
Porcelain at Tuscan Works, Longton, *c.* 1898 to present day.

Pleydell-Bouverie, Katherine: (1895–1985)
Studio potter.

Plymouth, Devon
Hard-paste porcelain factory established here in 1768; moved to Bristol 1773; eventually sold in 1781.
A number of different marks were used, principally variants on the conjoined numbers 2 and 4:

2_4

Poitiers, Haute-Vienne, France
Mark recorded:

A MORREINE
Poitiers
1752

Morreine was probably a modeller of figures in "terre de pipe" and Pierre Pasquier, "fabricant de faience émaillée". Felix Faulcon, a local printer, made faience here from 1776:

F·F·

Poole Pottery Ltd (*see* Carter, Stabler & Adams)

Poppelsdorf, Bonn, Germany
Earthenware made here from *c.* 1755; firm of Ludwig Kessel established in 1825.

Potschappel, *see* THIEME.

Pountney & Co: (*fl.* 1839–1969) English earthenware manufacturers at Bristol, Somerset.

Impressed   In blue   *c.* 1939+
c. 1815–35

Pouyat, J.: (*fl.* mid-19th century)
Started porcelain factory at Limoges in 1841, which has been continued by descendants.

Pratt, F. and R. & Co. Ltd: (*c.* 1818–)
Potters manufacturing earthenware at Fenton, Staffordshire; they specialized in multi-colour printing from contemporary narrative pictures.

**PRATT
FENTON**

Transfer-printed:
c. 1870 into 20th century

Pratt, William: (1753–99)
English master potter at Lane Delph, Staffordshire, *c.* 1780–99.

PRATT
Impressed

N.B. Other potters of same name used similar mark.

Premières, Côte-d'Or, France
Faience factory established here near Dijon in 1783, by one J. Lavalle or Laval, continued into 19th century by his descendants.

Either painted or stencilled

Proskau, Silesia, Germany
Faience made here from 1763 until 1850.

1763–69   1770–83   1783–93   1783

PROSKAU
IMPRESSED
1788–1850

Pulles, Georges: (*fl.* 19th century)
Imitator of Palissy wares, working at Paris.

PULL

In relief, incised, or painted in enamels

Purmerend, Holland
Factory making peasant art types of Dutch pottery.

Putten, J. van, and Company, Delft (*fl.* 1830–50)
Made earthenware in Delft tradition.

"P.V." mark
Found on earthenware figures of Shakespeare (after Scheemaker's statue in Westminster Abbey) and Milton, of late 18th-century date; perhaps for "Palmer: Voyez"; unconfirmed.

Quimper, Finistère, France
Faience made here from the end of the 17th century; stoneware was made during the 19th century.

P. P. Caussy (*fl.* 1743–82) Hubaudière (1782–)

Radford, Samuel (1879–1957)
Manufacturer of porcelain at Fenton, Staffordshire. Various marks incorporating SR monogram and crown. "England" added from 1891.

Raeren, Rhineland, Germany
Stoneware made here, *c.* 1560 until early 17th century.
Potters initials recorded include:
I.E. Jan Emens Mennicken (*c.* 1566–94)
I.M. Jan Mennicken (1576)
T.W. and T.W.K. Tilman Wolf "Kannenbacker"
Also, in 19th century:
H.S. Hubert Schiffer (*fl. c.* 1880)

Randall, Thomas Martin: (1786–1859)
Decorator of porcelain for London dealers; said to have started a soft-paste factory at Madeley, Shropshire (*c.* 1825), making imitation Sèvres.
Mark recorded:

Ratcliff, William: (*fl. c.* 1831–40)
Manufacturer of white and transfer-printed earthenware at Hanley, Staffordshire

Rathbone, Thomas & Co: (*fl.* 1810–45)
Made earthenware with distinct Staffordshire flavour at Portobello, Scotland.

or:

T. RATHBONE

Ratibor, Silesia, Germany
Cream-coloured earthenware made here by Beaumont of Leeds (1794–1803), followed by Salomon Baruch (1803); closed down in 1828.
Mark:
BEAUMONT or BARUCH
Impressed

Rato, near Lisbon, Portugal
Faience factory established here by Thomaz Brunetto in 1767; succeeded by S. de Almeida (1771–*c.* 1814).

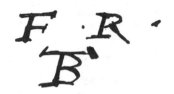

Fabrica Rato/Thomas Brunetto

Rauenstein, Thuringia, Germany
Hard-paste porcelain factory established here by the three Greiners in 1783; continues today as limited company.

Ravenna, Italy
Maiolica made here during the 16th century.
Mark recorded on piece not now accepted as genuine:

Reed & Taylor: (c. 1839–73)
Reed, James:
Reed, John: (until c. 1873)
English potters; successive owners of the earthenware factory called The Mexborough, or Rock, Pottery, at Mexborough, Yorkshire.

• R E E D •

Impressed   Transfer-printed

Registration marks:
These appeared on English earthenwares, and referred to the designs with which they were decorated; in two cycles, 1842–67 and 1868–83; consisted of a lozenge, with code-letters and numerals assigned by the "Registration of Designs" office; they were arranged thus:
Cycle 1842–67

Year letters 1842–67:

X	1842	P	1851	Z	1860
H	1843	D	1852	R	1861
C	1844	Y	1853	O	1862
A	1845	J	1854	G	1863
I	1846	E	1855	N	1864
F	1847	L	1856	W	1865
U	1848	K	1857	Q	1866

S	1849	B	1858	T	1867
V	1850	M	1859		

Month letters 1842–67:

C	January	E	May	D	September
G	February	M	June	B	October
W	March	I	July	K	November
H	April	R	August	A	December

Cycle 1868–83

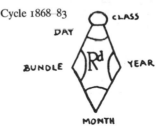

Year letters 1868–1883:

X	1868	U	1874	J	1880
H	1869	S	1875	E	1881
C	1870	V	1876	L	1882
A	1871	P	1877	G	1883
I	1872	D	1878		
F	1873	Y	1879		

Month letters 1868–83:

C	January	E	May	D	September
G	February	M	June	E	October
W	March	I	July	K	November
H	April	R	August	A	December

Note: in 1878, from 1st to 6th March, the registration letters were G for the month and W for the year.

Registration of marks
In 1764 an order regulating the use of marks was issued by the faience potters of Delft.
In 1766, when the Sèvres porcelain monopoly broke down, potters were authorized to produce porcelain with certain restrictions, provided they registered with the police the mark or marks to be used on their wares.
It is only after these enactions that the interpretation of marks becomes trustworthy.

Rendsburg, Holstein, Germany
Earthenware made here from 1765 to 1818.
Marks rarely found; recorded, on faience:
C.R. for Clar/Rendsburg, over initials of painter, and figures for year. (Christian Friedrich Clar, owner, later manager only, *fl.* 1765–98)
on cream-coloured earthenware:
RENI, or RF

Rennes, Ille-et-Vilaine, France
Lead-glazed earthenware (from 16th century) and faience (from 1748) made here.
Marks recorded:

J. B. Alexis Bourgouin
modeller (b. 1734)

Reval, Estonia
Faience made here by Karl Christian Fick
from c. 1775 until his death in 1792.

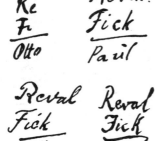

Reygens or Reygensbergh, Augustin:
Owner of De Vergulde Boot factory at
Delft, 1663–66.

Rhead, Charlotte (1885–1947)
Pottery decorator working for various
manufacturers. The backstamp "Lottie
Rhead Ware" appears on various wares
from the 1920s onwards.

Ridgway, J. & W.: (1814–c. 1830)
Brothers in partnership, manufacturing
earthenware at Hanley, Staffordshire.

Transfer-printed

Ridgway, Morley, Wear & Co.:
Manufacturers of earthenware at Shelton,
c. 1836–42 and, as Ridgway & Morley,
c. 1842–45.

Ridgway & Morley
c. 1842–45

Ridgway, William (& Co.):
Earthenware at Bell Works, Shelton, and
Church Works, Hanley, c. 1830–54.

Rie, Lucie: (fl. from 1938)
Studio potter working in London from
1938; Hans Coper working with her from
1947. Both their marks may occur on one
piece.

Hans Coper   Lucie Rie

282

Riley, John and Richard: (*fl.* 1802–28)
English manufacturers of china, stoneware, cream-coloured and printed wares, at Burslem, Staffordshire.

Impressed
c. 1802–28

Robert, Joseph-Gaspard or Jean-Gaspard:
(*fl. c.* 1750–*c.* 1795)
At Marseilles, made faience (from *c.* 1750) and porcelain (from *c.* 1770).
Marks:
On faience: letter R
On porcelain: JR as monogram

Robinson and Leadbeater: (*c.* 1864–1924)
English manufacturers of decorative parian wares at Stoke-on-Trent, Staffordshire.

Impressed *c.* 1885+

Printed *c.* 1905–24

Rogers, John and George: (*fl. c.* 1784–1814)
English potters making earthenware at Longport, Staffordshire; trading as John Rogers & Son from 1815 until 1842. Mark: name "Rogers" impressed.

Rome
Porcelain made here from second half of 18th century.
Marks recorded:
ROMA I MAG 1769
with crossed CC beneath a crown
(incised)
(For Carlo Coccorese, working for the Cuccumos factory, 1761–69. The factory closed *c.* 1781.)
G VOLPATO ROMA
(For Volpato factory, *fl.* 1785–1818)
Maiolica made at Rome from the 14th to the 17th century.

Cream-coloured earthenware made by the Volpato family 1785–1831.

Rörstrand, Sweden
Faience factory founded in 1726; in 1926 transferred to Gothenburg; in 1932 went to Lidköping. Continues.

Very early mark

1763

RORSTRAND   Rorstrand

Impressed
c. 1780

IRIS

RÖRSTRAND

Transfer-printed

From 1884   Modern mark

SWEDEN

GRATINA
UGNS · ELDFAST
OVENWARE
22

Modern mark

Rosenburg, The Hague, Holland:
Factory founded 1885 using the following marks:

Rosenthal, Selb, Bavaria, Germany
Factory established by P. Rosenthal in 1880; continues today.

Ross, James: (1745–1821)
Engraver; his signature appears on a number of pieces of Worcester porcelain.

J Rofs Vigornienfis sculp

Rossetti, Giorgio Giacinto: (*fl.* from 1729 to mid-18th century)
Faience painter working at Lodi (Ferretti factory, 1729) and at Turin (his uncle Giorgio Rossetti's factory, 1737). Various signatures recorded:
Lodi G Giacijnto Rossettij fecit
Laude Hijacintus Rossetus *f.* 1729
Fabricha di G. Giacinto Rossetti in Lodi
Fabrica di Gior: Giacin: Rossetti à Tarazzi in Lodi
Hyaci Rossettas

Rotterdam, Holland
Centre of tile-making industry; tile panels and pictures made here. Artists who signed their work include:
Cornelius Boumeester (*c.* 1650–1733)
Jan Aalmis (1714– after 1788)
Signature of independent porcelain decorator recorded:

F. L. S.
A Rotterdam
JW M̃: 1812

Rouen, Seine-Inférieure, France
Faience made here *c.* 1535–70; and from 1647 onward. Names connected with Rouen include: Masseot Abaquesne (q.v.)

(fl. 1545–c. 1551/64) followed by widow and son until c. 1570; Edme Poterat, who had monopoly from 1647 for fifty years. After this, many factories include:
Poterat and Letellier
Bertin, Fouquay, Heugue and Vallet
Guilliaud and Levavasseur
Pottier and Mouchard
Many marks recorded, of which large number must be those of painters or workmen.

Heugue Heugue
1698–early 19th century

Levavasseur
1700–

J. Bertin
c. 1700–1750

P. Caussy
1707–

Guillibaud factory
1720–50

Pinxit
·1736·
·CB·

Claude Borne

Borne
Pinxit
Anno
1738

Claude Borne

Fossé
c. 1740

Dieul, painter c. 1755

M. Vallet,
1756

P. Mouchard,
c. 1750

Letellier,
c. 1780

Rubati, Pasquale: (fl. 18th century)
Painter of maiolica at Clerici factory at Milan; set up rival establishment in 1759 or 1762.

Rubelles, Seine-et-Marne, France
Faience factory working from 1836 until 1858.

Rue Amelot, Paris
Hard-paste porcelain made here from 1784; factory survived until 1825.

In red
stencilled

In blue

In gold
c. 1820

Rue de Bondy, Paris
Hard-paste porcelain made here from 1781 (partnered by Guerhard from c. 1786. At Rue du Temple 1795, and Boulevard Saint-Martin 1825.

DIHL
Rue de Bondy

Rue de Crussol, Paris
Porcelain works started here by Englishman, Christopher Potter (1789).
Marks recorded:

Potter 4   B Potter 42

In underglaze blue

Factory said to have been transferred to E. Blancheron in 1792.

EB

or E. BLANCHERON in relief on biscuit pieces.

Rue de la Roquette, Paris
White faience made by Ollivier, during the second half 18th century

OLLIVIER A PARIS

Impressed

ollivier a paris

Hard-paste porcelain made here from 1773.
Souroux's mark:

S

In underglaze blue

Another factory, Les Trois Levrettes, was worked by Vincent Dubois from 1774 until 1787. Mark similar to La Courtille:

In underglaze blue

Rue de Reuilly, Paris
Hard-paste porcelain made here by Jean-Joseph Lassia from *c.* 1774 until 1784.

L

In colour or gold

L:

Rue des Récollets, Paris
Hard-paste porcelain cameos made here by Desprès (Desprez) 1793–1825, with mark DESPREZ.

Rue du Petit Carrousel, Paris
Charles-Barthélémy Guy had decorating establishment here in 1774; continued by his son Charles until 1800.

Stencilled in red
The name of the decorator, Perche, who was employed here, sometimes accompanies the mark.

Rue Popincourt, Paris
Hard-paste porcelain made here from 1772 by Johann Nepomuk Hermann Nast; continued by sons in 19th century

NAST   NAST a Paris

n ast.
p...

NAST   nast

Stencilled in red

Rue Thiroux, Paris
Hard-paste porcelain made here *c.* 1775 by
André-Marie Leboeuf; patron Queen
Marie Antoinette, whose monogram with
crown above was used as mark. After the
Revolution, factory in hands of Guy and
Housel (1797–98) and Leveillé, closing in
c. 1820.

Painted or incised, *c.* 1898+

Rye, Sussex, England
Earthenware made here during the 19th
century, at the Cadborough works; and at
the Belle Vue Pottery (1869 to early 20th
century), the latter using these marks to
1939.

In red

In blue,
red or gold

Also recorded:

Housel

Ruscoe, William: (*fl. c.* 1920–70s)
English artist potter: Stoke-on-Trent, Staffordshire (1920–44) and Exeter, Devon
(1944–70s).

Sadler & Green: (*fl. c.* 1756–99)
English transfer-printers, working at
Liverpool, Lancashire; decorated large
quantities of Staffordshire and Liverpool
earthenware; Wedgwood's Queen's ware
sent regularly to them; much of earlier
work in black, or black and red; Sadler
retired in 1770, Green continued to 1799.

SADLER
SADLER & GREEN

Saint-Amand-les-Eaux, Nord, France
Faience and earthenware made here in
18th century by Fauquez family.

Soft-paste porcelain made here by Jean-
Baptiste-Joseph Fauquez, 1771 to 1778.
Revived by J. de Bettignies of Tournay
c. 1818 until 1882.

Ruskin Pottery:
W. Howson Taylor, the proprietor, made
earthenware at Smethwick, near Birmingham, 1898–1935.

TAYLOR

Impressed *c.* 1898+

RUSKIN
RUSKIN POTTERY

St Clément, Meurthe-et-Moselle, France
Offshoot of Lunéville, working from 1757
to end 18th century. Revived *c.* 1824.

S. Clement

In blue   Stencilled in blue   Impressed on figures

Saint Cloud, Seine-et-Oise, France
Faience made here from *c.* 1670.

Soft-paste porcelain made here from *c.* 1693–1766 by the Chicanneau and Trou families.
Mark of the "sun-in-its-splendour" used from *c.* 1695 until 1722.

In blue

From *c.* 1722 until 1766, the mark included the initials of the factory and proprietor:

Incised in the paste
or painted in blue

St Petersburg, or Petrograd, Russia
Hard-paste porcelain made here from 18th century onward. Russian Imperial Porcelain Factory in regular production by 1758: continued under patronage of Catherine II.

In blue   Court inventory mark
Mark of Catherine II 1762–96

Paul I 1796–1801

Alexander I 1801–25

Nicholas I 1825–55

Alexander II 1855–81

288

Alexander III 1881–94	1900 Nicholas II 1894–1917	Soviet 1917– ?1991

Other less important factories were established by Babubin and Kornilov in the 19th century. Marks recorded:

Корниловыхъ

Korniloff
1835–

Б

Babunin
c. 1812–30

Saint-Porchaire, Deux-Sèvres, France
Earthenware made here, 1525–60.
Only one mark recorded:

Salt, Ralph: (1782–1846)
English ceramic decorator, and later (from 1828) a manufacturer of figures and "porcelain tablets" at Hanley, Staffordshire.

Impressed or relief moulded

Salvini, Florence
These marks occur on reproductions of Urbino/Gubbio lustres, and imitations of early maiolica styles:

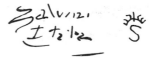

Samson, (Edme), & Co, 7 Rue Béranger, Paris
Made reproductions from 1845 onward; many pieces probably unmarked.

On reproductions of Chinese export porcelain. (Not accepted as Samson by some authorities)

On porcelain

On Japanese and Chinese

On Persian and Hispano-Moresque

On Meissen

On Meissen

Marks of many other factories were also used.

San Quirico d'Orcia, Tuscany, Italy
Maiolica made here from 1693 until c. 1724, and again later.

289

Sargadelos, northern Spain
Cream-coloured earthenware made here from 1804 until 1875.
Many marks used, mostly incorporating the name of the town.

Savona, Liguria, Italy
Maiolica made in Savona and Albissola near Genoa, 16th century to 18th century.
Marks of numerous workshops recorded:

Girolamo
Salomini or Siccardi

Conrade

Fortress mark
of Guidoboni

Sarreguemines, Lorraine, France
Factory for "faience fine" established here *c*. 1770 by M. Fabry and Paul Utzscheider; made imitation Wedgwood in the 19th century.

Sarguemines

SARREGUEMINES

**MAJOLICA
SARREGUEMINES**
702ᴾ

Pharos of Genoa
mark of Levantino

Luigi Levantino

Falcon mark of Folco

Fish mark of
Pescetto

Sun in its splendour
Salomini

On ware signed Agostino Ratti

Sceaux, Seine, France
Faience factory working here from *c.* 1735 until 1793.

Painted

Painted

The S.P. and anchor marks indicate the patronage (from 1775) of the Duc de Penthièvre, Grand-Amiral de France. Other initials, with conjectural meaning:
C.S. perhaps Chapelle/Sceaux
   Jacques Chapelle *fl.* here 1749–59
G.S. perhaps Glot/Sceaux
   Richard Glot, owner 1772–93
Soft-paste porcelain made at Sceaux, but surreptitiously. Marks:

Incised

Schaper, Johann: (1621–70)
Nuremberg painter of schwarzlot on faience.

Schaphuysen, near Crefeld, Rhineland, Germany
Slipware potters worked here using sgraffiato technique; wares dating from 1713 to 1795 recorded. Potters' names inscribed include:
Christianus Lappen 1713
Johann Franssen 1749
Paulus Hammelkers 1743
Gerrit Evers 1770
Gerrit Evers, 1795

Schierholz, C. G. & Sohn 1817–
Manufacturers of hard-paste porcelain at Plaue-on-Havel, Thuringia. Mark: a crown over shield with tree oak leaves.

Schlaggenwald, Bohemia, Czechoslovakia
Hard-paste porcelain factory established here 1792 by Paulus, Pöschl and Reumann; the letter S, painted or incised, was used as the factory mark. Factory owned by Lippert and Haas from 1803 until 1843; descendants continued the business.

Schleswig, Germany
Faience made here from 1755 to 1814.
Usual mark: letter S over initials of owners
and/or painters.

Johann Leihamer
(painter)
1758

Conrade Bade
(painter)
1764–91

Schlierbach
Earthenware made here from c. 1830.

Schney, Bavaria, Germany
Hard-paste porcelain made here from
c. 1783 to early 20th century. Mark: the
word SCHNEY impressed or the letter S
in blue. Later mark: St Andrew's cross
over letter S.

Closely similar to mark used by Samson of
Paris.

Schorndorf, Württemberg, Germany
Hard-paste porcelain factory established
here in 1904 under name of Bauer &
Pfeiffer, using following marks:

Marks of the Württembergische Porzellan
Manufaktur:

Schrezheim, near Ellwangen, Württemberg, Germany
Faience made here from 1752 until 1872.

Schütz, Lidwig:
Made decorative faience in the style of the
Renaissance, from c. 1871.

SCHÜTZ   L SCHÜTZ
CILLI   Cilly

Schwerin, Mecklenburg, Germany
Faience made here from 1753 onward.
Mark included the initial of the potter,
J. A. Apfelstadt (d. 1771), with name or
initial of the place over the painter's or
decorator's mark:

Scott, Anthony
Potter owning the Southwick Pottery, and
the Newbottle Pottery, at Sunderland, Co.
Durham.

SCOTT
Impressed

Scott Bros: (fl. c. 1786–96)
Made stoneware, red ware, and
ornamental pottery at Portobello, Midlothian, Scotland.
Mark recorded:

SCOTT BROS
Impressed

Seacombe Pottery:
Established 1851 near Liverpool (but in
Cheshire) by John Godwin. Closed by
October 1871.

LIVERPOOL

Printed

Impressed   Impressed, early 19th century

In 1841 the factory became part of the Villeroy & Boch company.

Seefried, Peter Antonius: (1742–1812)
Porcelain modeller and "repairer" working at Nymphenburg (*c.* 1756–66), then at Ludwigsburg (1766) and Kelsterbach (1767). Again at Nymphenburg, 1769 until 1810.
Mark perhaps his:
Letter S incised, repairer's mark occasionally found on Kelsterbach figures.

Segovia, Spain
Modern pottery made here by firm of Zuloaga.

Zuloaga

Selman (Seltman), J. & W.: (*fl. c.* 1865)
English manufacturers of bronzed and earthenware toys, at Tunstall, Staffordshire.

SELMAN

Impressed

Septfontaines, Luxemburg
The brothers Boch made earthenware here from 1766; Pierre-Joseph Boch became sole proprietor in 1796.

Impressed   Impressed

Impressed   In blue

Seville, Spain
Faience made here in 19th century in suburb of Triana; another factory was worked by M. Francesco de Aponte and Pickman & Co.

Sèvres, France
Factory at Vincennes, 1745; transferred to Sèvres 1756; moved to St Cloud in 1876. Soft-paste porcelain made 1745 to 1800; hard-paste porcelain from 1769 onward. Mark of crossed L's used in various forms at Vincennes, and from 1756 to 1793 at Sèvres.

Various forms of the crossed L's mark

Other examples, with date letters:

In blue;
year 1753

In red; year
1778; mark of
painter Dieu

In blue; year
mark 1759: mark
of painter Binet

In blue;
year 1780

In blue; year 1788
mark of gilder
Vincent, in gold

First Republic, 1793–1804:

E T.

1793–1804,
in purple, mark
of the gilder LF
in gold

G I

1793–1804,
in blue; mark
of the gilder GI
in gold

1793–1804,
in blue

In blue

RF.
de Sevres

In blue

First Empire, 1804–14:

M. Impl
de Sevres
7

Stencilled in red

Other 19th-century marks:

Printed in red
1810–14

In blue   In blue
           1814–24
      (Reign of Louis XVIII)

Sèvres   Sèvres   Sèvres
 24   25   27

In blue: 30   30
           1824–30
    (Reign of Charles X)

In blue 1830   Sèvres
                30

294

In gold or blue
1834

In chrome green

In blue or gold
1845

In red
Second Empire
1852–70

Destination marks:
in red

PAY DE BRETEUIL

CH DREUX

SÈVRES 1848
In red,
1848,
decoration mark

RF 49
In red,
1849, year
of decoration

S.51
In chrome green,
1851, year of
manufacture

Year marks 1753–77

A	1753	I	1761	Q	1769
B	1754	J	1762	R	1770
C	1755	K	1763	S	1771
D	1756	L	1764	T	1772
E	1757	M	1765	U	1773
F	1758	N	1766	V	1774
G	1759	O	1767	X	1775
H	1760	P	1768	Y	1776
				Z	1777

Year marks 1778–93:

AA	1778	FF	1783	KK	1788
BB	1779	GG	1784	LL	1789
CC	1780	HH	1785	MM	1790
DD	1781	II	1786	NN	1791
EE	1782	JJ	1787	OO	1792
PP			until 17th July, 1793		

Examples with year marks:

1763   1781   1782

Date signs used 1801–17:

Tg	1801	7	1807	tz	1813
X	1802	8	1808	qz	1814
II	1803	9	1809	qn	1815
÷	1804	10	1810	sz	1816
–//–	1805	oz	1811	ds	1817
W	1806	dz	1812		

Examples with date signs:

M N^le Sèvres –//–   M.Imp^le de Sèvres ÷   M.Imp^le de Sèvres W

1803 or 1805   1804   1806

Many artists' marks were used. The following is a selective list of some of the most important.

Marks or signatures of artists:

Aloncle, François: 1758
birds and animals

André, Jules: 1843–69
landscapes

Antheaume, Jean-Jacques:
1754
landscapes and animals

*Armand, Pierre-Louis-
Philippe:* 1746
birds and flowers

Asselin: 1764–1804
portraits, miniatures

Aubert, aîné: 1755
flowers

Bailly: 1753–93

Barbin, François-Hubert:
1815–49
ornament

Bardet: 1751–58
flowers

Barrat: 1769–91
flowers, garlands, fruits

Barré: late 18th century
flower sprays

Barré, Louis Désiré: 1846–81
flowers

Barriat, Charles:
1848–83
figures

Baudouin: 1750–90
gilder

Becquet: 1748
flowers

Béranger, Antoine:
1807–46
figures

Bertrand: 1750–1808
detached flowers

Bienfait, Jean-Baptiste:
1756–62
gilder and painter

Binet: 1750–76
flowers

*Binet, Mme (née Chanou,
Sophie):* 1779–98
flowers

*Boitel, Charles-
Marie-Pierre:*
1797–1822
gilder

Boucher: 1754
flowers and garlands

Bouchet, Jean: 1757–93
landscapes

Boucot, P.:
late 18th century
fruit and flowers

Bouillat: 1800–1811
flowers and landscapes

Boulanger, père: 1754–84
gilder

Boulanger, fils: 1770–81
flowers, pastorals, child
subjects

Boullemier, Antoine-Gabriel:
1802–42
gilder

*Boullemier, François-
Antoine:* 1802–42
gilder

Boullemier, Hilaire-François:
1813–55
gilder

Bulidon: 1763–92
flowers

*Bunel, Mme (née
Buteux, Manon)*
1778–1817
flowers

Buteux, Charles: 1760–
flowers and emblems

Buteux, jeune: 1759–66
flowers

Buteux, Guillaume: 1759
pastoral subjects and
children

Buteux, Théodore:
1786–1822

Cabau, Eugène-Charles
1847–84
flowers

Capelle, Mme: flowers
or
Capelle: 1746–
painter of landscapes

Capronnier, François:
early 19th century

Cardin: 1749–93
flowers

Carrier or Carrié: 1752–57
flowers

Castell: 1771–1800
landscapes, birds, hunting
scenes

Caton: 1749–98
pastorals, children, portraits

Catrice: 1757–74
flowers

Chabry: 1765–87
pastoral scenes

Chanou, Mme (née Durosey):
before 1800
flowers

Chapuis, aîné: 1756–93
flowers and birds

Chapuis, jeune: before 1800
flowers

Charrin, Mlle Fanny:
1814–26
figures and portraits

Chauvaux, aîné: 1752–88
gilder

Chauvaux, fils: 1773–83
bouquets

Chevalier: 1755–57
flowers
cf. mark of Boulanger, fils

Choisy: 1770–1812
flowers and ornaments

Chulot: 1755–1800
emblems, flowers,
arabesques

Commelin: before 1800
flowers and garlands

Constant: 1804–15
gilder

Constantin: 1823–45
figure subject

Cornaille, Antoine-Toussaint:
1755–93
flowers

Couturier: 1783
gilder

**Davignon, Jean-
François:** 1807–15
figures in landscapes

Degault, Jean-Marie:
1808–17
figures

Delafosse, Denis: 1805–15
figures (cf. Davignon)

**Derischweiler, Jean-Charles
Gérard:** 1838–88, gilder

**Despérais or Depé-
rais, Claude:** 1794–
1822, ornaments

Deutsche: c. 1815
ornament

Develly, Jean-Charles:
1813–48
animals in landscapes

Didier, Charles-Antoine:
1819–48
ornament

Dieu: various periods, 1777–
1810
painter of Chinese subjects
and flowers; gilding

K K. **Dodin:** 1754–1800
figures, portraits, etc.

Drand: before 1780
chinoiseries, gilding

D 7 **Drouet, Gilbert:** 1785–1825
flowers

Dubois, Jean-René: 1756–77
flowers

**Ducluzeau, Mme (née
Durand, Marie-
Adelaide):** 1807–48
figures, portraits

D.y **Durosey, Charles-Christian-
Marie:** 1802–30
gilder

D. D.. D **Dusolle:** before 1800
flowers

DT. **Dutanda:** 1765–1802
flowers

Evans: 1752–1805
birds, butterflies, landscapes

F **Falot or Fallot:** before 1800
birds and ornament

Fontaine: 1752–after 1800
emblems and flowers

Fontaine, Jean-Joseph:
1827–57
flowers

♡ **Fontélliau, A.:** 1747–80
gilder

Y. **Fouré:** 1749–62
flowers

Fritsch: 1763–64
figures, children, etc.

Fumez: 1777–1804
flowers

Gautier or Gauthier: 1787–91
landscapes and animals

G **Genest:** 1752–89
figures and genre

✝ ✝ **Génin:** 1756
flowers

g·g **Georget:** 1802–23
figures

Gd Gd. **Gérard, Claude-
Charles:** 1771–1824
pastoral subjects
and miniatures

γ. t **Gérard, Mme (née Vautrin):**
1781–1802
flowers

A A **Girard:** 1762–64
arabesque

DS **Godin:** 1792–1833
gilder, painter, ground-
layer or
Godin, Mme

Gomery: 1756
flowers

Gt **Grémont, jeune:** 1769–81
garlands and bouquets

X x **Grison:** 1749–71
gilder

jh. **Henrion, aîné:** 1768–84
flowers

hc **Héricourt:** 1770–77
garlands and detached
flowers (or "He")

Hilken: before 1800
figures

H **Houry:** 1747–55
flowers

h.Ɔ. **Huard:** 1811–46
ornament in various styles

Z Z **Joyau:** 1766–75
flowers

j. j **Jubin:** 1772–75
gilder

L Gⁱⁱ **Langlacé:** 1807–14
landscapes

*ʃ LR
LR* **La Roche:** 1759–1802
flowers

298

Léandre: 1779–85
children and emblems

Le Bel, aîné: 1766–75
figures and flowers

Le Bel, jeune: 1780–93
flowers
(landscape painter of this
name used this mark
1804–44)

Lecot: before 1800
gilder

Ledoux: 1758
landscapes and birds

Le Guay, Etienne-Charles:
various dates between
1778 and 1840
figures

Le Guay, Etienne-Henri:
1749–96
gilder

Le Guay, Pierre-André:
1772–1812
figures

Le Grand: 1776–1817
gilder (cf. Le Guay)

Levé: 1754–1805
flowers

Levé, Felix: late 18th century
flowers and chinoiseries

**Maqueret, Mme (née
Bouillat):** 1796–1820
flowers

Massy: 1779–1806
flowers

Méreaud, aîné: 1754–91
flowers and borders

Méreaud, jeune: 1756–79
bouquets

Micaud, Jacques: 1759
flowers and ornaments

Micaud, Pierre-Louis:
1795–1812
painter and gilder

Michel, Ambroise: 1772–80

Moiron: 1790–91
flowers

Mongenot: 1754
flowers

Moreau, D.-J.: 1809–15
gilding

Morin: 1754
sea-pieces and military
subjects

Mutel: various times,
1754–73
landscapes

Nicquet or Niquet: 1764–92
flowers

Noël: 1755–1804
flowers, etc.

**Noualhier, Mme (née Duro-
sey):** 1775–95
flowers

Parpette: 1755
flowers

Parpette, Mlle: late 18th century
flowers

Parpette, Mlle Louison: late
18th/early 19th century
flowers

Petit, aîné: 1756
gilder

Pfeiffer: 1771–1800
flowers

Philippine, aîné: 1778
pastoral subjects and
children

Philippine, jeune: 1787.

Pierre, aîné: 1759–75

Pierre, Jean-Jacques:
1763–1800
flowers

Pithou, aîné: 1757–90
figures and historical subjects

Pithou, jeune: 1760–95
figures and flowers

Pouillot: 1773–78
flowers

Prévost, aîné: 1754
gilding

Raux, aîné: 1766–79
flowers

Renard, Emile: after 1800

Robert, Pierre: first half 19th
century
ornaments

Rocher: 1758

Rosset: 1753
landscapes and flowers

Rousselle: 1758–74

Schradre: 1773–86
landscapes and birds

Sinsson or Sisson: 1773–95
flowers and garlands

Sinsson, Jacques: 1795–1846
flowers

Sinsson, Pierre: 1818–48

Sinsson, Louis: 1830–47
flowers

Sioux, aîné: 1752–92
flowers and garlands

Sioux, jeune: 1752
flowers

Swebach: 1802–13
military subjects

Tabary: 1751
birds

Taillandier: 1753–90
flowers

Tandart, Charles: 1756
flowers

Tardi: 1755–95
flowers

Théodore: late 18th century
gilder

Thévenet, aîné: 1745

Thévenet, jeune: 1752
flowers

Troyen: 1802–17
gilder

Vandé or Vaudé: 1753

Vavasseur, aîné: 1753

Vieillard: 1752–90

Vincent: 1752–1806
gilder

Weydinger, Pierre: late 18th
century–19th century
gilder

Xrouet: 1750–75
landscapes

Marks of Modellers and Repairers:

Bono

Bourdois: 1773

Chanou, Jean-Baptiste:
1779–1825

Collet: signed in full

Delatre: 1754–58

Duru

Fernex:
often attributed to Falconet
by older authorities

Le Riche, Joseph:
1757–1801

Letourneur: 1756–62

Le Tronne: 1753–57

Liance: 1769–1810

Pajou: 1751–59

Sewell & Donkin: (*fl. c.* 1780–1878)
Potters making creamware pink lustred wares, pierced baskets (Leeds-style) etc. at Newcastle-on-Tyne, Northumberland. Mark, "Sewell" alone, or name of firm:

SEWELL

Sharpe, Thomas: (d. 1838)
Potter working the Swadlincote potteries at Burton-on-Trent, Staffordshire (1821–38); firm afterwards trading as Sharpe Bros & Co.

T. SHARPE   THOMAS SHARPE
Impressed   Impressed

Shaw, Ralph: (*fl.* mid-18th century)
English potter working at Cobridge, Staffordshire; inscription recorded "Made by Ralph Shaw October 31, Cobridge gate MT 1740" (or 46); died 1754–59.

Shelley Potteries Ltd (1925–67)
Manufacturers of china and earthenware at Longton, Staffordshire. (The name "Shelley" was used by Wileman and Co. 1892–1925.)

CHINA
SHELLEY.
ENGLAND

c. 1945–

Shorthose & Co: (*fl. c.* 1817–22)
Firm, also known as Shorthose & Heath, making various earthenwares at Hanley, Staffordshire; specialised in printing. Marks recorded:

Siena, Tuscany, Italy
Pottery made here from 13th century; maiolica made 14th and 15th centuries to *c.* 1520; revived for part of 18th century.

Simpson, John: (*fl. c.* 1710)
English potter making "red dishes & pans" at Burslem, Staffordshire.
Possibly his mark:

Found on certain octagonal slipware dishes.

Simpson, Ralph: (1651–1724)
English potter working in Staffordshire; name found on various pieces, notably of trailed slip decoration, may be his:

Sinceny, Aisne, France
Faience factory established here by Jean-Baptiste de Fayard, working from 1733 onward.

In blue
The letter S sometimes occurs with the name "Pellevé" (manager 1737–)

Painters' initials or signatures:
B.T Pierre Bertrand

Alexandré Daussy
Pierre Jeannot
Joseph Bedeaux
LM Leopold Mélériat, 1737–75
"LJLC pinxit" Joseph le Cerf, *c.* 1772
Gh François-Joseph Ghail
Philippe-Vincent Coignard
Antoine Coignard
Antoine Coignard
André-Joseph le Comte
Examples:

A. Daussy   P. Jeannot   J. Bedeaux

F.-J. Ghail

Other factories, 19th century:
Lecomte and Dantier:
         L et D
Mandois:

Mandois

Sitzendorf, Thuringia, Germany
Porcelain factory founded by Liermann in
1845. Taken over by Alfred Voigt; continues to the present day.

Slee's Pottery, Leeds, Yorkshire
Established in 1888 for the manufacture of
cream-coloured wares to the patterns of
the Leeds Pottery; marks used were those
of the original factory, q.v.

Smith, Sampson: (1813–78)
English potter at Longton, Staffordshire;
began as decorator; specially noted for
earthenware "flat back" type figures
(1850+); business was continued by others
after his death; figure-making ceased in
1918, but revived *c.* 1948, using some of the
original moulds by Barker Bros, still trading as Sampson Smith Ltd until 1963.

Moulded in relief under some models

Smith, William, & Co: (*fl. c.* 1825–55)
Potters at Stockton-on-Tees, Yorkshire,
chiefly making imitations of Wedgwood's
wares (from *c.* 1824); in *c.* 1848 were
restrained by injunction from using the
latter's name (mis-spelt) on their products.
Marks recorded:

W.S. & Co's
WEDGEWOOD

W.S. & Co's
QUEEN'S WARE
STOCKTON

Sneyd, Thomas: (*c.* 1846–47)
English potter at Hanley, Staffordshire;
name found on red and other coloured jugs
crudely imitating the Portland Vase.
     T. SNEYD
     HANLEY

Solomon's seal mark
Five-point star:

Found on maiolica made at Savona, q.v.

Solon, Marc Louis: (1835–1912)
Ceramic artist; first worked at Sèvres,
developing the pâte-sur-pâte technique
(*c.* 1859); came to England, working at
Mintons (1870–1904) in the pâte-sur-pâte
technique there also.
Mark recorded:

He sometimes signed his early work "Miles" or M.L. Solon

Sölvesborg, Sweden
Faience factory founded here by Major Gabriel Sparre in 1773; later in hands of S. Fr. von Ziepel, closing down 1793.
Mark:
The letters S B, sometimes with a numeral.

Spode, Josiah (1733–97)
Founded factory at Stoke-on-Trent, Staffordshire, c. 1784, manufacturing earthenware, porcelain, stone china etc. Firm became Copeland & Garrett in 1833, and W. T. Copeland in 1847, under which name it continues to the present day. Old title Spode reintroduced in marks in 1970.

Printed in purple on felspar porcelain, c. 1815–27

Printed on stone china, in black c. 1805–15, in blue c. 1815–30

SPODE

On earthenware, c. 1805–33

In red, c. 1790–1820

COPELAND & GARRETT

c. 1833–47

Stevenson, Andrew:
Made earthenware at Cobridge, 1816–30.

Impressed 1816–30

Stevenson, Ralph: (*fl.* 1810–32)
English potter at Cobridge, Staffordshire; firm noted for blue-printed wares with American and other views, portraits of eminent men, etc.

Stevenson & Hancock: (*fl. c.* 1859–1935)
Owned china factory at Derby, England.

In red c. 1861–1935

Stockelsdorf, near Lübeck, Germany
Faience made here by Georg Nicolaus Lübbers, 1771–86; continued into the 19th century.

Stockelsdorf-Buchwald-Abraham Leihamer

Other initials recorded:
A J. A. G. Adler
S D. N. O. Seritz
C C. T. F. Creutzfeldt

Stralsund, Pomerania, Germany
Faience factory started here in 1755 by
J. U. Giese (d. 1780) with J. Buchwald;
leased to J. E. L. Ehrenreich in 1766;
production ceased 1786; revived later,
finally closing 1790.

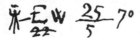

The arms of Stralsund, E for
Ehrenreich, the price, and the date

Strasbourg, Alsace, France
Faience made here in the 18th century by
the Hannong family. Marks:
P H for Paul Hannong, proprietor 1738
(d. 1760)
J H for Joseph Hannong, proprietor
1760 (d. c. 1790)
Painters' initials, with numerals, often
accompany these monograms.

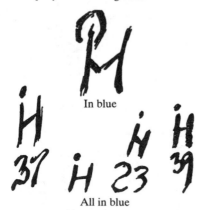

In blue

All in blue

Artists' marks recorded:
H M **Henri Montoson** 1754
J H **Joseph Hannsmann** 1745
N M **Nicolas Mittmann** 1749–53

Porcelain made at Strasbourg c. 1752 and
c. 1768 by Hannong family.

Sulzback-Philippsburg, Germany
Faience made here 1751–74, and porcelain
1771–74.

CT in monogram, for Carl Theodor, with
or without the Electoral hat.

Swansea, Glamorganshire, Wales
Earthenware made here (c. 1764–1870)
and porcelain (c. 1815–17), and a porcelain
incorporating soapstone (after 1817 to
1823), at the Cambrian Pottery, under
different owners: trading as Haynes, Dillwyn & Co (1802–10); Dillwyn & Co (1810–
17); T. J. Bevington & Co (1817–24); and
Dillwyn again (1831–c. 1850); finally in
hands of David Evans, followed by his son.

Marks much copied

Talavera, Spain
Tin-glazed earthenware made here from
c. 1560 to c. 1720, and again c. 1761.
Similar industry at Puente del Arzobispo,
mid-17th century until 19th century.

Blue and white faience made during the
19th century. Marks used included the
name TALAVERA.

In black   In purple-brown   In blue

In brown

Talor (Tallor), William
English name recorded on large Toft-style slipware dishes, one being dated 1700.

Tata, Hungary
Earthenware made here from *c.* 1756–58 until after 1811.
Mark: T incised or painted in blue.

Taunay, Pierre-Antoine-Henri: (*fl.* 1745–78)
Porcelain painter and colour preparer at Vincennes and Sèvres.

Taylor, George
English name recorded on a slipware posset-pot, dated 1692, and on a dish.

Taylor, William Howson: (d. 1935)
Potter who founded the Ruskin Pottery at Smethwick, Staffordshire, in 1898; closed down 1935.

Tebo: (*fl. c.* 1750–75)
Perhaps English rendering of French "Thibaud". There is evidence that a repairer at Bow (from *c.* 1750) who signed T. A. Tebo worked at Worcester in the 1760s and the mark occurs on Plymouth porcelain 1768–70. The following marks, formerly incorrectly attributed to Tebo, are now thought to be those of John Toulouse.

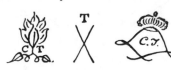

Teichert, E.: (founded 1884)
Firm working at Meissen, using for mark word MEISSEN.

Teinitz, Bohemia, Czechoslovakia
Earthenware made here from 1801 until 1866, by Count Wrtby and F. L. Welby.

Impressed

Terchi, Bartolomeo: (*fl.* 18th century)
Italian pottery painter; at S. Quirico d'Orcia, Tuscany, 1714–*c.* 1724; at Siena 1727, and at Bassano *c.* 1744.

Tettau, Franconia, Germany
Porcelain factory founded here in 1794.

In purple or blue

Thieme, Carl: (*fl.* 19th century)
Founded hard-paste porcelain factory in 1875 at Potschappel, Dresden, making imitation Capodimonte wares, etc.

Thompson, Joseph: (*fl. c.* 1818–56)
Manufacturer of earthenware at Hartshorne, Derbyshire; sons continued trading as Thompson Bros. in 1856.

J. THOMPSON
Impressed

Joseph Thompson
Wooden Box
Pottery
Derbyshire
Impressed

Thooft & Labouchere, Delft, Holland
Working during 19th century, making traditional wares.

Taken from firm's advertisement 1895; usually rendered very freely:

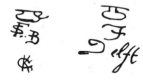

Thornhill, Sir James: (1675–1734)
English baroque painter; not ceramic artist, but there are some tin-glazed earthenware plates (British Museum) perhaps painted by him at Delft in 1711. Signed:

Thoune, Switzerland
Factory founded here in 19th century making pottery. Continues to present day.

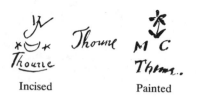

Incised   Painted

Incised

Tiefenfurt, Silesia, Germany
Hard-paste porcelain made by P. Donath from 1808, at the Schlesische Porzellanfabrik.

Tinworth, George: (1843–1913)
English modeller at Doulton's Lambeth (London) factory, from 1867.

Incised

Tirschenreuth, Bavaria, Germany
Porcelain factory established here in first half 19th century.

Tittensor, Charles: (*fl.* early 19th century)
English figure-maker and black-printer; in business at Hanley, Staffordshire (1802–c. 1813); at Shelton (recorded in 1818 and 1823).
Mark recorded:

Impressed

Tittensor, Jacob: (*fl. c.* 1780–95)
Marks recorded:

Incised   In relief

Toft, James: (b. 1673)
Probable maker of dishes bearing his name: dishes dated 1695 and 1705 are known.

IAMES TOFT

Toft, Ralph: (b. 1638)
Name occurs on large Toft-style dishes, two being dated 1676 and 1677; a posset pot is dated 1683.

RALPHOFT

Toft, Thomas: (d. 1689)
Name occurs on 35 large dishes, 2 jugs, and a posset pot; wares decorated with trailed slip, the dishes having trellis rim borders with the name; uncertain whether the name indicates maker or recipient, more likely the former.

thomas:tofI

THOMAS TOFT

thomas TOFT

A A A a

Variations in letter A
in Toft signature

Tooth & Co Ltd: (*fl.* late 19th century)
Potters at Burton-on-Trent, Staffordshire, established 1883. Firm continues to present day.

H

Toulouse, Haute-Garonne, France
Faience made here in 17th and 18th centuries. From 1829 to 1848 made by François and Antoine Fouque, collaborating with Antoine Arnoux.

Toulouse, John. See Tebo.

Tournay, Belgium
Soft-paste porcelain made here from 1751 to 1796 by F.-J. Péterinck; owner from 1797 to 1799, C. Péterinck-Gérard; Bettignies family worked the factory *c.* 1800 to 1850.

In gold or colour
1751–56

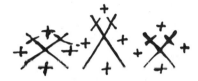

In blue, red, brown, or gold, 1756–81

Treviso, Italy
Soft-paste porcelain made here, 1759–77; by Andrea and Giuseppe Fontebasso, 1795–1840.

F. F.
Treviso, 1799

G.A.F.F.
Treviso

G.A.F.F. for Giuseppe Andrea Fratelli Fontebasso.
Signature of painter Gaetano Negrisole occurs with dates of early 1830s.

Tunnicliffe, Michael: (*fl.* 1828–41)
Potter making earthenware toys and figures at Tunstall, Staffordshire.

Impressed

Turin, Piedmont, Italy
Hard-paste porcelain made here between 1737 and 1743; examples rare.
Maiolica made here from 16th to 19th centuries.

In blue
For the Rossetti factory, started 1725.
G.A.A. (underlined) for G. A. Ardizzone (recorded in 1765)

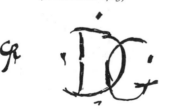

In black

For a 19th-century potter, D. Gionetti.

Turner, John: (1738–87)
English potter at Stoke-on-Trent, Staffordshire (from c. 1756); at Lane End, now Longton (1762–87); firm trading as Turner & Co in 1803; closed down 1806.

TURNER   TURNER & CO
Impressed   Impressed

Turner's Patent

In red: 1800–1805
on stoneware

Twigg, Joseph & Bros: (*fl.* 19th century)
Potters making decorated earthenware at Swinton, Yorkshire, from 1839; Twigg family carried on until 1881.

      TWIGG'S

Impressed

Twyford (Twiford), Joshua: (*c.* 1640–1729)
Potter said to have made red and black "Elers" ware and salt-glazed stoneware at Shelton, Staffordshire.
Mark ascribed:

On piece in British Museum, London

Val-Sous-Meudon, Seine-et-Oise, France
White earthenware made here from 1806 until 1818, by Mittenhoff & Mouron.

Valenciennes, Nord, France
Hard-paste porcelain factory started here by J. B. Fauquez in 1785; assisted by brother-in-law Lamoninary, 1800–1810.

In blue: for Fauquez, Lamoninary, and Valenciennes

Vallauris
Pottery made here in 19th century by Jerôme Massier and Company.
Found impressed:

Varages, Var, France
Faience in Moustiers and Marseille style made here from late 17th to early 19th century. One mark cited: "Fait par moi E. armand à varages 1698". Factory mark: letter V rather freely drawn:

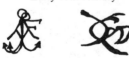

Venice, Italy
Maiolica made here from *c.* 1570 until mid 18th century
Workshops of 18th century include;
The Bertolini brothers (first half);
The Manardi brothers (1669–1740)

Early 18th century

18th century

Venice: Cozzi factory
Factory established 1764, making porcelain; maiolica a subsidiary; closed 1812.

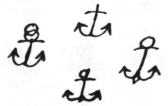

In red (Figures rarely marked)

Venice: Hewelke factory (*fl.* 1758–63)
Porcelain factory established at Udine 1758–61; at Venice from 1761 to 1763; owned by Nathaniel Friedrich Hewelke and his wife, Maria Dorothea, from Dresden.

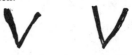

Incised, and covered with
a brown-red pigment

Venice: Vezzi factory (*fl.* 1720–27)
Factory founded by Francesco Vezzi (1651–1740) in 1720; closed in 1727 under his son Giovanni Vezzi.
Forgeries of wares and marks are known.

In blue

In red, blue or gold   in red

In colour

In underglaze blue   In red   In red

In underglaze blue: other
equally fantastic forms are recorded

Lodouico Ortolani Veneto dipinse nella Fabrica di Porcelana, in Venen...

Verhaast, Gijsbrecht: (*fl. c.* 1690)
Delft landscape painter.
Signature recorded on some plaques:

G Verhaast.

Vianna do Castello, Portugal
Faience made here from 1744.

V VIANNA V

Vienna, Austria
Hard-paste porcelain factory founded here
in 1719 by Du Paquier assisted by S.
Stölzel; passed through various hands,
closing in 1864.
Marks:
Du Paquier period (1719–*c.* 1744), no
marks except an occasional pseudo-
Chinese one.
Shield mark used from 1744 until 1864.
1744–49 Painted in red, black or purple
overglaze colours, impressed or
incised
1749–80 Painted in blue
1820s Drawn almost as a triangle
Later, more elongated shape, either im-
pressed or in blue
Factory rejects marked:
On wares sold undecorated:
a cross cut on the wheel across
the blue shield mark
On decorated rejects:
Letter A in green or red, over the
blue mark
Year marks:
From 1783 to 1800, the two last figures
After 1800, the three last figures

Impressed   In blue   In blue

Some later 19th-century Viennese factory
marks:

KNESL
WIEN

Impressed

Artist's mark recorded:

Viktoria Porzellanfabrik (1833–)
Factory run by Schmidt & Co. at Carlsbad,
Austria.
Marks: "GEMMA" in shield beneath
crown; "Victoria Austria" with crown;
"Victoria Carlsbad Austria" in garter with
winged figure.

Villeroy and Boch: (founded 1841)
Firm founded by families of Villeroy and
Boch, to amalgamate the factories at Wal-
lerfangen, Septfontaines, and Mettlach;
new factory built at Dresden in 1853.
Merzig absorbed into the business 1879,
and Schramberg 1883.
BB
In blue
J. F. Boch and
Buschmann

Mettlach   Mettlach   Septfontaines

310

Mettlach   Dresden

    Schramberg   Schramberg

Mettlach   Wallerfangen

   Dresden   Dresden

Mettlach   Mettlach   Mettlach

Villers Cotterets

These words used as mark on ware made at Chantilly (c. 1770) for the Château of Villers Cotterets.

Vinovo, near Turin, Italy

Porcelain (hybrid hard-paste) factory established here in 1776, closing 1780. Re-opened 1815, worked by Giovanni Lomello.

Incised or painted in blue

Cross of Savoy

Painted in blue

In blue
1780–1815
Initials D G for Dottore Gioanetti (1729–1815)
Initial L for Lomello (fl. 1815–20)

Viry family: (fl. later 17th century)

Faience painters at Moustiers, and at Marseilles.
Inscriptions recorded:

"Fait à Marseille chez F. Viry 1681"
"Fay a St iean du desert Viry" (on a piece dating from c. 1690)

Viry, Gaspard:

Faience painter at Moustiers.
Inscription recorded:

Vische, near Turin, Italy

Porcelain factory set up here by the Conte de Vische in 1765; production ceased after 1766.
Mark on pieces in Turin Museum:

Vista Alegre, near Oporto, Portugal

Hard-paste porcelain factory established here by J. F. P. Basto in 1824, surviving to present day.

Viterbo, Umbria, Italy

Inscription recorded on a maiolica dish:
"In Viterbo Diomeo 1544"

(inscription forms part of decoration)

Vizeer or Viseer, Piet: (d. 1762)

Owner of De Dunstenaar (The Artist) workshop at Delft, 1735–62.

Volkstedt, Thuringia, Germany
Porcelain factory established at Sitzendorf *c.* 1760; moved to Volkstedt 1762. Acquired 1800 by Wilhelm Heinrich Greiner and Carl Holzapfel who continued until 1817 or later.

Marks:
Crossed hayforks from Schwarzburg arms used with a line across after 1787

Greiner & Holzapfel
1799–1817

Beyer & Boch
decorating from 1853
manufacturing from 1890

Volpato, Giovanni: (d. 1803)
Founded earthenware and porcelain factory at Rome *c.* 1790; continued by descendants until 1832.
Mark occasionally found on figures:
G. VOLPATO. ROMA
Impressed

Voyez, Jean: (*c.* 1735–*c.* 1800)
Modeller and manufacturer, of French extraction, working in England; with Wedgwood (1768–69); recorded at Cobridge, Staffordshire (1772); probably modelled for the Ralph Woods of Burslem; no mention after 1791 in London.

**J VOYEZ
1788**

Vron, Somme, France
Painted tiles made here, end of 18th century.
VRON
Impressed

Vyse, Charles (*fl.* 1911–23)
Manufacturer of earthenware figures and stonewares in London. Marks include "C.V."; "C.V.Chelsea"; signature in script; "Vyse" and a date; "C.V" monogram with date.

Waldenburg, Silesia, Germany
Hard-paste porcelain made here by Carl Krister, beginning in 1831.

In green

Waldershof, Bavaria, Germany
Hard-paste porcelain factory established here by Johann Haviland in 1907.

Walker, Agatha
Studio potter

Wallendorf, Thuringia, Germany
Company formed here by members of the Hammann and Greiner families, to make hard-paste porcelain. Gotthelf Greiner went to Limbach 1772; Hammann's factory closed 1833.

In blue
Mark often confused with that of other factories, including Meissen.

Wallerfangen, Saar Basin, Germany
Earthenware factory established here in 1789 which passed to Villeroy and Boch.

Impressed

Walton, John: (*fl.* early 19th century)
English maker of pottery figures, from the first decade of the 19th century until 1835, at Burslem, Staffordshire.
Mark, usually on the back of the figure, occasionally underneath; also occurs on recent reproductions.

Impressed

Not to be confused with other figure-makers of the same surname:
Walton, James: (*fl.* 1848–51) Hanley
Walton, Joshua: (*fl.* 1830–35) Hanley
Walton, William: (*fl.* 1846) Shelton

Warburton, Francis: (*fl.* 1800 onward)
Made cream-coloured earthenware, first in partnership with brother Peter (1800–1802) at Cobridge, England: later at La-Charité-sur-Loire, France. Factory taken over by Le Bault in 1803.
LA CHARITE
Impressed

Warburton, Peter: (1773–1813)
Maker of cream-coloured earthenware at Cobridge, Staffordshire; at first in partnership with Francis Warburton, until 1802; afterwards on his own account; partner in New Hall company (between 1804 and 1810).

Impressed

Warburton family: (*fl.* 18th century)
Manufacturers of earthenware at Cobridge, Staffordshire; factory worked by John Warburton (*c.* 1802–25) and continued by his widow, and his son Thomas (lasted more than a century).
WARBURTON
Impressed

Washington, Robert Johnson: (b. 1911)
Studio potter

Watcombe Pottery Co., South Devon
Ornamental terracottas, *c.* 1867–1901. Continued as Royal Aller Vale and Watcombe Pottery Co., 1901–62.
Among marks used:
WATCOMBE
TORQUAY

Printed
c. 1875–1901

Wattisfield, Suffolk, England
Earthenware made here during second half of 18th century; pottery taken over (1808) by Thomas Watson; worked continuously by his descendants. Thomas Harrison (1844) made brown earthenware here.

Impressed, *c.* 1948–

Wedgewood. See William Smith & Co.

Wedgwood: European imitations
Mark recorded:
WEDGWOOD
Impressed
Found on cream-coloured earthenware made at Hubertsburg, end 18th/early 19th centuries.
Also used at Bodenbach in Bohemia, 19th century, and at Schmidt's factory, Bayreuth.

Wedgwood, Josiah: (1730–95)
English potter at Burslem and Etruria, Staffordshire, making all kinds of wares (except bone china and porcelain); in partnership with Whieldon (1754–59); trading as Wedgwood & Bentley (1769–80); factory inherited by Wedgwood's second son, Josiah; continues today.

JOSIAH WEDGWOOD
Feb. 2nd 1805

wedgwood WEDGWOOD

Wedgwood & Bentley: Etruria

WEDGWOOD
WEDGWOOD

Wedgwood

W. & B.

Wedgwood
& Bentley
356

WEDGWOOD & SONS   WEDGWOOD

Wedgwood
& Bentley

Wedgwood
Wedgwood

WEDGWOOD

WEDGWOOD

Twentieth-century marks include, where appropriate, the name of the pattern. Examples:

Printed:
dated 1956

Factory mark printed in grey-green; other marks painted in red; dated 1958

Other marks

A system of date marks was introduced in 1860; it consisted of three capital letters representing month, potter, and year respectively.

Month letters 1860–64:

J	January	Y	May	S	September
F	February	T	June	O	October
M	March	V	July	N	November
A	April	W	August	D	December

Month letters 1864–1907:

J	January	M	May	S	September
F	February	T	June	O	October
R	March	L	July	N	November
A	April	W	August	D	December

Year letters 1860–97:

O	1860	A	1872			N	1885
P	1861	B	1873			O	1886
Q	1862	C	1874			P	1887
R	1863	D	1875			Q	1888
S	1864	E	1876			R	1889
T	1865	F	1877			S	1890
U	1866	G	1878			T	1891
V	1867	H	1879			U	1892
W	1868	I	1880			V	1893
X	1869	J	1881			W	1894
Y	1870	K	1882			X	1895
Z	1871	L	1883			Y	1896
		M	1884			Z	1897

Year letters 1898–1930:

A	1898	N	1911	A	1924
B	1899	O	1912	B	1925
C	1900	P	1913	C	1926
D	1901	Q	1914	D	1927
E	1902	R	1915	E	1928
F	1903	S	1916	F	1929
G	1904	T	1917	G	1930
H	1905	U	1918		
I	1906	V	1919		
J	1907	W	1920		
K	1908	X	1921		
L	1909	Y	1922		
M	1910	Z	1923		

Marks from 1930 onward:
A new and simpler method was introduced consisting of a figure to indicate the month, a letter for the potter, and two figures for the year.
Examples:

WEDGWOOD 2 0 56

Impressed
February 1956
"O" for E. R. Owen, modeller 1947

WEDGWOOD 2 A 58

Impressed
February 1958
"A" for Austin Arnold modeller 1904–47

Wedgwood & Co. (Ltd): (1860–1965)
Manufacturers of earthenware and stone china at Tunstall, Staffordshire. Not to be confused with Josiah Wedgwood & Sons Ltd. "& Co." in the mark is the distinguishing feature of this firm. "Ltd" was added in 1900. The name of the body or pattern is often included.

WEDGWOOD & C?L?.
ENGLAND.

Weesp, Holland
Hard-paste porcelain made here from 1759 until 1771; business transferred to Oude Loosedrecht (1771) and then to Amstel (1784).

In underglaze blue

Wemyss ware: See HERON, ROBERT & SON

Whieldon, Thomas: (1719–95)
English potter at Fenton Low (or Little Fenton), Staffordshire; gave his name to a distinctive type of earthenware, notable for its range of colours, or rather the coloured glazes. No marks were used at this pottery.

Wileman family: (second half 19th century)
English manufacturers of china and earthenware at the Foley Potteries, Stoke-on-Trent, Staffordshire; established 1860 by Henry Wileman; continued by sons (1864–67); in 1867 C. T. Wileman took over the china, J. F. Wileman the earthenware, trade; reunited 1870 (C. J. Wileman retired); soon after trading as Wileman & Co. See also SHELLEY POTTERIES LTD.

Transfer-printed

Wilson, Robert: (d. 1801)
English potter making cream-coloured earthenware and "dry" bodies at Hanley, Staffordshire; partner with James Neale, trading as Neale and Wilson, eventually succeeding him; succeeded by David Wilson & Sons; firm bankrupt in 1817.

NEALE & WILSON

Impressed

Impressed

Witteburg
Minor faience factory.

Wohlfart, Friedrich Carl: (*fl.* 1766–71)
Painted porcelain (scenes of gallantry etc.) at Frankenthal (1766), Pfalz-Zweibrücken (1767–68), possibly at Ottweiler (1768–71), and at Höchst (1771).
Inscription recorded:
"Wolfart pinxit" on tureen at Hamburg.

Wolfe, Thomas, the younger: (1751–1818)
Potter making porcelain at Liverpool (1792–1818) and various earthenwares at Stoke-on-Trent, Staffordshire (1784–1818).
Mark recorded on cream-coloured earthenware:

Impressed

Wolfsburg, Carl Ferdinand von: (1692–1764)
Amateur porcelain hausmaler, *fl.* 1729–48.
Signatures recorded:
"C. F. de Wolfsbourg pinxit 1729"
"Carolus Ferdinandus de Wolfsbourg et Wallsdorf Eques Silesiae pinxit Viennae Aust. 1731."

Wolfsohn, Helena: (*fl.* 19th century)
Owned factory at Dresden, where Meissen porcelain, bought in the white, was decorated.

Used indiscriminately, until prevented by injunction *c.* 1880.
Subsequent marks used:

In blue

Wood, Enoch: (1759–1840)
English potter making earthenware, cane ware, black basaltes, etc, at Burslem, Staffordshire (from 1784); trading as Wood & Caldwell (1790–1818); later took sons into

the firm, who continued as Enoch Wood & Sons until 1846.
Marks:

E. WOOD
ENOCH WOOD
SCULPSIT
Impressed or incised
WOOD & CALDWELL
There are several variations.

Impressed

Wood, Ephraim: (1773–after 1830)
English potter making figures; enameller, gilder, and lusterer of earthenware; at Burslem, Staffordshire.
Marks recorded, which may stand for Ephraim Wood or Enoch Wood:

EW
1788

Impressed:
on a "Fair Hebe" jug

WOOD

Impressed: on early 19th-century figures: bench sign and circles probably workmen's marks

Wood, Ralph: (1715–72)
English potter (established 1754) at Burslem, Staffordshire; business continued by son, Ralph Wood II (1748–95) and grandson, Ralph Wood III (1781–1801) until 1801; noted for figures and Toby jugs.

R. WOOD
Impressed

Ra Wood

Impressed

Ra Wood
Burslem

1770 Ralph Wood

Incised
Rebus mark (of three trees) occurs on some Wood figures:

Wood, Robert: (1650–1717)
English potter making slipware at Burslem, Staffordshire; a posset-pot (Hanley Museum) is lettered THE BEST IS NOT TOO GOOD FOR YOU ROBBORT WOOD.

ROBBORT WOOD

Slip

Worcester
Porcelain factory established here by Dr. John Wall (d. 1776) and others in 1751. In 1783 bought for Joseph and John Flight (d. 1791); Robert Chamberlain left to form a rival company; in 1792 Martin Barr joined the firm, the successive partners being:
Flight & Barr 1792–1807
Barr, Flight & Barr 1807–13
Flight, Barr & Barr 1813–40
In 1840 amalgamated with Chamberlain. Later owners were Chamberlain and Lilly (1848), joined by W. H. Kerr in 1850; Kerr & Binns from 1852; Worcester Royal Porcelain Co, 1862 onwards.
Marks:

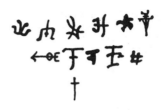

About 1755–65

1765–80

1760–90	1765–80	1770

In blue 1783–89	In red 1789–92	In red 1792–1807

1791–1807	Incised	1820

B.F.B.	F.B.B.
Barr Flight & Barr 1807–13	Flight, Barr & Barr 1813–40

Printed
Kerr & Binns

Impressed
1852–62

Printed
James Hadley
& Sons
1896–1903

James Hadley
& Sons

Impressed:
since 1862

Worcester Royal Porcelain Co.
1862–

73

51

c. 1862 to present-day standard printed or impressed mark. Numerals under the main mark are the last two of the year of decoration, 73 for 1873 etc.

Amended printed or impressed mark; *c.* 1876–91 crescent instead of "C" in centre.

Standard printed or impressed mark after 1891; wording around not found on earlier version.

Wouters, Joseph: (*fl.* later 18th century) Made cream-coloured earthenware at Andenne, in Belgium, from 1783.

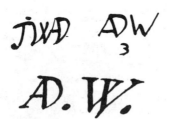

Wright, John: (early 18th century) Name recorded on large Toft-style slipware dishes (dates 1705–07); perhaps his initials on slipware posset-pot (British Museum) in inscription: ANN DRAPER THIS CUP MADE FOR YOU AND SO NO MORE I.W. 1707

Wright, William: (early 18th century) Name recorded on Toft-style slipware dishes, one being dated 1709.

Wrisbergholzen, Hanover, Germany Faience made here *c.* 1737 to *c.* 1830. Mark: WR in monogram form, with or without a painter's initials.

Wrotham, Kent, England Slipware pottery made here and nearby, in 17th and 18th centuries; no dated pieces after 1739 are known. Mark, the word WROTHAM, often in conjunction with the initials of the potter or eventual owner.

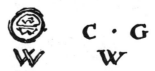

Potters recorded at Wrotham include:
Hubble, Nicholas: (d. 1689)
Ifield, John (d. 1716)
Livermore, Nicholas: (d. 1678)
Richardson, George: (*c.* 1620–87)

Würzburg, Lower Franconia, Germany Hard-paste porcelain made here by Johann Caspar Geyger, from 1775 to 1780.

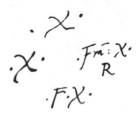

Xanto Francesco, Avelli da Rovigo: (*fl.* 1530–42) Maiolica painter of Urbino. Signature frequent and various, from simple X to full signature:

Yvernel: (*fl.* mid-18th century)
Painter of flowers and birds, at the Vincennes-Sèvres factory from 1750.

Zell, Baden, Germany
General pottery established here *c.* 1820 by J. F. Lenz.
Mark: ZELL impressed
Factory continued using these marks:

(Mid and late 19th century)

Zerbst, Anhalt, Germany
Faience made here from 1720 until 1861

Ziegler, Jules-Claude: (1804–56)
Made salt-glazed stoneware at Voisinlieu near Beauvais, France, from *c.* 1839.

Zieseler, Philipp: (*fl.* mid-18th century)
Painter, working at Höchst *c.* 1749, and at Fürstenberg from 1759. The initial "Z" may be his mark.

Zillwood, W.: (*fl.* early 19th century)
Potter at work in the Salisbury, Wiltshire, area; initials "ZW" sometimes found incised. Wares include spurious early dates.

Zimmermann: (*fl.* 18th century)
Signature recorded on an example of Münden faience (otherwise unknown): "Zimmermann 1777".

Zopf or Zopff, Georg Friedrich: (*fl.* mid-18th century)
Painter said to have worked at Stralsund *c.* 1757, and at Eckernförde *c.* 1766.
Mark at Eckernförde thought to be his, the initials "Z" and "J".

Zurich, Switzerland
Porcelain and faience made here, *c.* 1763; faience and lead-glazed earthenware made *c.* 1790 to end of 19th century.
Marks recorded:

In blue, 18th century

Also the cursive letter "Z" found incised, on soft-paste porcelain (very rare).

Japanese Marks

Marks on Japanese ceramics take various forms and include: stamps or seals giving the name of the potter or the place of manufacture; a reign mark in Chinese characters; a mark of commendation. These marks are not always easy to interpret. Individual potters sometimes used more than one name, and names could be passed down from master potters to their pupils; an immense number have been recorded.

In general, Japanese ceramics were rarely marked before the 19th century, although reign marks in Chinese characters may sometimes be found in 17th- and 18th-century blue and white Arita porcelain. All marks beginning "Dai Nippon" ("Great Japan") indicate a 19th- or 20th-century date.

Marks of origin

Dai Nippon Seto Sei
(Made at Seto in Great Japan. 19th century. The first two characters in the right-hand column read "Dai Nippon")

Dai Nippon Kutani Zo
(Made at Kutani in Great Japan)

Marks of commendation

Jiu (long life)

Fuku (happiness)

Chinese Imperial Reign Marks

Imperial reign marks on Chinese ceramics came into regular use at the beginning of the Ming Dynasty. They were usually painted in underglaze blue or overglaze red enamel, on the base of the piece, and consist of a group of six or four characters which are read from the top right downwards. They may be in normal Chinese script (*kaishu*) or the more angular, archaic script (*zhuanshu*, or seal script).

Reign marks should be treated with caution. Out of reverence, Chinese potters sometimes used the marks of an earlier reign. The Qianlong reign mark, for example, was often used on ceramics of later date, and Kangxi and Ming reign marks are also found on Guangxu pieces.

Other marks on Chinese porcelain, less easy to decipher and not given here, include potters' marks, marks of dedication, good wishes and commendation, various symbols and two-character date marks.

Ming Reign Marks 1368–1643

Hongwu 1368–1398	Chenghua 1465–1487	Jiajing 1522–1566
年製 洪武	化年製 大明成	靖年製 大明嘉

Yongle 1403–1424	Hongzhi 1488–1505	Longing 1567–1572
年製 永樂	治年製 大明弘	慶年製 大明隆

Xuande 1426–1435	Zhengde 1506–1521	Wanli 1573–1619
德年製 大明宣	德年製 大明正	曆年製 大明萬

Tianqi
1621–1627

啟年製　大明天

Chongzhen
1628–1643

年製　崇禎

Ch'ing Reign Marks 1644–1909

Shunzhi
1644–1661

治年製　大清順

Quianlong
1736–1795

隆年製　大清乾

Kangxi
1662–1722

熙年製　大清康

Jiaging
1796–1820

年製　嘉慶

Yongzheng
1723–1735

正年製　大清雍

Daoguang
1821–1850

光年製　大清道

Xianfeng
1851–1861

大清咸
豐年製

Xuantong
1909–1912

大清宣
統年製

Tongzhi
1862–1874

大清同
治年製

Hongxian
(Yūan Shih-kai)
1916

洪憲
年製

Guangxu
1875–1909

大清光
緒年製

Books for Further Reference

METALWORK

BRADBURY, FREDERICK *Guide to Marks of Origin on British, and Irish Silver Plate . . . and Old Sheffield Plate Makers' Marks. . . .* Northend, Sheffield, 11th edition, 1964.

BRETT, VANESSA *Phaidon Guide to Pewter.* Phaidon, Oxford, 1981.

COTTERELL, H. H. *Old Pewter, its Makers and Marks, In England Scotland and Ireland.* Batsford, London, 1929.

CULME, JOHN *Gold and Silversmiths, Jewellers and Allied Traders 1838–1914*, 2 volumes. Antique Collectors' Club, Woodbridge, 1987.

ENSKO, S. G. C. *American Silversmiths and their Marks.* Robert Ensko, New York, 1937.

FALLON, JOHN *Marks of London Goldsmiths and Silversmiths c. 1697–1837.* Tuttle/David & Charles, Newton Abbot, revised edition 1988.

GRIMWADE, ARTHUR *London Goldsmiths 1697–1837. Their Marks and Lives.* Faber, 3rd edition, 1990.

MONTGOMERY, C. F. *A History of American Pewter.* Praeger, USA, 1973.

PEAL, CHRISTOPHER *Pewter of Great Britain.* John Gifford, London, 1983.

PICKFORD, IAN (editor) *Jackson's Silver and Gold Marks of England, Scotland and Ireland.* Antique Collectors' Club, Woodbridge, 3rd edition, 1989.

PICKFORD, IAN (editor) *Jackson's Silver and Gold Marks*, pocket edition. Antique Collectors' Club, Woodbridge, 1991.

RIDGWAY, MAURICE *Chester Goldsmiths from Early Times to 1726.* Sherratt, 1968.

RIDGWAY, MAURICE *Chester Silver 1727–1837*, Phillimore, 1988.

STARÁ, DAGMAR *Pewter Marks of the World*, Hamlyn, 1974.

FURNITURE

BEARD, GEOFFREY and CHRISTOPHER GILBERT *Dictionary of English Furniture Makers 1660–1840.* Furniture History Society/W. S. Maney, 1986.

HEAL, SIR AMBROSE *The London Furniture Makers (1660–1840)*, Batsford, London, 1953.

KJELLBERG, PIERRE *Le Mobilier Français du XVIIIème Siecle.* Les Editions de l'Amateur, Paris, 1989.

LEDOUX-LEBARD, DENISE *Le Mobilier Français du XIXéme Siecle.* Les Editions de l'Amateur, Paris, 2nd edition 1988.

MACQUOID, PERCY AND RALPH EDWARDS *The Dictionary of English Furniture.* Revised edition by Ralph Edwards. Country Life, London 1954, reprinted by the Antique Collectors' Club, Woodbridge, 1983.

TAPESTRY

GOBEL, HEINRICH (trans. Robert West) *Tapestries of the Lowlands*, Hacker, New York, 1974.

THOMSON, W. G. *A History of Tapestry.* Hodder & Stoughton, London, revised edition 1973.

CERAMICS

CUSHION, J. P. AND W. B. HONEY *Handbook of Pottery and Porcelain Marks.* Faber, London, 4th edition 1980.

DAVISON, GERALD *A Guide to Marks on Chinese Porcelain.* Bamboo, London, 1987.

GODDEN, GEOFFREY *Encyclopaedia of British Pottery and Porcelain Marks.* Barrie & Jenkins, revised edition 1991.

Handbook of British Pottery and Porcelain Marks. Barrie & Jenkins, London, 1978.

Ceramic Art of Great Britain 1800–1900. Revised and re-illustrated edition of Jewitt's classic work. Barrie & Jenkins, London, 1972.

GRAESSE, J. AND E. JAENNICKE *Führer für Sammler von Porzellan und Fayence.* . . . Klinhardt & Biermann, Braunschweig, Berlin, 21st edition, 1967.

HASLAM, MALCOLM *Marks and Monograms of the Modern Movement.* Lutterworth, Cambridge, 1977.

RÖNTGEN, ROBERT E. *Marks on German, Bohemian and Austrian Porcelain 1710 to the Present.* Schiffer, Exton, Pennsylvania, USA, 1981.

SANDON, HENRY *Royal Worcester Porcelain.* Barrie & Jenkins, London, 3rd edition 1978.

SANDON, HENRY AND JOHN *Grainger's Worcester Porcelain.* Barrie & Jenkins, London, 1990.

WHITER, LEONARD *Spode: A History of the Family, Factory and Wares from 1733 to 1833.* Barrie & Jenkins, London, revised edition 1989.

Collectors especially interested in research relating to individual English factories are directed to the work of Geoffrey Godden (published by Barrie & Jenkins) on Coalport, Caughley, Worcester, Lowestoft, Minton, Ridgway etc.

Index